STOLEN

BLOOMSBURY CIRCUS
Bloomsbury Publishing Plc
50 Bedford Square, London, WC1B 3DP, UK
29 Earlsfort Terrace, Dublin 2, Ireland

BLOOMSBURY, BLOOMSBURY CIRCUS and the Bloomsbury Circus logo
are trademarks of Bloomsbury Publishing Plc

First published in Swedish in 2021 by Romanus & Selling as *Stöld*,
this edition published by agreement with Ahlander Agency
First published in English in 2023 by Scribner Canada, an imprint
of Simon & Schuster Canada, Inc.
First published in Great Britain 2023

A catalogue record for this book is available from the British Library

ISBN: HB: 978-1-5266-5998-9; TPB: 978-1-5266-5997-2;
eBook: 978-1-5266-5996-5; ePDF: 978-1-5266-5995-8

2 4 6 8 10 9 7 5 3 1

Printed and bound in Great Britain by CPI Group (UK) Ltd, Croydon CR0 4YY

To find out more about our authors and books visit www.bloomsbury.com and sign up
for our newsletters

STOLEN

A Novel

ANN-HELÉN LAESTADIUS

Translated from the Swedish by
Rachel Willson-Broyles

BLOOMSBURY CIRCUS
LONDON · OXFORD · NEW YORK · NEW DELHI · SYDNEY

PART I

DÁLVI

WINTER 2008

CHAPTER ONE

Okta

Elsa didn't turn around. She straightened her spine and concentrated on finding her rhythm, but still she had to glance at her skis to make sure they stayed in the tracks. It was a little too dark to head out, but she was so eager.

Her cheeks were windburnt. From the corner of her eye she caught a glimpse of her dark hair sticking out from beneath her hat and turning silvery gray with frost. Her eyelashes had changed color too, and she could feel the cold moisture when she blinked. It was like she was becoming a different person.

The lake was crisscrossed with snowmobile tracks leading home and away. To neighbors and cousins. To the reindeer corral. She followed the widest track. She'd found her rhythm, and her skis swished beneath her. She was nine years old. A big girl now. With skis of her own, not hand-me-downs from Mattias.

She poled onward, her arms strong and powerful, with each glide long. She knew the house would soon be a tiny dot behind her. The lake gave way to forest, but she wasn't afraid. She was never afraid, because she knew exactly where she was and could always find her way home. She didn't usually go beyond the lake. But now she was big.

It was early January, so the sun had found its way back, but it hardly rose over the horizon before dipping down again, leaving a pink shimmer in the sky. Today the clouds absorbed the light faster than she'd expected, but it wouldn't be pitch-black for a while yet. She would make it there before dark. The snow weighed down the firs and birches. It looked like they were all bowing to her, welcoming her home. To think, that they recognized her even with her frosty silver hair and new skis.

She heard the reindeer and skied faster, though her thighs were stiff. Her breath came faster too, stinging her throat. She must not lick her dry lips or they would redden and crack. She didn't like the taste of blood.

No one was there now, she knew that. Mom, Dad, and Mattias were at home. It wasn't time to feed the reindeer yet, but she was going to surprise them. Get the pellets ready, haul out the bags, and maybe even go in and scatter some of the feed. Hold the reindeer lichen in her hand so the animals would flock around her, not the least bit afraid.

The sound of a snowmobile starting up halted her in her tracks. Such disappointment. She wasn't the first one here after all. The snowmobile was idling. She pushed off with her poles, almost silent, then grabbed the trunk of a pine and peered around it.

It was him.

She never said his name.

In his mouth, between taut lips, was something soft and downy. In his hand, a bloody knife. Elsa squeezed her poles so hard her cold knuckles ached inside her mittens.

He took the piece of ear from his mouth and stuffed it into the pocket of his grimy yellow pants, the kind road construction workers wore. The wide reflective strips flashed as he passed in front of the snowmobile's headlights. The dead calf lay next to the fence, just outside the corral. He bent down— for what? To take it with him? Her throat betrayed her and he looked up. His eyes were searching, quick and deft, until he found her. Maybe he wouldn't recognize her with her silver hair?

It looked like he was swearing, stomping toward her in his boots. His tongue bulged behind his upper lip, pressing against the snus to release the nicotine.

Then he grinned and pointed at her, holding an index finger to his thin lips—shhh—before drawing his finger across his throat.

Death. She knew that meant death.

He went back to the snowmobile, took a pair of black gloves from his pocket, and swung his leg over the seat. He was unaware that he had pulled out more than just the gloves. The small, downy ear fluttered through the air and landed in the snow. It bore the mark that proved the calf belonged to their herd.

He revved the engine, releasing the stench of exhaust, but also something undefinable that made Elsa's nose crinkle.

She skied on shaky legs to where the man was last standing, removed her mitten, and picked up the ear. She wiped the snow away and got blood on her palm. It wasn't the whole ear; he'd cut off just the outermost part, where the marking was.

She glanced at the dead body by the fence.

It was Nástegallu—Elsa's reindeer. The white patch between her eyes, and her unusually long legs. Drops of blood covered her soft fur. Elsa's reindeer, without her earmark to show where she belonged. Elsa couldn't cry, couldn't scream. There was a frightening clamor in her head. The thought that one day she would kill the man who did this.

CHAPTER TWO

Guokte

Mom and Dad were whispering above her. She was tucked into the snowmobile sled, wrapped in a blanket. Her skis were under the reindeer pelt. No one was even thinking about how she'd skied all the way to the corral; no one said a word about it. Elsa closed her eyes. The snowflakes that brushed her face melted fast and the silvery frost in her hair was gone. She was herself again.

Her parents, her Enná and Isa, had found her sitting beside her reindeer. They asked what had happened, but she was mute. Inside her mitten she squeezed the little piece of ear. The blood had congealed but the fur was still soft. She didn't show it to them, even when they exclaimed, upset, that "that bastard" had taken the ears, all of one and half of the other. Sometimes you were required to show the ear markings to prove your ownership of a reindeer if it had been run over or killed by a predator. But she wouldn't let anyone have this ear. Her Nástegallu was dead.

Mom sat down beside Elsa and pulled her close. Enná was crying. Her mom always cried. She tried to stay calm, to wait until they were back home so she could shut herself in her bedroom where she thought no one could hear.

Dad and Mattias were taking gentle care of her reindeer. It had been dark for a long time, and Elsa couldn't see everything they were doing, but she could hear them mumbling.

"She must have seen them, or else they would have taken the reindeer," Mattias said.

"Oh no, they just want to kill and make sure we see it."

Dad walked around, aiming his flashlight at the snowmobile tracks. Elsa could have pointed out which way he'd gone and which tracks were his, but she couldn't lift her hand. It was as if the ear kept her still, weighing down her arm. She had seen the man make the sign for death, so she knew this was serious.

The beam of light bounced over snowbanks, sagging trees, and snowmobile tracks. Dad bent down and took several pictures on his phone. They had photographed Nástegallu too, before they moved her. Elsa was sure they had called the police, but they all knew no one would come tonight.

"We have to go now, Nils Johan. She's freezing," Mom said.

Elsa wasn't freezing, but she was trembling. Mom held her tighter and rubbed her whole body with a firm hand. It didn't help.

Dad hit the gas so fast they fell backwards on the sled. Mattias passed them on his snowmobile. He sped out into the drifted snow, his engine roaring through the forest. Elsa knew he was angry. You could always tell by the sound of his snowmobile. Soon his taillights were just two red points far across the lake.

Her hand fumbled under the reindeer pelt and found her skis. She felt their smooth surface. She would never ski to the corral again.

CHAPTER THREE

Golbma

Mattias found reasons to peek into Elsa's room all evening. She studied him, her big brother. Stuoraviellja. Seven years her elder, no longer a child but not grown either. In between—"gasku," as Áhkku liked to say. Her grandmother had a word for everything, but only in Sámi. In Swedish, Áhkku felt she had too few words, but sometimes she couldn't speak Sámi without having to mix in some Swedish.

The adults said Mattias was like Mom; he was tall like her, and they said he was so grown up. Elsa thought he had the face of a little boy. Mom and Mattias had the same dark hair and the same eyes, but Mattias's eyes were more watchful.

He dug through the wardrobe in the corner of Elsa's room but wouldn't say what he was looking for.

"Did you see him?" he asked without turning around. "Was it Robert Isaksson?"

She lay under the covers, the ear in her hand. She couldn't hold it too tightly, because then it got sweaty and wasn't as alive and as soft as it should be. But she didn't dare let it go.

"You have to talk, or they'll think you've gone crazy and need to go to the hospital," Mattias said, stomping around the room.

It was sweaty under the covers because Áhkku had turned up the heat in the room. She thought heat was the remedy for everything, rather than snuggling and being close, because she had trouble lifting her arms when she gave a hug. It was unsettling to hug someone who didn't hug back, but if Elsa lifted her grandmother's arms for her, she could keep them there. And sometimes her fingers moved across Elsa's back, almost shyly.

No one had mentioned yet that it was Elsa's reindeer, the one she had marked herself with the little knife she always had on her belt. Her fingers stroked the cuts in the ear. She could draw the ear marking, cut it in her mind, the marking that was hers, theirs, the family's. She let her index finger slip across the small edge of the cut, remembering how difficult it had been to make. The larger, round cut had been simpler, as had the one that cleaved the very tip of the ear by just under half an inch.

She truly did want to tell Mattias everything, but he would do something stupid—she knew it. That's what always happened back when he was in school. It was in self-defense, but no one cared and he was always to blame. According to Áhkku, Mattias was just like Áddjá at that age. Grandpa used to get into fights at school too. But Mattias would never be able to beat up a grown man. And never *that man*. He was tall, taller than everyone else, with broad shoulders and huge hands.

Stalking back and forth, Mattias rubbed his scalp with the tips of his fingers.

"All you have to do is nod, unna oabba. Nod so I know it was him."

Elsa lay perfectly still to keep herself from nodding by accident. To be on the safe side, she closed her eyes. But that made Mattias angry; she heard him snort. It was best to peek again.

Maybe she couldn't talk anymore. That's how it felt, as if the words would no longer allow themselves to be said. That scared her, because it was important to be able to talk at school. She cleared her throat, testing it out a little, and Mattias fixed his eyes on her. She didn't want to disappoint him, but she didn't want him to die either.

"Why did you have to go out there by yourself?" he snapped.

She swallowed hard, willing herself to think about something else.

CHAPTER FOUR

Njeallje

That evening, Dad cracked open the door to her room. Elsa shut her eyes and breathed calmly, as though she were sleeping. She knew it was him, had recognized his footsteps. He closed the door again, gingerly, but it still creaked.

When she could no longer hear anyone outside her door, she sat up in bed and let her eyes adjust to the dark. She pulled off her nightgown, which was stuck to her back. Goose bumps rose on her skin as she slipped silently out of bed and tiptoed to the window facing the lake. The wind blew hard, whining between the houses scattered around the lake. The streetlamp at the crown of the village had the hiccups. Its light flickered. The township had decided to stop lighting the lamps along the road that ran past their house. It was too expensive—that was the only explanation Elsa had heard—so only the more populated part of their village was well lit. At their house, which was farthest out and by the lake, Dad had installed lights that automatically turned on when someone entered the property. Now and then Elsa liked to sneak out onto the front steps when the darkness got to be too scary. The floodlight illuminated the whole yard so that no one could hide.

The house wasn't large. She and Mattias each had their own room, and Mom and Dad had their bedroom, although Dad mostly slept on the living-room floor on a mattress he rolled up every morning. Elsa could hear him snoring out there, and if she woke up at night to no snores she grew frightened and had to get up. Sometimes it turned out Dad was standing by the stove, holding a cup of coffee even though it was the middle of the night. His face was gray; his stubble was turning gray. All of him was getting grayer.

Áhkku and Áddjá lived next door. If she pressed her nose to her window, she could see part of their house. It was small too. Áhkku said it had been built by the state sometime in the fifties when reindeer herders were allowed to have a domicile and own property. Elsa didn't know what "domicile" meant, and Áhkku spit the word out when she said it. Elsa wasn't supposed to hear this sort of thing, but she did.

Áddjá had painted the house a sunny yellow. He wanted to build additions, but the men in town who made decisions about houses said no, so he built an equally yellow storage shed and often slept there. When Elsa stopped to think about it, not many adults slept together. But then again, the dads were often away for long stretches, following the reindeer on their natural migration paths.

Between the houses was the wooden goahti where they smoked meat. The chunks of smoked meat were suspended in long rows to dry in the wind in a cage on top of the roof of the shed. Elsa's mouth watered when she thought about the finished product, goike biergu. In their yard sat four-wheelers, trailers, two cars, two snowmobiles, and, under a tarp next to the shed, another old snowmobile that they really ought to sell. Their closest neighbor besides Áhkku and Áddjá had complained that their yard "looked like shit." Elsa had heard them call it "the Lapps' place." The neighbors liked to mow their lawn and plant flowers. They liked quiet, so when Gabo barked they got even grumpier. But dogs bark, everyone knows that. Elsa wished Gabo was in her room now so she could bury her nose in her fur. She should have brought her to the corral, sicced her on him.

Gabo was a mutt, but most of her was Australian shepherd. She was the best herding dog they'd ever had. She could smell danger a mile away.

Elsa leaned her head against the windowpane. She could feel the wind buffeting the walls of the house. Maybe it wanted to move them out of the way too, blow them somewhere else.

She heard mumbling from the kitchen and tiptoed over to the door, where she pressed her ear to its cool, white surface.

"We'll have to take shifts in the corral tonight." Dad's voice was sharp. He often sounded like that when he was on the phone.

"Every goddamn trace is blowing away as we speak, and of course the police say they don't have time to come." He paused for a moment. "I know it's Sunday, but since when did the police stop working on Sundays?"

There was silence, and then he spoke in a low voice. She could only hear the occasional snippet.

"It was Elsa's . . . found . . . Ears were gone . . . in shock."

Her cheeks felt hot. This was the first time someone had said it was her reindeer. It was like they'd been hoping she hadn't realized which one it was. But of course she knew. She was nine years old. She recognized her own reindeer.

Dad said his name: Robert Isaksson. Goose bumps covered her arms.

"No, Elsa didn't see him."

She threw herself under the covers and squeezed the rough duvet, which was new and uncomfortable. She hadn't lied. Not saying anything wasn't the same as lying. All she had to do was remain quiet.

CHAPTER FIVE

Vihtta

It smelled like coffee and wet dog in the kitchen, but Gabo had been let back outside. Elsa stifled a yawn as she sat down at the kitchen table with Dad and Mattias. As usual, Mom couldn't sit down in the morning. She was too antsy to sit with them at supper too. But she wasn't as bad as Áhkku, who always stood at the stove, frying another round of suovas or testing the potatoes with a skewer.

"I'll be right there," Mom always said when Elsa asked her to come to the table.

But by the time she finally arrived everyone was finished eating.

Right now she was rummaging in the freezer, trying to find the bread she'd baked last week. The coffeepot was whistling on the stove. Dad hurried out of his seat with an open-faced sandwich hanging from the corner of his mouth, the slice of cheese almost falling off. He pulled the pot off the burner. Mom shot him a look of irritation. She was good at giving him nasty looks. There were a lot of glances flying across the table that morning. Dad shook his head, probably unaware of what he'd done wrong. Men were seldom aware, as Áhkku often told Elsa. Áhkku was even better at nasty looks. She did everything just a tiny bit better than Mom.

"You'll have to come along to the police station," Dad said gruffly.

Elsa froze, her glass of milk at her lips, and looked at him. There were dark circles under his eyes and the whites of his eyes were red, but his chin was smooth and almost shiny. He had shaved.

"Why?"

"You have to tell them where you found the reindeer."

She glared at him.

"Right, your reindeer," he clarified. "I just want them to understand what you've been through. Maybe you even saw someone? Or . . . ?"

He ran out of air at that point. He couldn't bring himself to look her in the eye.

"This time they killed the reindeer just to harass us. And the police won't understand the difference. They'll think this is only about the money, if they even believe it's our reindeer." Mattias's voice trembled, but not because he was about to cry. He was angry, and Elsa didn't dare look at him.

"Stop it!" Dad snapped. "Not now." He nodded discreetly at Elsa.

"But it's true!" Mattias was rocking back and forth on the pine chair, balancing his juice glass in his hand.

Mom cleared away the butter, wrapped the cheese in a plastic bag, and dropped the cheese slicer in the sink. She put away the milk and juice, wiped up the crumbs, and took out coffee cups for herself and Dad.

Elsa drank her milk very, very slowly. She wondered exactly how illegal it was to lie to a policeman. Prison-illegal, or just a little illegal? According to Mattias, the police always lied to them, so why couldn't she do the same thing? She thought of the ear, which she'd hidden under the bed for the time being, buried beneath her clothes. She'd held it for a while before falling asleep, but she didn't want to risk keeping it in bed since Mom always woke her up in the morning.

The wall clock ticked loudly. Mom sat down.

"I think we should say it was Mattias who found it. She's too little."

The legs of Mattias's chair hit the floor, and he slammed his juice glass on the table.

"Definitely! I'll do it."

Elsa gazed longingly out the window at the big road. If only she were standing there right now, waiting for the bus with Anna-Stina, with no reason to think about the police or how she'd lost what was hers.

Mom rubbed her temples, and Elsa looked at the gray strands that grizzled her dark hair with silver streaks. Maybe Mom was on her way to becoming someone else too, like Elsa in the forest, because she didn't quite recognize her anymore. She cried a lot, and shouted even more, mostly at Mattias, who hunched his shoulders and slunk away.

People sometimes called Mom "rivgu," a word spoken by malicious tongues, a word to describe women who weren't Sámi. Mom wasn't from the village—she was "Marika from town." Elsa didn't believe all this rivgu stuff; after all, Mom spoke Sámi, sewed gákti herself and wore them too, and she was a reindeer herder. But she'd said she had to learn all of this when Dad decided he wanted to marry her.

"He'd made up his mind, yes sir, and you know that when Dad makes up his mind no one can change it," she laughed.

It had been a long time since she reminded Elsa how they fell in love. Now there was mostly just tension in the air.

Once Mom married Dad, and Mattias was born, the rivgu talk diminished. Mom also started to wear a gákti. Áhkku had explained that people didn't always use rivgu in a mean way; you had to listen carefully to how they said it. It might just be that someone was clarifying that she didn't have Sámi roots, because it was important to know who was related to whom. Still, Elsa didn't like the word "rivgu." And Mom had said people didn't know what they were talking about.

"I am Sámi too," she had whispered in Elsa's ear one night, back when she still read her bedtime stories.

Elsa, who had never suspected anything different, had absorbed this information in silence. And Mom had suddenly looked scared as if she'd told a secret.

"You're too little," she'd muttered.

"We're the same," Elsa replied firmly.

Mattias claimed it was impossible to remember anything from before you were six, but Elsa did.

She'd also heard that rivgu talk out in the village, when someone mentioned Mom in passing. When she came home and asked about it, Mom laughed at the old ladies and their gossip. It wasn't a real laugh, though, because Elsa knew how it sounded when it came bubbling up from your belly.

At around the same time, Elsa had realized that Áhkku and Áddjá actually had other names, and that Mormor and Morfar, her mother's parents, did too. "Áhkku" and "Áddjá" could mean a grandparent on either side of the family, but the Swedish words for grandparents couldn't.

Elsa had always been best at Sámi, better than at Swedish, so her tongue felt most at home with Áddjá and Áhkku. There, it was easy to talk and say what you wanted. It was difficult with Mormor and Morfar in town. School is where she learned to grow comfortable with Swedish. Even though it was a Sámi school, she had classmates who preferred to speak Swedish.

Once Dad arrived at her side and cleared his throat, she could no longer bury herself in her memories.

"Elsa is coming with me. If we start lying now, and it gets out, we'll never be believed or get any sort of justice."

He didn't wait for Mom's reaction. He just stood up suddenly to rinse out his coffee cup.

Mattias shrugged and sighed. Mom stared at Dad's back, and Elsa felt like her breakfast was coming up. She swallowed it back down.

Dad went to the bedroom, and Mom stood up and left the kitchen too.

"Elsa! Your room smells funny. Did you leave a piece of fruit or a wet towel in your bag again? What is that?" Mom asked with a displeased wrinkle on her forehead.

The ear! It must smell. She hadn't noticed it herself.

"Yeah, maybe I forgot something. I'll check," she mumbled.

Mom moved on to the bedroom and Elsa hurried to her room. Maybe it was a little smelly. She would have to take the ear out to the shed as soon as she got home from school. It would dry properly out there. She quickly emptied her little green box of necklaces and placed the ear in it. Then she put the box on the bookcase and laid two books on top of it. Surely that would keep any bad smells from leaking out.

She went back to the kitchen. Annoyed muttering came from Mom and Dad's room.

She leaned across the kitchen table so she could see the bus stop through the window. The sign was almost completely snowed over. The plow had come by that morning, piling the snow into huge banks.

Anna-Stina was standing on her own. There were only two girls in the village who went to the Sámi school, Anna-Stina and Elsa. The rest went to the Swedish village school, which was next to the Sámi school. Anna-Stina was two years older than Elsa, in the fourth grade, but they still got along. They didn't have a choice since there was no one else around.

She made up her mind, hurried into the hall and put on her coat, stuck her feet into the still-too-big boots without tying them, wrapped her scarf twice around her neck, tugged her red hat low on her forehead, grabbed her mittens in one hand and her school bag in the other—and she was out the door. The snow on the steps crunched under her boots and she jumped over the last one. The approaching bus echoed across the forest. The morning was so quiet that the bus could be heard from miles away. The cold nipped at her cheeks and her lungs contracted. It might be almost twenty below.

Anna-Stina waved as she made a dash for the road.

CHAPTER SIX

Guhtta

Mattias started the Phazer snowmobile, then pulled his neck gaiter over his nose and his hat way down over his forehead and ears. Only his eyes were exposed, and they teared in the cold air until he put his goggles on. He felt a chill and his movements grew stiffer, despite his outerwear. He wasn't freezing, though.

"Your helmet!" Mom called, just as he was about to take off.

"Eh!"

If he'd stayed at home for a second longer, he would have broken something. He was so goddamn tired of all of them. So fucking weak! Everyone knew who was stealing and killing their reindeer, but did they do anything about it? No!

He squeezed the throttle hard, and the sound of the engine and all the rumbling power beneath him was just what he needed. He carved a track between the birches, ducking and leaning into the curves to keep from getting stuck in snowdrifts. On the river he could go even faster.

He aimed for the dip to make the snowmobile fly. More than four hundred pounds of machine launched into the air. The snow swirled around him as he landed, and he had to tense every muscle to maintain control. It was his longest jump ever, and no one was around to see.

"Fuck!"

His roar echoed through the surrounding forest. He sped up, facing a long lane of snowmobile tracks. The river wound through the villages, tying them together. In the summertime he liked to drive the snowmobile on the river. Not even then did his heartbeat quicken; he knew what he was doing. He knew how much gas it took to keep him afloat. There was nothing he couldn't handle. He'd been driving snowmobiles since he was five, and the older he got, the more often he snuck out on his own. Sometimes it upset Mom, but Dad understood because he'd done the same when he was Mattias's age. In a calm voice he told his wife that Mattias needed to be able to drive. She protested—it was illegal. And she didn't stop protesting when he turned fifteen and it became legal. She was still just as upset every time he went out.

He slowed down as he approached the next village. Smoke rose from chimneys. He heard dogs barking as he passed a few of the houses. Otherwise the quiet was deafening; it was that particular silence that descended when snow blanketed the villages.

There was no real plan; he just wanted to go by the house, see what that bastard had done with the reindeer he killed. But there was always the risk that Mattias wouldn't be able to stop himself. He didn't get into fights if he could help it, but sometimes there was no choice. His belly was full of that smoldering sensation again. It wasn't a good idea to go on his own. He should call someone. It was common knowledge that Robert Isaksson was crazy, just like his father, who was a drunk. But there were two of them, and he was all alone. As this thought took root, he hesitated, which made him even more furious.

The Phazer hummed, idling. He pulled down his gaiter and leaned to the side, rocketing out snot.

What did it help, seeing his house? The police wouldn't give a shit this time either.

"Fuck!"

He yanked the handlebars sharply to the right. He turned homeward again, watched the speedometer soar.

CHAPTER SEVEN

Čieža

A sour smell wafted from the wet snow pants and sweaty fleeces hanging on the hooks outside the classroom. Through the window came voices, laughter, and shouts from the playground in Sámi and Swedish. Elsa dressed slowly, pulled her gray knit sweater over her head so her hair stood up around her face like a floating electric halo. Her bangs were slicked to her forehead.

She could see him out there—Markus, who was related to *him*. Mondays were the worst because they had recess at the same time. What if he knew what she had seen? Blood on the knife, the ear in his mouth. What happened to people who had seen too much? She had read what someone had written on Dad's Facebook. *The only good Lapp is a dead Lapp.* After that, she stopped reading Dad's page, even though she really wanted to see when he posted pretty pictures from the reindeer forest.

In the third kitchen drawer by the dishwasher at home, Mattias said there were documents from the police. In that drawer were all sorts of things you might need for various emergencies. Bandages, tape, scissors, Tylenol, magnifying glasses, fishing lures, blister kits, and bottle openers. You had to be careful with the red-and-yellow lures, to keep from getting caught on the hooks. Elsa had seen Dad operate on Mom after she got one stuck in her thumb when they were fishing in the river. You had to get rid of the barbs by clipping the hook where it bent, with pliers, and then pulling out the straight part that was caught in the skin.

Elsa had never seen the police documents, but she thought it might be a good idea to look at them now. Once, a police officer had come to their house and written details of their conversation in a notebook. They were talking about a slaughtering spot, which was weird because it wasn't even slaughtering season. That was the first time she'd heard a name that would pop up over and over again. He was dangerous, but she couldn't figure out why. Now she knew.

Robert Isaksson from the next village over was a reindeer killer.

She had asked Mom and Dad about the police officer in their kitchen. They had forced a little laugh, saying, "It's nothing, unna oabba." Unna oabba, little sister. When you were the littlest, you didn't need to know everything. It was as simple as that. They seldom called her Elsa, neither her parents nor Mattias. She was their unna oabba.

Markus was staring at the window. Elsa quickly slid down the bench, her heart galloping wildly. He was looking for her! If only Mattias still went to school. He would have protected her. She knew Mattias and Markus had fought the year before. Markus had had a lot of friends on his side, and they'd all kicked Mattias. He had a fat lip for a whole week. Dad filed a police report and called the school, but all he got in response was that boys will be boys.

She tied her laces with trembling fingers. The minutes ticked by. Recess would soon be over. Maybe she wouldn't have to go outside.

By now Markus had climbed the snowbank outside the window, and when he breathed on the glass it made a fog that slowly faded away until he was visible again. He was glaring at her. Under his chin was a cluster of pimples. He didn't make any threatening gestures. No, he just stared at her until she looked down at her feet.

A snowball struck the windowpane with such force that the sound thundered down the hallway. She jumped. Markus turned around, laughing, and vanished down the snowbank. Elsa kicked off her boots, pulled her legs onto the bench, and tucked herself into a little ball. She wrapped her arms around her calves and pressed so hard that she squeezed the air out of her lungs. Her forehead rested against her hard kneecaps.

"What are you doing?" Anna-Stina was at the other end of the hallway.

"I have a stomachache."

"Should I get a teacher?"

Elsa shook her head.

"Did something happen?"

Elsa pictured her reindeer, wished she had brought the ear to school. She longed to feel its softness in her palm. Suddenly she was crying. Her cheeks were wet, her nose was running, and deep down in her throat, it hurt, ached.

Anna-Stina took a few tentative steps forward. Elsa lay down on the bench, as if she no longer had the strength to sit up. Sweat broke out on her forehead; it took effort to cry this hard.

The classroom door opened and out came Marja, her teacher. She sank to her knees and brushed the hair out of Elsa's face.

"Mii lea dáhpáhuvvan? Anna-Stina? What's wrong?"

"I don't know. I just got here." Anna-Stina's voice was tiny.

Elsa was small for her age. Marja had no trouble picking her up and carrying her down the hall to the teachers' lounge. Elsa let her arms drop, her body suddenly lifeless. Marja smelled faintly of cigarettes. Elsa had always suspected that her teacher secretly smoked in the classroom. During recess she always opened the windows wide, even when it was freezing out. Elsa usually shivered when she came in and sat down on her cold chair.

As Marja lay her down on the red sofa in the teachers' lounge, many anxious faces flickered by. She heard them speaking in Sámi and Swedish. Someone said they ought to call her parents. Elsa shook her head vehemently. Marja stroked her hair. And once again the tears came pouring out.

"Oh, sweetheart, honey, what's wrong?"

Elsa grabbed the back of Marja's neck and pulled her closer. She whispered, "My reindeer was killed."

"What happened? Did it get run over?"

"No. She was murdered." When she said it aloud, it was so enormous that she tried to suck the words back in. She changed her mind but it was too late. Marja's eyes had already gone wide.

"Murdered?"

"Don't say it loud. Don't tell anyone!"

Marja dried Elsa's wet cheeks with her palm. She had reindeer too; she understood. Not everyone did, but Marja understood.

"I don't know if someone killed her. But she was bloody. And dead." She couldn't look her teacher in the eye as she told the lie.

Marja clenched her fist, but then she relaxed and stroked Elsa's forehead. "You're warm. You should have stayed home today."

Elsa nodded. Suddenly she was so tired and had to close her eyes. "Can I stay here until the bus comes?"

She opened her eyes, just for a moment, and saw Marja checking her watch.

"Don't you want me to call your parents to come get you?"

Elsa shook her head but kept her eyes closed.

"Well, get some rest then, and I'll come get you later."

She grabbed Marja's wrist. "Don't say anything about my reindeer. Not to anyone."

Marja nodded but looked displeased.

The hum of activity in the teachers' lounge was soothing and numbing. Elsa tried to stay awake, but it was impossible. It was like lying under the kitchen table when the grown-ups were talking. And the sofa, which smelled dusty, was so soft.

CHAPTER EIGHT

Gávcci

When Elsa woke up, Áhkku was there. She was a tiny old woman, not even as tall as the measuring tape in Mom's sewing kit. She was wearing a speckled knit hat, and the zipper on her blue down coat was halfway undone. Áhkku had pulled a chair up to the sofa and was perched on it, her feet dangling. She was wearing her best shoes, nuvtthahat, which she had sewn herself out of white reindeer hide.

She didn't look concerned in the least, the way all other grown-ups did when something wasn't right.

"What are you doing here?" Elsa asked.

Áhkku nodded back toward Marja, who was standing at the kitchenette counter and dipping a teabag into her mug.

"She called."

Elsa sat up and began sucking on a chunk of her hair. Anna-Stina always said it was gross to suck on your own hair, but Elsa often forgot and did it anyway.

"What did she say?"

"That you probably have a fever."

Áhkku leaned over and felt Elsa's forehead, then shook her head. Mom usually used her lips, pressing them softly to Elsa's skin.

"Let's go now," Áhkku said. She seemed eager to leave.

"Marja said you went here together. Back when it was a nomad school."

Elsa should have known not to say anything. Áhkku didn't want to talk about the nomad school. She thought it was unnecessary when people wrote books or even talked about the church and state-run schools the children of reindeer herders had been forced to attend. She often muttered that nothing good could come of dragging all that up again.

In the hallway, Áhkku began to breathe faster. She opened her coat, fanning both sides back and forth.

"Well, hurry up, go get your things."

Elsa took Áhkku's hand and tugged at her. Her knuckles felt like the sandpaper Áddjá kept in the garage.

"Don't you want to see my drawing? In my classroom?"

Elsa looked down the dark hallway. What if Markus was there? She pressed the light switch and the fluorescent tubes popped and flickered overhead as they came on. Áhkku grabbed the wall for support; tiny beads of sweat had appeared on her upper lip.

"Please," said Elsa. "You'll just have to stand here anyway. You can't leave me."

Áhkku nudged her between the shoulder blades and began to walk. Elsa immediately found the bounce in her steps.

Outside her classroom, she pulled on her snow pants and her coat, smiling at Áhkku all the while. Her socks bunched around her toes as she stuffed her feet into her boots. She took Áhkku's hand again and opened the door. The drawings hung in a row across the room. Elsa ran over and pointed.

"That's you! See?"

But Áhkku wasn't looking. Her gaze was steady on the floor, and she was gripping the door frame, her hands like claws.

Elsa was surprised, but she stood on tiptoe and pulled loose the pins that held her drawing in place.

"Look! That's you," she said, holding the paper close to Áhkku's face.

Áhkku peered with one eye and nodded. Maybe she didn't like that Elsa had drawn her in her black gákti. She should have chosen the blue one. She let her hand fall and walked back to the wall, her steps slow. The drawing ended up crooked after she pinned it up again, but it would have to do.

The cold hit them when they went outside. Elsa's nostrils felt dry and she had to cough. Áhkku was already in the car, and the exhaust turned into a mushroom-shaped cloud. The seat was cold and ice crystals had formed on the inside of the windshield. Áhkku attacked it with the scraper and muttered in a low voice as the frost flew down onto their legs and the gearshift. She got out and scraped the outside just as violently. She bellied onto the hood but still couldn't reach the middle of the windshield. A white string of ice remained. The heat was on full blast but it didn't help. The air was still ice-cold. Now Áhkku was scraping the rear window, even though Áddjá said it wasn't allowed. Back in the car, she didn't put on her seatbelt and stayed in first gear for too long. Áhkku couldn't see over the steering wheel; instead she peered through it like an owl.

It was black as night outside, even though it wasn't even dinnertime. Áhkku yanked off her hat and Elsa could see that her hair was all sweaty. She had coiled her long braid into a bun at the nape of her neck.

It was unclear whether Áhkku actually had a driver's license. One day she simply began to drive, Dad had said. Áhkku claimed she'd taken an intensive driving course in town a long time ago, but didn't drive until she thought it was absolutely necessary. And that time coincided with when Áddjá broke his leg in a snowmobile accident the same year Mattias was born. No one seemed to know if her story was true. Dad liked to say that they'd find out once she got stopped at a checkpoint. It hadn't happened so far. But then again, the police didn't much care about the villages.

"Your father called. We're going to the police station."

Áhkku finally had a clear view through the windshield, and she pressed the gas harder. Snow-heavy firs and birches bowed to them as usual, but they could hardly see them as they sped down the road. The snowplow had cleared the roadway, which looked wider than it was. Just a bit too far to one side and they might end up in the ditch. But Áhkku didn't care about that. She drove down the center of the road and made everyone else swerve around her.

An oncoming truck dimmed its high beams but Áhkku didn't bother to do the same. How else could I see if there's a moose? she typically murmured to herself. It's enough for one of us to dim our lights. The truck flashed its lights to remind Áhkku to turn hers down. When she didn't, he turned his high beams back on and it was like they were seeing the white light that would take them to heaven. The truck had headlights above and below the cab. Elsa and Áhkku felt like they were being struck by lightning, and they closed their eyes as the truck thundered by.

"What an idiot!" Áhkku snapped.

Elsa was blinded and couldn't see anything, even though her eyes were open again.

"I don't want to talk to the police."

"You only have to say that you found the reindeer, and where it was."

"That's all?"

Áhkku cast a quick glance her way.

"Is there more?"

Elsa curled her lips over her teeth and bit them from the inside.

"Did you see him?"

Áhkku had almost caught up with another car, and didn't dim her high beams this time either. The other driver tilted their rearview mirror and appeared to be waving a hand in irritation.

"Did you?"

Elsa counted how many people she had lied to at this point. Áhkku was a Christian as well, so it might be extra bad to lie to her.

"No."

They drove past the village and Áhkku was looking at her house instead of the road.

"Áddjá hasn't plowed the yard."

Elsa couldn't tell as they whizzed by. Motion sickness began to creep in and she looked for a salty candy in her coat pocket.

"Can't Dad just say I found the reindeer? Mom said that's what we were going to say."

Áhkku snorted.

"I told him it doesn't matter if you talk to the police, or if he does. They won't care either way."

CHAPTER NINE

Ovcci

The police station was in the center of town, past the community center. It was surrounded by snowbanks and the lights were on in three ground-floor windows that faced the street. Áhkku parked careless and crooked just outside the three-story red-brick building. Dad's Kia was a little farther on, and he was leaning against the passenger door with his arms crossed. His fleece hat was pulled low on his forehead, and his breath made white puffs in the cold air. The temperature had fallen fast and was approaching thirty below. It hurt to breathe, and Elsa pulled her scarf over her nose before opening the car door. Áhkku didn't lock the car. She just slammed the door as hard as she could and rounded the front, hurrying toward Dad without waiting for Elsa, who trudged after her, kicking up snow from the sidewalk.

Dad held the station door open; Áhkku walked through first, with Elsa following slowly after. She stared stubbornly down at the shiny black stone floor. With a little luck maybe she would crash into something, fall down, hit her head, and pass out. If she was really lucky, she would lose her memory altogether.

Dad stood by the counter, which came up to his chest. Elsa could tell he was standing slightly on tiptoe, in his big boots, to appear taller. She often did the same thing when the gym teacher at school divided them up into teams by height.

Elsa wasn't visible over the gray counter. Maybe the police officer could see her reindeer antler-print hat. The antlers were reflective if you shone a light at them.

There was a buzz like at the clinic when the window at the reception desk opened. Dad introduced himself in an authoritative voice she didn't recognize.

"Do you have an appointment?" asked the woman behind the counter.

Elsa didn't like her tone. That's how it sounded in some places, when they came in wearing gákti. But none of them were wearing gákti right now, although Dad had his leatherwork belt on. It hung slightly askew, low down on his hip, and had round eyelets in white, yellow, and red. He'd come straight from the corral. His knife wasn't hanging from the belt. You took that off; even if you were just getting gas, you knew to leave your knife in the car. And of course, you couldn't bring a knife into a police station.

"I spoke with Martin Henriksson this morning and said that I would be coming by with more information for a police report."

"Concerning?"

Elsa backed up a little so she could see the woman, who was aiming a sour look at Dad. She had sharp black lines around her eyes, and her dark hair was pulled back in a tight ponytail.

"A reindeer that was killed at the corral."

"Name?"

"Nástegallu."

Elsa's voice was clear and steady. Dad, Áhkku, and the woman looked at her. Dad closed his eyes for a moment and took a deep breath.

"It means 'white spot,'" she clarified.

The woman clucked her tongue.

"I meant your name."

Dad responded in a less authoritative voice while the woman typed at the keyboard.

Elsa lowered her head and leaned against the counter. She felt like spitting on the floor.

"I'm not sure he has the time. In which case, I can take the information," the woman said.

Elsa glanced up at Dad and shook her head. She would never speak to that person again.

"We need a good officer," Dad began.

"I see."

Elsa thought her voice sounded like sheets of ice creaking against each other in the spring, when the thaw had begun and the current wanted to open up the river.

"I just mean we need an officer who has experience with children. My daughter is a witness."

Elsa suddenly needed to pee so badly that she couldn't wait. She took a few steps toward Áhkku and whispered that she needed to go to the bathroom.

"Where's the bathroom?" Áhkku asked loudly.

She didn't like speaking Swedish; she had trouble making the intonation and the consonants come out right. According to Áhkku, Swedish was missing the melody of the heart.

The woman sighed and pointed past the red chairs in the hallway. Elsa stumbled over and yanked the door open, barely managing to pull down her snow pants in time. She sat there for a long while, then got up and washed her hands three times. She looked in the mirror and stuck out her tongue, spat a big glob onto the floor.

When she came out, a policeman was holding open the door to a long hallway. Dad was already on the other side, but Áhkku was waiting for her. Elsa looked up at the officer, who was over six feet tall. He held out a cool, dry hand that enveloped her skinny fingers.

"Elsa, is it?" he said with a smile.

Her eyes opened wide. The policeman had braces. He had to be as old as Dad, and he had braces. She couldn't wait to tell Anna-Stina.

The hallway was long, with doors on either side, some open, some closed. Music was playing somewhere. Elsa tried to look into each office. To think there were so many police officers in town. No wonder they never had time to come to the village, if they all had to sit in offices and type on their computers.

Martin Henriksson's office was the very last one down the hallway. He sat behind his desk with Dad across from him. There was only one other chair, so Elsa sat in Áhkku's lap. It had been a long time since she'd sat in anyone's lap, and Áhkku tensed her thigh muscles as if she were trying to make Elsa bounce right off.

They learned that Henriksson was new at the station. That was why the room was so bare, the bookcase almost empty, and the windowsill without flowers. He had just moved home again after going to school in the south and working in Stockholm. Elsa waited on tenterhooks to spot his braces again, but Henriksson hardly opened his mouth when he spoke.

"So . . . ," he said, pressing a key on his keyboard. "Further information, was it?"

Dad nodded. He had taken off his fleece hat and opened his coat. Elsa wasn't about to take off her hat. She was ready to pull it down over face if necessary. Áhkku liked to talk about God's trials and how everything happened for a reason. Elsa had decided a long time ago that God wasn't for her, and when Nástegallu died she was totally convinced of it. She wanted to scream at Áhkku and ask why *her* reindeer had to be killed. What was the reason behind Elsa having to sit here and be interrogated by a policeman? And be forced to lie. It came over her again: she was about to lie to a policeman and a Christian áhkku. She couldn't even look at Dad.

"So, Elsa, I hear you're nine years old. So you can read and write, of course," said Henriksson.

She snorted. She could read and write by the time she was five. Áhkku stiffened under her bottom and pinched her in the back.

"Yes."

"What's your favorite subject in school?"

Elsa pursed her lips. Why did he want to know that? When she didn't respond, Henriksson smiled and she stared into his mouth.

"I was best at recess!" he said cheerfully.

"That's not a subject," she muttered.

He closed his mouth and she sank back against Áhkku, who gave a start.

"And you have reindeer. Is that fun?"

She nodded, and Áhkku seemed to hold her breath.

"As I understand it, you skied out to the reindeer paddock by yourself on Sunday. Well done! Because it's a long way to go, isn't it?"

Elsa looked down at her hands. The skis were back home in the garage, and she hadn't touched them again. Didn't even want to look at them. But she missed them.

"Can you tell me what happened that afternoon, when you were skiing? Was it cold? Were you chilly?"

Martin Henriksson leaned back in his leather office chair, which came all the way up to his head. The muscles of his upper arms tensed under his pale blue shirt. His dark hair was styled in a crew cut, and Elsa wondered if it would feel like petting a hedgehog.

Now she was thinking too much again, and forgot what had been said. Luckily, Henriksson repeated his question.

"It was pretty cold. But I wasn't chilly. I was sweating."

"Sure, that's what happens when you go skiing," said Henriksson. "Was there anyone around when you got there?"

She heard laughter in the hallway. And here she'd thought everyone at a police station was angry and strict.

"Are there children in the jail?" she asked in a thin voice.

Her knuckles turned white as she grabbed the arm of the chair. She almost had to pee again.

"No, absolutely not. Children can't go to jail."

She swallowed hard. Then the only one left to punish her, if she lied, was God. And she didn't believe in God anyway.

"There was no one there," she said firmly.

Dad and Henriksson exchanged glances, and Henriksson rubbed his chin and nodded slowly.

"Okay. Well, what did you see when you got there?"

Now it wasn't lying anymore, but it was still hard to say.

"Mu miessi," she whispered. "My calf."

Henriksson leaned forward and rested his elbows on the desk. He was too close, and she pressed back against Áhkku, who in turn pressed herself back into the chair.

"Tell me about it."

"She was bloody. Dead."

Dad's knee was bouncing up and down. When he did that at home, the whole kitchen bench would shake.

"Did you go up to it?"

Elsa nodded and looked straight at Henriksson. Now it was true, everything she was saying.

"And what did you see?"

"She had been killed. There was blood on her fur. Her eyes were afraid, even though she couldn't see anymore."

Dad's knee stopped abruptly.

"And that made you sad," said Henriksson, tilting his head to the side.

She nodded and had to look away from him.

"Where was your reindeer?"

"On the ground, next to the fence. Outside the corral."

"Not inside it?"

"No, outside."

"So someone purposely took the reindeer out of the corral to kill it," Dad said, resting a heavy hand on her shoulder. "Elsa was forced to see her reindeer, dead."

Henriksson didn't look convinced.

"Could someone have left the gate open?"

"Not a chance," Dad said, letting go of her shoulder.

Henriksson turned his gaze to the computer screen.

"Wounds on the throat, it says here. From a knife, you say. But couldn't the animal have gotten too close to a sharp part of the fence?"

"Out of the question," said Dad. "And that doesn't explain how it ended up outside the corral. And without its ears." Dad leaned to the side so he could shove his hand into his pocket and take out his phone. He looked through his pictures and handed the phone to Henriksson.

"And we found fresh snowmobile tracks, like I said."

"Yes, those are snowmobile tracks, I can see that."

Elsa listened carefully, because Henriksson's voice wasn't the same now. Not like when he was asking her about school.

"Right, we called you, the police, but no one came."

"We were busy dealing with a car accident in town. And also, our snow-mobile helmets were past their inspection date."

Dad's jaw muscles tensed; he took a deep breath.

"I'll get you the pictures. We know for certain that these tracks aren't from any of our snowmobiles."

"But it can't be that easy to just go in and take a reindeer from the corral. They're timid—at least as far as I recall. I spent a lot of time around the corrals as a kid. My best friend had reindeer," said Henriksson.

"If you have food in your hand, they'll come," Dad said, his voice rough and tired.

"Is it such a good idea to feed the reindeer? How does it affect the meat? I heard it's not as good."

Dad didn't respond. He took his phone back and pressed his lips together.

Elsa felt Áhkku's heart beating against her back, faster and faster. But she was sitting perfectly still.

"If you'd come out with us yesterday, you would have seen which direction these tracks were going," said Dad.

Elsa thought of how Nástegallu would come when she held out the reindeer lichen. And she finally got to pet her.

"Unna oabba, leat go sihkkar ahte it oaidnán ovttage?" Dad asked in Sámi. Are you sure you didn't see anyone?

She shook her head without looking up.

"Mus lea gožžahoahppu," she whispered. I need to pee.

"Fas?" Again?

"You know I don't understand Sámi, right?" said Henriksson.

"She needs the bathroom," said Dad.

"There's one next to my office. Go right ahead."

She slid off Áhkku's lap and walked, her legs unsteady, out of the office and into the bathroom. It smelled bad, and she had to hold her breath. Dad's voice flared up and she pressed her ear to the wall, but couldn't hear any better. She flushed an empty toilet and quickly washed her hands.

When she came back out, Áhkku was already walking down the hallway. Dad was standing stiffly beside Henriksson, and they were conversing in low voices. When they shook hands, it looked as if they were trying to beat each other at arm wrestling. Then Dad folded a sheet of white paper in his hand.

"What's that?" Elsa asked.

Henriksson offered his big hand again.

"You were a big help, Elsa. Maybe you'll want to become a police officer someday. We need brave girls who aren't afraid to ski on their own in the dark."

She rolled her eyes, even though that wasn't allowed. She tried to squeeze his hand as hard as he'd squeezed Dad's.

Henriksson closed the door behind him, and she and Dad walked down the hall together.

"What is that piece of paper?"

"It's a copy of our police report. Another theft."

"A theft? But she was killed, not stolen. Shouldn't it say killed, or murdered?"

"It's hard to explain."

"Will the police catch whoever did it?"

They arrived at the glass door where Áhkku was waiting.

"No, that might be hard to do."

They walked past the reception desk and the woman fixed her eyes on Elsa, who glared back.

"Did you and the policeman get in an argument?" she asked Dad once they were outside the station.

"No, but I agree with you—it shouldn't be called theft. It should have said something else. And they should have come out to the corral." He fell silent and unlocked the car door with a chirp.

"Thanks for this, Enná. See you."

Áhkku nodded but didn't move. Elsa wanted to give her a hug, but instead she just leaned against her upper arm. Áhkku smiled. "You did a good job. Not everyone can talk to the police."

She left before Elsa could respond. Dad opened the car door, and as he belted her in, as if she were little again, he rested his forehead against hers.

Good thing it's dark, black as night, so no one can see the tears, Elsa thought. And it was a good thing that children can't go to jail. She would tell Anna-Stina tomorrow.

CHAPTER TEN

Logi

The kicksled creaked beneath her. It went fastest in the center of the road, where the surface had been plowed and packed into hard ice. Elsa wasn't technically allowed to use the kicksled in this part of the road, but she could hear the cars coming from far away and could make it into the ditch before they approached. She shoved off with her right foot, her left foot balancing steady on the runner. She held on tight to the handles, closing her eyes as she kicked as hard as she could, and zoomed down the road. It felt like she was flying.

School was closed for the day, and she was riding the kicksled back and forth, waiting for Anna-Stina to wake up. She always slept in late.

The sun peeked out from behind foggy clouds, barely clearing the treetops. The snowmobile tracks leading to the corral were like a wide street across the ice. Mom had wanted her to ski there instead, but Elsa couldn't put them on again. Maybe she never would. She didn't say so, just shook her head sullenly, closed the door, and dashed to the kicksled.

On her seventh pass, she heard snowmobiles in the distance—Dad and Mattias were on their way home. They'd gone out to the corral early that morning. They were almost always there, these days. Since Nástegallu died, they mostly came to the house to eat. Dad slurped meat stew and ate Mom's gáhkku in silence. Mattias did the same, but with headphones on. Elsa and Mom were quiet too.

The snowmobiles pulled slowly into the yard. Dad and Mattias took off their helmets and sat for a moment, speaking in low voices.

"You know you're not allowed to kicksled down the middle of the road!" Dad called.

She slowly slid toward the ditch, still kicking, but the runners got caught and she could no longer fly. Anna-Stina had to be awake by now. Elsa turned onto the road on the left and pushed the kicksled up the hill. This was the best hill in the village to ride down. But Mom and Dad said it was super dangerous, because it ended up on the big road. You could always skid at the last second and run into the snow in the ditch, though. When it was soft and fluffy, it was like falling into a cloud. But parents didn't understand things like that.

ANNA-STINA WAS STILL SLEEPING, but her mother, Hanna, invited Elsa in with the same warm smile as always. It smelled like freshly baked cinnamon buns with a hint of the meat stew that had been simmering for hours. The kitchen window had fogged over.

Anna-Stina's uncle, Lars-Erik, whom everyone called Lasse, was sitting in his usual spot with a view of the hill Elsa had just come up. He had a coffee cup in his hand and a tin of snus in front of him on the table. You might think an eanu would be old, but he was only a few years older than Mattias. Sometimes the two of them hung out, waking up the whole village when they motocrossed to the river rapids. Sometimes he helped Dad, and during those times Mattias wasn't as surly or difficult. Lasse was the youngest of four siblings, a surprise baby—a váhkar, as they said. But when you were the youngest of four, and the third boy, it was hard to become the head of a household with a vote in the reindeer collective. Hanna was the oldest of her siblings, but of course there was no chance that the girl in the family would take over her father's reindeer lands or become head-of-household. But it all worked out when she married the neighbor boy, who was also from a family of reindeer herders.

Elsa had asked Mattias why Lasse couldn't work with the reindeer as much as everyone else did, and he had told her that Lasse wasn't very rich in reindeer; he didn't have enough of them to make a living that way. But when she asked why Hanna wasn't allowed to become head-of-household, he only rolled his eyes in response.

Some people said Lasse was happy enough with how everything had turned out, and now and then he left the village and didn't return for weeks. Sometimes he was very tan when he came back. Sometimes he returned with lots of money and would take Mattias out for pizza in town. Elsa was never allowed to tag along. But now he had his eyes on her. He grinned and she couldn't help but laugh. He was the funniest out of all the grown-ups. Maybe because he wasn't entirely grown up yet. He rebelled with motocross, and stayed up all night, gaming with Mattias.

He took out his phone and showed her a picture of a big sand dragon on a beach surrounded by palm trees.

"Think I can make one just like this on our beach this summer?"

She shook her head, grinning.

"I made this one when I was in Crete, I swear."

She giggled and shook her head again.

"You did not!"

"You'll see, next summer when the beach turns up."

The softest sand was hidden in the river like a treasure only the villagers knew about. When the meltwater from the mountains had run through and the rains had abated, the river had a chance to subside. And then it appeared. The beach. First as a shadow beneath the water, and finally as a small island that grew larger by the day. The sun warmed and dried the sand until it was golden. Then they hopped in boats and set out for the island. They lay on towels, closed their eyes, and pretended they were in another country. When they got attacked by horseflies, they splashed into the icy water for some relief. There were sun-warmed puddles, into which the children released sticklebacks they'd caught in their nets. Elsa thought the water in those puddles must be warmer than the Mediterranean.

Hanna's glass clinked as she stirred chocolate powder into milk. Elsa smiled, took the glass, and drank it in huge gulps.

"Do you have a boyfriend yet, Elsa?"

Lasse sometimes had a walleye, like now, but she knew to look at his right eye, because that one was holding still. Not drifting off like the other one.

"No way! I don't like any boys."

"That's good. No one is good enough for Elsa, princess of the village!"

Hanna sighed. "You're so full of crap."

"I'm hungover," Lasse whispered to Elsa.

Even though she didn't understand, she nodded as if she did. Lasse whispering to you was a big deal, so you had to nod and look serious. He laughed again as Hanna snapped a dish towel above his head.

The cinnamon buns were swirls of heaven, Elsa thought as she gobbled down her third one.

Hanna sat down next to her and ran a hand over Elsa's long, dark hair, which reached just past her shoulder blades. The back of her neck felt shivery.

"I heard about your reindeer," she said gently.

Elsa stared down at the table, at the crumbs she ought to scrape together with her palm.

"It's really too bad," Hanna continued.

Lasse grunted. "Too bad doesn't cover it. Messed up, is what it is."

The princess of the village nodded quietly but didn't look up.

"But it was brave of you to go to the police," Hanna said, her voice rising a perky octave.

"The police. What a joke!"

"Lasse," Hanna said in a low voice.

"Yeah, yeah," he sighed.

Then they heard footsteps on the stairs. Anna-Stina was wearing her pink nightgown and the bright red ragg socks she'd knitted in crafting class.

The girls cuddled up next to each other on the bench. Anna-Stina's eyes were puffy and she gave a big yawn. Elsa pressed up against her; she was warmer than the sun.

Lasse got up and stretched, groaning as he did.

"Well, I'm off. Thanks for the coffee, sis."

"Where are you off to?"

"You never know. But there are plenty of people waiting for me. Doors open everywhere."

He winked at Elsa, who couldn't make up her mind whether to wink back. He was already in the hall, the moment gone. She heard him whistling as he was putting on his shoes and coat.

"See you, cuties!" he called before he opened the door and the cold air swept through the kitchen.

Hanna leaned over the table, wiped some of the fog from the window, and watched him go. She was shaking her head slightly but also smiling. Elsa knew he was skidding off so that snow flew up behind the green Volvo.

HALF AN HOUR LATER, Elsa and Anna-Stina were lying side by side, their faces flushed with the effort of digging a snow cave. By strict order from Hanna, their feet remained outside the opening. There had to be legs to pull on in case the snow collapsed on top of them.

Inside their cave the air was dull and it was quiet. The only sound came from their tiny gasps. The ground was cold beneath their backs, but their sweat was still warming. When Elsa moved, a hot gust escaped her collar.

"I saw a grown-up with braces," she said.

Anna-Stina rolled her eyes and Elsa shrank. It was hard to surprise someone who was going to turn eleven soon.

"So what? I've seen lots of grown-ups with braces."

Elsa ran her mitten along the wall of snow.

"I went to the police station yesterday."

This time Anna-Stina turned her head.

"Is that a lie?"

"No! It's true. I got interrogotated." She hesitated. "Questioned."

"It's called 'interrogated.'"

But Anna-Stina wasn't acting superior this time, only eager for Elsa to get to the point.

"Was it because of your reindeer?"

She nodded.

"The police asked what I saw."

Elsa took off her mitten and dug in the pocket of her snowsuit until she found the ear. She both did and didn't want to take it out.

"So what did you tell them?"

"That Nástegallu was dead and bloody."

"Dad thinks it was Robert Isaksson."

Her hand stiffened around the ear. She didn't like hearing his name and didn't like that Anna-Stina was the one saying it out loud.

For generations, Elsa and Anna-Stina's families had belonged to the same reindeer collective, the same čearru. They were cousins—not first cousins, but it didn't matter, a cousin was a cousin. At home, Elsa's family had the genealogy book that showed how all Sámi families in their area were related, close or distant. She and Anna-Stina each had their own page, and you could determine their family relation by way of numbers and codes. Even though Mom had shown her, Elsa didn't know how; it was too complicated. The important thing was, Anna-Stina was her cousin, her oambealli. To have your name in a book, imagine that! Elsa liked to take it out and run her finger over her name and birthdate. And follow the steps back to Áhkku and Áddjá and their parents and back through centuries she couldn't even imagine. Mom was in a different Sámi family book, but her family didn't want to acknowledge it. Still, it was proof that Mom wasn't a rivgu. She existed, just like everyone else. But there seemed to be a difference, between existing and not existing. No one had explained to Elsa how the invisible borders had been drawn, and she didn't ask either.

"I'm sure it's Robert. He's the one who shoots reindeer, chases them down on his snowmobile, and tortures them. Once someone cut the uterus out of a cow. While she was still alive. And beat the calf to death."

Elsa stared at Anna-Stina. Cutting out the uterus, where a calf was waiting to be alive?

"I know," she said, her voice full of spirit even though her heart was pounding and her ears were ringing.

"Yeah, everyone knows. They're filling their freezers with reindeer meat. Selling it."

Elsa slowly pulled her hand from her pocket, leaving the ear behind. She closed the zipper.

She'd heard about reindeer getting killed, but not like this. Had Nástegallu been tortured before the knife went through her fur and reached her beating heart? Elsa got dizzy and felt like she couldn't breathe. They must have run out of oxygen in their snow cave. She quickly sat up and scooched forward until she was out and could take deep, cold breaths. Anna-Stina wriggled out backwards like a centipede, which normally would have made Elsa burst into laughter.

"What's wrong? You're all pale."

"Nothing."

"What did they do to Nástegallu?"

"Stabbed her with a knife."

"I once saw the intestines on the outside of a reindeer they cut open."

Elsa stood up and ran for the kicksled. Anna-Stina called after her. But she was already going fast, and she knew the downhill slope would take care of the rest.

CHAPTER ELEVEN

Oktanuppelohkái

H anna stood at the kitchen window, watching Elsa run to the kicksled and hurtle down the hill. Anna-Stina stayed behind, staring after her. Hanna recognized the angry, hurt look on her daughter's face all too well.

She opened the window and called out.

"What's going on? Why did Elsa go home?"

"How should I know?"

"Come inside."

Angry little feet stomped into the hall, and outerwear ended up on the floor instead of being hung on the hook. Her daughter's nose was running and her cheeks were bright red. She sat down on the kitchen bench, a haughty look on her face and defiance blazing from her eyes.

"You have to be nice to Elsa. Remember, she's younger than you."

"But I am nice!"

"So what happened?"

"Nothing."

Hanna gave her a kind smile; she knew just how to wheedle something out of her daughter.

"Come on, sweetie. Tell me what happened. I won't be mad."

Which was true, she was seldom mad; she would never dream of raising her voice to her own child or anyone else's. But she didn't like it when Elsa and her daughter fought, and when they did she came close to using a sharp tone of voice. She had the urge to protect that serious little honeybun from her own daughter, who could, unfortunately, be domineering.

"I only said that it's Robert Isaksson who kills reindeer. Well, it's true! I don't know why she got like that."

"Well, she's really sad about her reindeer. Don't you understand that?"

"But she started it! She's the one who told me she went to the police station."

Hanna handed her a sheet of paper towel. Anna-Stina looked offended but grabbed it and blew her nose noisily.

"What did you say, exactly?"

"I said he cuts reindeer open and takes out the calves."

Hanna stared at her for a moment.

"That was maybe a little brutal."

"But it's true, I know it is! I've seen their intestines."

"But sweetheart, she's only nine. You shouldn't say such scary things to her."

"Well, it's not like it's my fault there are idiots who kill reindeer!"

Hanna slowly shook her head. She suddenly felt close to tears and had to turn around. This wasn't like her.

"You're right about that, honey."

"Now I don't have anything to do! There's no one to hang out with!"

Anna-Stina's whining struck at Hanna's guilty conscience. Always this issue of friends, living far away from them and spending so much time on her own. She looked at the clock—she'd probably have time to drive Anna-Stina to the next village.

"Do you want to go see a different friend?"

"I don't want to live here! I never have any friends!"

Hanna let her wallow in self-pity. Just last week she had a whole gang of girls over for a visit, giggling in her room. But it was always quickly forgotten, and there was drama every time her loneliness set in. Every lonesome second in this house was drama to Anna-Stina.

"So maybe you should call and apologize to Elsa?"

Her daughter snorted. No, an apology was not on the table. It seldom was.

Hanna curled up on the bench beside her daughter, put her arms around her slender body, and stroked her hair. She would probably begin to resist in a few years, refuse to accept hugs, so Hanna took every chance she got.

"But next time I'm sure you'll remember that you're older so you know a lot more. And there are some things a little nine-year-old doesn't need to hear."

CHAPTER TWELVE

Guoktenuppelohkái

N othing could make Elsa go to the corral, no matter how much they pleaded. And once the snowmobiles left the yard, she was determined. First she went to the shed and checked on the ear, which she'd hidden in the far corner behind Dad's toolboxes, where she knew cold air came in through the cracks in the floor. There it would dry quickly and lose its odor. Each day she went to the shed to feel the soft fur and see if it was finished drying. Often she took the ear with her, just so she could feel it for a while.

Once she checked the ear, she went inside, full of just as much purpose, and opened the third drawer down by the dishwasher, cautiously removed the fishing lures, and found the bundle of documents at the very bottom.

There were difficult words and many numbers, but she read what was there and looked for Nástegallu's name, but couldn't find it. She did recognize the description, though, and she read it aloud.

"Deceased reindeer found at reindeer corral, outside the fence. Knife wound to the heart. Ears cut off. The complainant's minor daughter found the reindeer. Snowmobile tracks present."

Her mouth stumbled over the words, and she didn't understand what "minor" meant or how to pronounce it. She smoothed the paper out against the kitchen counter but it wanted to curl up again. She ran her index finger over the word "daughter." It wasn't like seeing your name in a family book. Why didn't they write that the reindeer's name was Nástegallu?

She continued to flip through the documents even though her body felt uncomfortable; the discomfort got worse when she read about a pregnant cow who had been chased down by at least one snowmobile. The tracks indicated that the chase had gone on for about five hundred yards. The cow had been run over and one of her hind legs broke. It said that she died of internal injuries.

Her hands trembled as she made her way, whispering, through the next page.

"Someone chased down ten of the owner's reindeer with snowmobiles, ran them over and killed them, and removed them from the scene. The complainant went out to check on the reindeer. In the forest he found traces of blood, antlers, and fur. Two snowmobile tracks, one pulling a sled, led down to the river and in the direction of the next village."

The next village. Where *he* lived. She held the paper so tight that it crumpled. They had found blood, antlers, and fur. Ten reindeer. Why hadn't anyone told her?

Perhaps that was the time Dad came home from the forest and was so angry that he punched the door of the shed. He had a bruise on the knuckle of his middle finger for days.

At the bottom of the page, Dad had written something in pencil; she recognized his round handwriting. *Preliminary investigation closed!!* She didn't know what that meant.

She had to lie down on the cold kitchen floor. She was small and, some might say, downright skinny. When she lay on her back, her hipbones stuck out like two sharp mountain peaks on either side of her sunken belly. She could, if she wanted to, dig her fingers up under her rib cage. But Mom didn't like that. Now she could see a pulse jumping right between her ribs. Fast, fast, fast.

When she sat up again, she knew what she had to do. She put her shoes back on and went out to the shed. She took the ear, and in Mom and Dad's bedroom was last summer's bealljebinnát, the small pieces of ear they saved after earmarking the calves, all strung on a sinew thread. She had sat beside Áhkkú when she was stringing them on. "It's so the calves can stick together," she'd said. Elsa had solemnly handed her the bits of Nástegallu's ear and told Áhkku that they should be at the end of the thread, so she knew which ones they were.

You couldn't go around bragging about how many calves you had marked, Áhkku said, so the bealljebinnát must not be hung anywhere in plain sight. But today Elsa lay them out on the kitchen table and stroked the soft little bits of fur. When she came to Nástegallu's, she took the ear, which was almost completely dry, and held it close. It was as if lost puzzle pieces snapped into place, becoming whole again. Nástegallu was whole again. That was how she felt, even though she knew it wasn't true.

CHAPTER THIRTEEN

Golbmanuppelohkái

They shuttled back and forth, taking turns around the clock. Dad, Mattias, Anna-Stina's father, Ante, and her uncles on both sides, and Elsa's dad's brothers. The men and the boys. It was so quiet once they left the house, but somehow it was just as quiet when they came home again. They made sandwiches and stood by the kitchen window to eat them, their eyes gazing into the distance. It was as if they were looking past the snow-mobile trail on the ice, past the trees, straight into the reindeer grounds. As though they were out there even though they were home. They were never truly home. They stood in the yard, loading up sleds, gassing up the snow-mobiles, pressing one nostril closed as they rocketed snot out the other. Their fingers were stiff; some of them would probably never completely straighten out again. Body parts ached at night and Dad limped in the morning. But even worse was the fact that sleep was never deep enough.

Elsa lay on the sofa, stretching out her legs until her toes brushed the white coffee table. The prickly blanket was red with a big reindeer on it. Mom didn't like it, but it had been a fortieth birthday gift from her home-care colleagues, so she couldn't exactly get rid of it—what if they dropped by for coffee? It was an insult to all the actual Sámi handicrafts they had around the house. All the duodji Áddjá had made. And Áhkku and Mom sewed the most beautiful gákti. Elsa had never had to use a hand-me-down one; she always had new ones. She could sew too, her fingers almost as deft as the grown-ups'. She had the patience for it, as well.

Dad's phone buzzed on the living-room table, and he shouted from the bedroom that she should answer it. Elsa hadn't even said hello before the voice spat and hissed into her ear.

"It's all your fault! Your family's goddamn reindeer! I'll kill every last one of them."

She held the phone away from her face, hardly able to breathe.

"Our new car is a total loss and I'll be damned if the wife hasn't got whiplash! And do you even care? No, because now you'll get a payment for your goddamn dead reindeer!"

She threw the phone onto the sofa and stared at it, squeezing herself into the corner among the pillows.

"Isa, come quick!" she called.

He hurried in, sliding her way in his sock feet and grabbing the phone.

"What's going on?" A pause. "I understand, but . . ."

He went to the kitchen, but Elsa could still hear the enraged, metallic rasp from the phone pressed to his ear.

"Where did you hit it?"

His voice was steady, but he was losing his patience.

"I'm sorry to hear that, but . . ." Another pause. "Yes, I know, but you have to understand that you're threatening me, and I will be filing a police report."

Mom had just come in and was fluttering about, unable to keep still. One moment she was in the kitchen shushing Dad, and the next she was in the living room, turning up the TV.

"Sure, go ahead and report me. Go right ahead," Dad said.

Silence. For a moment. Then came the muttering. Mom and Dad. It came in waves, quiet but with heft on the consonants, sometimes a word or two that went above a whisper. Mom's shushing, always her, never him.

The sound of shoulders wriggling into a snowmobile suit, a zipper going up, and then the chilly draft of air coming in to touch Elsa's bare arms and disappearing just as suddenly. The headlights of a car sweeping across the living room.

"Who was that?"

Elsa asked loudly enough for Mom to hear in the kitchen. There was sniffling. Of course. So Elsa must not sniffle too. That would be one too many people crying.

"Just someone from the village, unna oabba."

"Not the next village?"

"No."

That was all she said.

Half an hour later, blue lights flickered across the living-room walls. Elsa quickly leapt to her knees, grabbed the back of the sofa, and pushed herself up to see. An ambulance, with lights but no siren. Good thing it wasn't past five yet, because then the ambulance wouldn't have come. At five the paramedics packed up and went home; then you had to wait for the ambulance from town and that could take over an hour.

The reindeer herders always put out warnings when there might be reindeer running loose near the corral. Black garbage bags fluttered and snapped in the wind, attached to the orange reflective stakes that lined the road. But still some drivers shifted into higher gear. Far from all of them— most of them slowed down, turned on their high beams, and kept a sharp eye on the forest. But others got angry. Why should they have to look out for the Lapps' goddamn reindeer? Yes, that was when it slipped out, that "Lapp" slur.

She pulled the blanket over her head, thinking that tonight she would check the front door an extra time. Sometimes Dad, who was up the latest, didn't lock it. Áhkku never locked it. She also put the broom in the door when she left home, to signal she was out, instead of locking up. Elsa had noticed that sometimes Mom trudged over to their yard late at night and locked the door with their spare key. Especially that summer when there were rumors about organized gangs robbing houses in the villages.

Mom rifled through kitchen cupboards, filled pots with water, turned on the radio, but didn't manage to turn it off before the reporter talked about the accident on their road, one person with minor injuries. Elsa didn't learn how the reindeer had fared, because by then Mom had turned it off. The pan sizzled and the scent of frying suovas spread through the house.

The front door opened and Áhkku came in. Without taking off her shoes, she sat down on the old storage chair closest to the hall, the one under the clock. That chair was for people who came for a visit, without quite visiting. Mom liked to say that sometimes you just wanted to belong for a little while, to have a place where you could sit quietly and feel less sad and alone. It didn't happen as often anymore. Not since old Per-Niila had gotten too poorly to come. He used to look in a few times each week, until he turned ninety-four. He would sit there sipping his coffee from the saucer, as the old folks did, saying nothing but watching Elsa carefully as she sewed at the kitchen table. Saying "hmm" now and then, and reaching out with his cup to ask for another refill before he went on his way, and sometimes he waved at her. But he was probably the last of his kind and now it had been months since he'd come by.

"It was the Johanssons," Áhkku said.

"Yeah," Mom said, lowering her voice. "They called, furious."

Elsa removed her blanket and went to the kitchen; now she wanted to hear. For real. She sat on the kitchen bench and looked first at Mom and then at Áhkku, but they didn't say anything. Mom turned her back.

"They had to put the reindeer down," she said.

"They always drive too fast on that straightaway," said Áhkku.

"Yeah."

Mom fried the suovas, and grease spattered on the fan on the wall. Áhkku took out a bag of ribbons to be sewn onto the holbi, the broad hem of a gákti. She held them up and Mom nodded, grabbing them on her way to the fridge. She dropped the bag on the counter next to the microwave.

"Set the table, unna oabba," she said.

Áhkku had bandages on her index finger and thumb. Sometimes her knife slipped. When she was sick of the softer crafts, she picked up the knife to do some woodcarving. And if she cut herself it didn't matter because Áddjá had the ability to stanch blood. You weren't supposed to talk about it much, how Áddjá could think about how the blood should stop flowing and then it happened. It was only natural, nothing remarkable about it, but Mom often said that there was no need to talk about it with other people, or anyone at all, in fact. Áddjá could also blow on hurting spots and the pain would stop. Sometimes people came to his house for help, and lots of people called. But that was stuff you weren't supposed to talk about.

"Did you cut yourself again?" Elsa asked as she set the table.

"Oh, only a little bit."

They heard engine sounds in the yard, but Dad didn't come inside.

"Well, I'll go see," said Áhkku.

Two little puddles were left behind by her chair. Mom wiped them up with a paper towel and sighed.

Dad drove out of the yard again and Áhkku didn't return. Elsa saw her make an agile leap over a snowbank and head home.

Mom was making a racket with some ladles that didn't fit in the second drawer.

"Well, guess it's just you and me," she said, holding out the frying pan and poking the thin rounds onto Elsa's plate.

"You can peel the potatoes yourself."

"I'll eat the peels."

"No, you practice peeling now."

The boiled potato burned her thumb and tears sprang to her eyes.

CHAPTER FOURTEEN

Njealljenuppelohkái

"Robban, hey man! Long time no see!"

Robert stopped mid-motion as he was pulling his wallet from his back pocket to pay for his betting ticket.

Some people called him Robert, others Isaksson, but in that case there was a chance they meant Pop. Robban, though—no one had used that nickname for probably twenty years, since he was around twenty years old. He frowned and looked over at the magazine rack.

"Petri."

Right, he recognized the guy. Petri Stålnacke. He hadn't changed much, a little round, his legs short and stout, a thick, dark shock of hair, and big eyes.

"I'll be damned. Haven't seen you since that forestry job," Petri said with a smile.

"I've been here the whole time."

"But they never did make a timberman out of you, did they?"

Robert didn't want to get bogged down in the past, so he changed the subject.

"What are you doing here?"

"I'm in the market for a cabin," Petri said. "You don't know anyone who's selling, do you? Or a piece of land, maybe?"

"What business would you have up here? Do you still live in town?"

"Yeah, I'm still there. I work in the mine. But I'm getting sick of spending weekends in town and it's such a drag only visiting Ma in the village so I thought I would find a place of my own."

"So you pick our village."

"It's good fishing I'm after, and I know what a great river you've got for salmon."

Petri mimed casting out a fishing line.

"Yeah, I caught a forty-pound one this past summer," Robert said.

"Forty! I'll be damned. Wonder why I haven't seen you around, I've been fishing here a few summers in a row now."

"It's a long river, and I've got my spots."

Petri chuckled and nodded. "Sure, I can imagine."

Robert swiped his debit card.

"So where do you work, then?" Petri didn't seem to want to give up.

He took his time putting the card back in his wallet. "Disability leave. My back."

"Oh, shit, that's too bad. Has it been long?"

Robert looked around to see if anyone was listening, feeling his irritation grow.

"Yeah, it has. It's a chronic thing."

Petri shook his head, a sympathetic look on his face. "Oh no. That's no good."

Robert put his wallet in his back pocket and pressed his tongue against the snus tucked behind his upper lip. He didn't like being pitied, yet he kept standing there with Petri. It was kind of hard to dislike the guy. He wasn't the smartest, but he was kind. Just as he remembered him.

"I'm all right. I pick up some odd jobs on the side. As much as I can get away with, without someone alerting the insurance agency."

Petri laughed. "I get it."

"I'm afraid it's the wrong time of year to be looking for a cabin."

"I thought maybe someone might have gotten tired of theirs, in the middle of winter like this."

Robert allowed himself a crooked smile. "Yeah, who knows."

"Let me know if you get wind of someone who wants to sell, will you?"

Robert nodded. Sure, he could keep an ear out.

"So where do you live?"

"A little ways into the forest, not right in the village."

Petri smiled. Was he expecting an invitation? Robert said the polite thing.

"You should drop by for a cup of coffee sometime. It's up past the hill back here, after about a quarter mile you take a right and drive to the end of the road. A red house with a big barn."

Hardly anyone ever came for a visit. And Pop wouldn't let them in if they did. Whenever he saw a car coming, he was out in the yard in no time. Robert would probably have to do the same if Petri got it into his head to stop by.

"No niin," he said, and gave Petri a quick nod as he left the store.

CHAPTER FIFTEEN

Vihttanuppelohkái

A smooth piece of bright blue woolen fabric lay on the kitchen table, and on top of it the ribbons they'd bought in the next village. They'd been trying to decide how to arrange the ribbons on the holbi, which was red. Some of the ribbons shimmered in the overhead light, while others were matte, but the white would look good against the red. It was pitch-black outside, and their faces were reflected in the windowpane. Elsa had never liked being so clearly visible, while she herself couldn't see anyone looking in.

She sighed and ripped out the stitches that she had sewn wrong. Her work was seldom good enough. Mom put on her reading glasses, which made her eyes big. Their fingers brushed each other lightly as Mom helped her remove the stitches. She smiled at Elsa, who seized the opportunity to lean against Mom's upper arm. They re-pinned the red ribbon with blue glitter. Not too much glitter, Mom had said, that wouldn't be right. But Elsa liked glitter and always snuck in a ribbon that Mom would frown at and remove. Elsa would wear this gákti to the Winter Market in Jokkmokk. They were usually working against the clock, sewing until the night before they had to leave. Polishing the silver brooches and sometimes crying with exhaustion. All those scrutinizing eyes, Mom always said. Elsa didn't understand; for her it was better than Christmas Eve, better than her birthday, to show up in her new clothes and see those eyes on her. Anna-Stina would have a new gákti too. Their choir would be singing at the market. She hadn't heard from Anna-Stina since they built the snow cave. She hadn't been at school, either. The flu, someone said.

Mom held pins in her mouth and worked with a steady hand, only slightly trembling if Áhkku was watching.

"This is probably pointless," she would sigh. "You grow so fast, by next year it'll be too small."

But Elsa didn't want her older cousins' hand-me-downs. Especially since now she would get to sing in the choir too.

The low clatter of the sewing machine sped up and slowed down. The seams had to be straight. When Mom reached for the measuring tape, the faint odor of sweat wafted by. Her hair was unwashed and she put it up with a brown butterfly clip. Strands of her bangs fell over her cheeks. The palest cheeks in town, Áhkku liked to say.

The phone rang, and Mom lifted the blue fabric and, with a little smile in the corner of her mouth, answered. She leaned back on the kitchen bench, removed the hair clip, and laughed. It was Siessá, Aunt Ella. It had to be for Mom to sound like that. Elsa knew the rhythm of their conversations: when Mom was listening quietly and tossing in an occasional "nu go lea" or just a "juoa" of agreement, or when she was the one talking and hardly pausing for a breath between sentences.

Siessá had taken Mom under her wing when Dad decided to marry her. She was Dad's sister, and had left their reindeer collective for her husband's, which was farther south. But for a long time she was still there, looking after Mom, teaching her how to tie her shoe bands properly and how tight the buttons on her belt should be, and letting her speak a little backwards Sámi without correcting her too harshly. Otherwise it was only the dogs and Mattias who were allowed to hear Mom's whispering Sámi, and anyone could do that—anyone could call a dog or ask a child to look at the light or come eat. But Siessá gently encouraged Mom and didn't correct her like the language police, she said. Elsa had always wondered who those people were, and was greatly surprised to learn that one of them was Áhkku. Mattias had laughed out loud when she asked where Áhkku worked as a police officer. And then nothing more was asked or said about that, either.

Siessá lured and coaxed the words out of Mom, and one day she stopped whispering and spoke up.

Siessá looked like Áhkku, short and skinny, but with Áddjá's sharp nose and bushy eyebrows she was something different. And no one laughed like her, at everything, for way too long. She had fled from Áhkku's Christian nonsense as soon as she was able, when she had to leave the village to go to high school in town. People said she had lost some of her laughter there. There were holes in the story that Elsa tried to fill in, but when her questions weren't answered her imagination took over. Siessá's laugh came back as soon as she came home again, was all anyone said. In the summer, when they went up to the mountains to mark the calves, it was Siessá who welcomed the grounds with her laugh. She only said that when she was feeling extra bold, because as Elsa and everyone else knew it was the other way around—the grounds welcomed *them*, and it was important to feel gratitude for what nature gave them and the reindeer. Elsa knew exactly where everyone had walked before her, what these places were called, and what they meant. Above all she knew what it was like to wait to see her reindeer—her special boazu, the one among the thousands in the big herd. She could only pick out a reindeer like Nástegallu because of her unique markings. Dad and Mattias could recognize many more. But now she would never get to look for Nástegallu again.

Elsa grabbed one of the sparkliest ribbons and began pinning it to the holbi, next to a yellow ribbon. Anyone could see it looked prettiest that way. Siessá wouldn't have protested; she would have said that Elsa could do as she liked. But Enná had to be cautious, because she might be called rivgu again at the drop of a hat.

Mom laughed aloud beside her and Elsa's heart sang.

CHAPTER SIXTEEN

Guhttanuppelohkái

It was early morning when Elsa and Mom boarded the bus to town. It was barely half-full and Elsa smiled to herself when she spotted open seats at the very back. She liked to sit by herself and imagine that she was grown up and traveling somewhere on her own. Mom sat at the front so she could chat with the friendly bus driver, the one with the big mustache. There were two of them; the other one wasn't as cheerful and never offered more than a curt nod in greeting.

Each day the bus passed through the village, taking children to their schools and villagers to town in the morning, and bringing them back in the afternoon and evening. On the way into town, the bus traveled through villages big and small. Some didn't look as they once did. Paint was flaking on porches, and old shop signs were bleached by the sun and battered by the rain and snow. Barns had sagging roofs and windowpanes as thin as the most fragile crystal flutes. But there were also villages where optimistic newcomers painted their houses a brilliant white, got out their trampolines even before Midsummer, and bought a kerosene-powered mosquito fogger that ran around the clock all summer long. Outside those homes stood cars, four-wheelers, kicksleds, and tractors, and in the dog run was an eager companion just waiting for moose-hunting season.

They didn't take the bus to town often, but on a day like today, when it was snowing heavily, Mom preferred not to drive. There was a party for Elsa's aunt in town, but there wouldn't be many in attendance because the corral needed guarding. No one had said so out loud, but Elsa understood.

She rested her forehead against the cold window and exhaled until there was a foggy patch she could draw on.

When the bus stopped in one of the villages, Robert Isaksson got on. Elsa saw his yellow work pants and his black knitted cap that was perched off-kilter on his head. But she didn't have time to get up, to run to Mom. She shrank into her seat, listening as the steps came closer. She had never heard his voice, but now he greeted someone in Finnish, a few rows ahead of her. A man rumbled his answer in both Swedish and Finnish, which meant that they had to continue in Swedish. They knew each other, of course, and were aware of which language the other preferred. In the villages you knew, simple as that. They knew one another's language, whether they were related or not, and whose dad had beat up whose in the schoolyard.

From between the seats she caught a glimpse of his pants and a black coat. He didn't sit down beside the other man but spread himself out across the opposite seats, on the other side of the aisle. His hard consonants shot out in a rat-a-tat as he talked about hockey. He tossed in a few Finnish words that were simple enough for Elsa to understand. He extended one leg into the aisle; his boot was black and the laces were untied. He gesticulated a lot as he spoke, and he frequently scratched the back of his head through his cap, which he didn't remove.

Elsa leaned cautiously to the side, looking for Mom. The bus driver turned up the radio when the news came on. Two reindeer were run over, said the reporter.

"Voi helvetti! Last week Johansson almost died and now this again. When are they going to get those goddamn reindeer under control?" he said irritably.

"Oughtta keep the shotgun in the car to shoot them."

"No niin, tietenki. I'd do it in a heartbeat."

Elsa looked down the row of seats and to the side, and there was Anette, who was a substitute teacher at the village school. She gave an audible sigh and shook her head.

Then there was silence, aside from a tin of snus opening and closing.

"You don't usually take the bus, do you?"

"No, ei! But I had to this time," Robert said. "The goddamn ignition is acting up. I don't quite trust it, so I left the car with a friend here in the village and I'm heading into town for parts. We'll see how fast he can fix it when I get back this evening."

Streaks of light appeared over the river as they crossed the bridge. The snow wasn't as heavy and they could have taken the car. If only they were in the car right now.

There were ice-crystal patterns on the bridge railing. A woman on a kicksled, just past the abutment, veered as far onto the shoulder as she could.

Elsa heard them talking again, their muttering soft but threatening.

"The Lapps shot a moose on our land and hauled it over to their side."

They were riling each other up like wolves. She put her hands over her ears; she didn't want to hear any more.

Suddenly he stood up and glanced across the seats, and she pressed her forehead to the window and stared out. From the corner of her eye she could see that he was wriggling out of his coat.

"Turn down the heat!" he shouted to the driver.

She thought she could smell him, the gasoline and cigarettes. It was as though he was crowding in on her, using up all the air on the bus.

Soon he would spot her, and then what would he do? She had to make herself tiny, almost invisible. She lay down across the seats, drawing her knees to her chin. She was small enough to curl up, but her shoes were probably still visible. She held her breath until her lungs were ready to burst.

CHAPTER SEVENTEEN

Čiežanuppelohkái

Once she was certain he was no longer lingering outside, Elsa walked slowly down the bus. The driver's teeth were hidden beneath his mustache.

"Oh, no school for you today?" He smiled.

"No."

"Nice to have a day off then?"

"My auntie is turning forty, so we're going to help out before the party."

"Forty? Well, that sure deserves a celebration."

She wanted to tell him that Dad and Mattias couldn't come because they had to guard the reindeer. But she didn't know what the bus driver thought of that kind of thing, so it was best not to talk about it. In fact, it was best not to talk about most things, if you asked Mom. No good could come of bringing up your business around people you didn't know. So Elsa just smiled and said goodbye before jumping over the front steps and out of the bus.

Mom was talking to Anette; the concern was visible on both their faces. Elsa kicked at the snow, bent down to try to make a snowball, but the snow was like sugar.

A police car cruised slowly by, and she was almost sure that Henriksson was in the passenger seat. Dad hadn't mentioned what happened after their visit to the police station, but there had been talk about how Robert would have to be caught in flagrante. She would have to ask Anna-Stina what "in flagrante" meant. If she could muster up the courage. She still couldn't stop thinking about gutted calves lying dead on the ground.

Elsa stepped into the snow that bordered the sidewalk and stomped around until she had made a heart. She was just about to make an angel in the middle when Mom called out that under no circumstances was she to lie down in the snow. She could hear that they were talking about racists and nutjobs. Mom muttered something inaudible and Elsa cartwheeled in their direction to hear better.

"We think Robert Isaksson was the one who killed the reindeer at the corral."

"No doubt about that! Who else would it be? And Elsa, did she see him?"

Elsa cartwheeled right into a snowbank and found herself sitting with snow on her hat.

Mom shook her head.

"Too bad. But isn't it strange that he didn't take the reindeer?"

Mom turned and looked Elsa right in the eyes, as though she were seeing her for the first time in a long time. Elsa threw herself onto her back and let her arms flap as though she were possessed, her legs too.

By the time Mom was standing over her, arms crossed, Elsa's muscles were stiff with effort and she was panting.

"What did I say? No snow angels. Now you're all wet."

"Am not. The snow is dry."

Mom reached out a hand and pulled Elsa to her feet. The snow fell off her like grains of rice. Only the back of her knitted hat had any snow, and Mom brushed it off a little too hard.

The snow crunched beneath their boots as they walked toward the center of town.

"Who's racist?"

"You shouldn't eavesdrop."

"What does 'nutjob' mean?"

"Elsa, that's enough."

THE AUTOMATIC DOORS AT ICA SLID open with some difficulty because of the snow. Mom grabbed either door and shoved them apart. It was warm in the grocery store and it smelled like freshly baked bread. Elsa longed to go back to the time, not so long ago, when she could ride in the cart. Mom cruised between counters and shelves, selecting liters and liters of milk and cream. Once the cart was full enough not to tip, Elsa hung on one side until Mom snapped that she was too heavy to turn the cart. She stopped, closed her eyes for a moment, and apologized—she was tired, hadn't gotten enough sleep.

"Why didn't you get enough sleep?"

"That's just what happens sometimes. I'm sure it was the full moon."

"There wasn't a full moon."

"Well, almost."

Mom texted her sister, who would be picking them up.

"Why doesn't Auntie do the shopping herself?"

"What is with you and your thousands of questions today?"

Elsa grabbed a Twix bar and tossed it into the cart. Mom kept pushing. Elsa tossed in three more. Mom didn't stop, but she did give a loud sigh.

Next to the checkout was a rack of newspapers. Elsa read the boldest headline. "Three reindeer tortured to death." She tugged on Mom's arm and pointed.

"Don't even ask."

"But where did it happen?"

"I don't know."

Mom placed their groceries on the conveyor belt. Elsa fingered the newspaper, trying to flip to page four unnoticed. Mom's hand was on her shoulder, firmly guiding her away.

"Bag these. Heaviest things at the bottom."

She took out her purse and looked for the debit card, punched in the PIN, and didn't speak to the cashier at all. The receipt was long and she stuffed it into her coat pocket. They bagged their groceries in silence.

"But, Mom . . ."

"Not here."

When the doors jammed again, Mom, who was now carrying three bags, turned to the girl at the cash register with a snarl in her voice.

"You need to clear this snow away!"

She began wedging one shoulder in the gap and using the weight of her body to ram the doors open. Elsa kicked at the frozen mounds of snow.

"It's turned to ice."

"I know."

Auntie flashed her high beams from across the road. She drove a little Honda, and her head almost touched the roof. Auntie was tall, and often wore her henna-dyed hair up in arrangements that made her look even taller.

They hurried across the road. Mom tossed the groceries in the trunk and Elsa hopped into the backseat. Auntie smiled and extended her hand so they could touch.

"Sweetheart. Unna oabba! It's been ages."

Unna oabba was the only thing Auntie could say in Sámi, and it always made Elsa's stomach weak. Auntie's name was Angela, but Elsa always called her Auntie.

She was younger than Mom, and seemed to come from a different world. Mom would always mutter that she was from the exact same world as them, but wasn't quite made for small-town life. She was destined for something bigger, somewhere far away.

Mom yanked the lever and the passenger seat flew back with a lurch.

"So nice of you to do the shopping. I mean, I'm just so stressed out, with the venue and all that. And I have to make it to the salon and I haven't even put on my makeup yet."

The car was cold as ice and flowers of frost had formed on the inside of the backseat windows. Elsa used the nail of her index finger to etch her name in it.

"Why is it so cold in the car?"

"I don't know, something's up with the thermostat."

Auntie made a sharp U-turn and sped up the little hill.

"Party tonight, unna oabba!"

Their eyes met in the rearview mirror and Auntie winked.

"You know we'll have to head back before then," Mom said.

"You're such an old lady. You could stay for the party, you know."

"No, I can't, and you know it."

"That's what happens when you marry a reindeer herder. It's like being single eighty percent of the year, Sis." Auntie laughed her hoarse laugh and clapped Mom on the shoulder. "Just kidding!"

"I appreciate it an awful lot."

That made Auntie laugh even harder.

"But seriously, Marika, she's got her grandmother and grandfather, she could have spent tonight with them."

Elsa wrote a bad word in the frost. Her index finger ached. Grandmother and grandfather. Those names felt wrong in her mouth. She knew Áhkku had offered to watch her, but she didn't dare tell Auntie. She was sure Mom had her reasons.

Auntie was different, not like anyone else in their family. No kids and no man in her life. Or way too many men, Elsa had heard people say. Worst were the whispers about how none of them had stuck around long enough and that's why she had no kids and now it was too late.

When they got to the apartment building, they hugged and Mom said happy birthday. Elsa couldn't stop staring at Auntie's multicolored finger-nails with glitter at the tips. They were long and must make it totally impossible for Auntie to use her hands. She pinched Elsa's cheeks and kissed her forehead. Even her hands smelled like perfume and a little like vanilla ice cream.

Her apartment was on the second floor of a three-story brick building that had blue balconies. The walls were white, there were pictures hung everywhere, and the lamp in the living room was covered in billowing feathers. The rugs in the hall and the kitchen were gray, but the one in the living room was purple and so fluffy that Elsa had to take off her socks to feel it between her toes.

Mom and Auntie stayed in the kitchen, and it wasn't long before the hand mixer was going. It was time to bake. Auntie sighed and said there was no need; she'd bought a chocolate mousse cake from Coop.

Elsa lay on the sofa and pulled a big, soft, white blanket over herself; her head sank deep into a pink sofa pillow. Everything her fingertips gently stroked was soft. Mom complained about stinky garbage and soon the apartment door slammed. Auntie came in right away and collapsed on the sofa next to Elsa, who giggled.

"I could lie here all day," Auntie whispered.

"Me too."

Elsa swallowed the lump in her throat and clung tight to her aunt. Auntie laughed at first, but then she hugged her just as tight, and they lay there in silence. It wasn't fair that she was so alone and didn't get to have any children of her own to sing to her on her birthday. The apartment door opened and closed again. Auntie grinned and pulled the blanket over their heads. They heard the sigh, and Mom's firm soles on the living-room floor, but she let them be. Soon the hand mixer was humming again.

Elsa wanted to tell Auntie about her eighth birthday party, how no one showed up. That she had also been the lonely one. No one dared to come because Mom had called around to say that Elsa had thrown up in the middle of the night. No one from her class had been invited anyway, and Mom had frowned at that, but Elsa had stood her ground, saying that she only wanted to invite her cousins. And then no one came at all, even though she wasn't throwing up anymore. But at the stroke of three, there was a knock at the door. In stepped Lasse with one gold party hat on his head and one in his hand. A little fanfare that made her and Mom stop short and look at each other in astonishment. Without a word he stepped forward and fastened the hat on her head and flicked her nose lightly, then bowed.

"A princess without her hat is no princess at all! Ollu lihkku ráhkis, Elsa! Happy birthday!" And from his coat pocket he fished out a small pink package with gold ribbon and handed it to her. From his other pocket he fished out a mask.

"I borrowed this from my dentist. Not because I'm afraid of germs, but to protect you from mine."

Elsa could recite his words as though they were lines from a movie.

Inside the package, which was—to be honest, Lasse had to confess—from Anna-Stina, was the silver ring she'd wanted more than anything else. When Mom presented the cake, Lasse poured sequins all over the table, and they sparkled and fell to the floor and into Elsa's lap and she laughed until she could hardly breathe. Then he poured some in her hair too.

All afternoon he told stories that probably weren't entirely true, but he made Mom laugh so hard that she had to wipe her eyes. Elsa had never seen her laugh like that before. It was like she was a different mom. One she wanted to keep forever.

CHAPTER EIGHTEEN

Gávccenuppelohkái

When Nils Johan and Marika got married, neither Elsa nor Mattias existed yet. But that didn't mean Elsa didn't know all about that day. She had forced Mom to tell her what it had been like, in great detail, many times over. The older Elsa got, the more she asked to hear the story. And these days, when she thought about the wedding, it almost felt like she had been there too.

The young couple had put up gigantic tents in the middle of the village, enough to fit five hundred guests. There wasn't room for all of them in the church, but everyone could get food in the tents and Mom shook hands with so many people she'd never seen before. She didn't wear white, but nor did she wear a gákti—she didn't dare. She'd had a dress made that resembled a gákti, with blue fabric that had narrow bands of red and yellow at the hem, around the V-shaped neckline, and at the ends of the sleeves. Not the broad bands like on Dad's family's gákti, but as close as possible. This wasn't just about doing things right; it was also about not insulting her own family. In her family there were those who had long since shed both their given surnames and their ancestral roots. But each time Elsa asked why they would do that, Mom responded with an evasive "That's just the way it was."

Siessá, who had become almost like a sister, had polished the risku and fastened it at the center of Mom's chest. Elsa liked this part of the story, when Mom told her about the brooch that jingled whenever she moved, and how proud and joyful she felt to hear it jingling for her as it had done for all the women in Dad's family. The risku was becomingly small. The women on the northern Norwegian side wore the largest brooches, and their gákti were the most sparkly and their ribbons were wider than anyone else's.

Mom's family vanished among all the colors. They sat in the first row on the left side of the church and the rest of the relatives were in the two rows behind them, like a little gray stain in a sea of blue and red. But they sat with their heads held high, proud and moved. Who was better than whom could have become the subject of a heated debate, but on that day everyone fell in line. Even Mom. Still, there was whispering in the pews, because you could never please everyone. Someone had asked if Marika knew what she was getting herself into, but, as Mom said, Nils Johan was the one. They'd danced all night long and walked hand-in-hand through the village at the break of dawn.

Elsa had seen the wedding pictures and was grumpy that Mom couldn't have waited for her. It was the party to end all parties, the kind they only threw on Dad's side. Elsa had been to other massive family festivities, walked around in a new gákti with her shoe bands wound so tight up her calves and her brooches pinned on a shawl that sat not an inch out of place. That was how she liked it.

ELSA STOOD IN THE doorway to Auntie's living room and there was no comparison between a party on Dad's side and one on Mom's. Sure, Grandma was wearing her good floral blouse and Grandpa was wearing black jeans instead of blue ones, but it was nothing like how a party *could* be. Elsa would have liked to wear her flowered gákti, but whenever she brought up wearing gákti when they were going to town, Mom's face always got tight and she pretended not to hear. Parties in town could be fun, but they were simply different. It took more than glitter on your fingernails to have a good time.

Auntie waved Elsa over, and even though she was too big, she sat down in her lap. They giggled and their arms got tangled as they tried to eat some cake. Her tongue wasn't fighting her as much anymore; Elsa could quickly switch between Swedish and Sámi.

At the party were Grandma, Grandpa, Mom and Auntie's cousins, and their aunts and one uncle. Just as well that Dad wasn't there, because things always went sour between him and Mom's uncle. They always ended up talking about reindeer and road salt or hunting and land use. It was like the air was made of barbed wire.

Auntie looked at the clock for the tenth time. She lifted Elsa off her lap and began to collect plates and spoons. Grandpa chuckled and said, "Oh, I see you want to get rid of us."

They hadn't sung for her yet, and Elsa found this so sad she could die on the spot. It was no birthday without the birthday song, and the thought that Auntie had woken up alone, and stayed that way until Elsa and her mother arrived, was unbearable. So Elsa began to sing softly, not loud enough for the buzz of voices to fall silent. She sang from her belly and suddenly everyone else stopped talking to join in. Auntie came hurrying back from the kitchen exclaiming "Oh, unna oabba!" and took Elsa's hand while they sang. They shouted the customary four "hoorays," and Auntie curtseyed deeply and laughed aloud.

There. Now Elsa could go home without an ache in her chest. Grandma picked her up, pinched her skinny collarbones, and sighed, shooting Mom glances, to no response.

"When are you going to come stay the night with us again? It's been so long," Grandma said, braiding Elsa's hair.

"Soon."

Grandma took hold of her wrist, her thumb and index finger encircling it with room to spare.

She frowned. "You're nothing but skin and bones."

Elsa looked at her wrist and tried to encircle Grandma's, but she couldn't reach even halfway. She was like a nicely baked bun: warm, soft, and sweet-smelling.

"She looks just like me when I was little, don't you remember?" Mom said, stroking Elsa's arm.

"You're still scrawny. That's why you have more wrinkles than me."

Grandma laughed so that her round belly bounced, and Mom stuck out her tongue but smiled.

Elsa felt sleepy; Grandma's soft arms had lured her in many times. Her eyelids drooped, and she had to close her eyes.

Mom and Grandma waited for her breathing to slow.

"I think she was crying under the blanket today," Auntie whispered in passing.

"Things have been a little hectic recently."

"You have to let her talk to someone about the dead reindeer. It was such a shock," said Grandma.

"If I have to take her to a counselor every time we find a dead reindeer, I'll have to get a punch card."

"Do you know who did it?"

"The police refused to come out to the corral. There were snowmobile tracks. I'm sure they could have followed them all the way to his house."

"You've lost weight, Marika."

"I'm no thinner than usual."

"Nils Johan shouldn't have taken her to the police. By the way, what happened with that?"

"The preliminary investigation was closed. Or, as they put it, 'no grounds to proceed.'"

Elsa's eyelids fluttered but she didn't move. She had to remember to ask Anna-Stina what "no grounds to proceed" meant.

CHAPTER NINETEEN

Ovccinuppelohkái

T he low rumble of the Lynx spread through the yard. The sound, and even the smell of gasoline, gave Elsa butterflies. It was only eight below, but it would be even colder in the headwind. Anna-Stina was already on the sled that Lasse pulled behind the snowmobile. He was goofing around as usual, making Mom smile. Elsa put on her leather mittens and Mom tied the leather strings of her hat into a neat bow under her chin. The fox fur stroked her cheeks, forehead, and chin. She was starting to outgrow her snowmobile suit; its legs had inched up over her ankles.

"Don't go too fast," said Mom.

"But Makki, that's the whole point!"

Lasse was the only person who called her Makki, but then again he gave everyone nicknames they hadn't asked for.

Elsa tucked herself close to Anna-Stina; they were small enough to sit next to each other and stick their legs out straight. There was already a tickle in Elsa's belly, and she fumbled for a firm grip on the reindeer pelts. You weren't allowed to hold on to the edge of the sled, because your fingers might hit a sharp snowbank.

Lasse drove out onto the ice, but not onto the snowmobile trail that led to the corral. He squeezed the gas and made Elsa and Anna-Stina fall back and giggle aloud. The snowmobile darted across the ice, making broad curves along the shore where the plastic rowboats were moored in summer.

Now and again, Lasse glanced back to make sure that both girls were still there. Anna-Stina waved, urged him to go faster, they could handle it. As he sped up, snow sprayed out from the tracks. He chose one of the narrower trails that led to the forest on the other side of the lake. They couldn't go as fast in the forest, and they had to protect themselves from the birch branches. Elsa closed her eyes too, just to be safe. The sled bounced and they were thrown around, giggling. Soon they reached the next lake, and he sped up again.

When they came to a new section of thick forest, they heard the sound of another snowmobile approaching. Elsa turned her head and saw Mattias. She recognized the way he stood to drive. With his arms stretched out, and sometimes with one knee on the seat as he forced a curve or when he didn't want to get stuck in the deep snow. Anna-Stina's eyes opened wide and she gave a huge smile. Lasse and Mattias exchanged grins. One of the longer stretches of ice was ahead of them. They would go crazy fast. It was always a competition.

Anna-Stina and Elsa tried to hold hands, but it was hard in their stiff leather mittens. Elsa decided to grasp the frame of the sled after all, since there were no snowbanks on the ice. Anna-Stina did the same, and they held their breath. The snowmobile engines roared across the lake as they rode neck-and-neck. Soon there was no more lake, and neither made any move to slow down and let the other win. Elsa wanted Mattias to win, wanted to see him happy. Sure enough, he was the winner, and he pumped a fist in the air before driving, with a lighter touch on the gas, in among the firs and birches.

Lasse followed, going a little too fast. He steered into the loose snow and leaned to the right to force the snowmobile through the curve without getting stuck. It worked, and now he was ahead of Mattias. The next open area would be a clear-cut, licking its wounds beneath the blanket of snow. There were only a few trails here; they didn't usually go this far when Anna-Stina and Elsa were with them. The girls didn't recognize places Lasse and Mattias knew, and they gazed around, trying to create mental maps of new ground. Suddenly Elsa was struck by a birch twig. She whimpered and held her cold leather mitten to her cheek.

The ride across the clearing was bumpy, and Mattias took off faster than Lasse could with the sled behind him. Her insides seemed to be jumping around inside her, and her back protested, but Elsa wasn't about to complain. Anna-Stina looked equally determined. Mattias took a long arc back around the clearing and came up alongside Lasse. They gestured, pointed, and chose another new trail. Slowly they passed hollows in the snow and took a closer look—reindeer had lain down here. Elsa liked the way they seemed to have trampled paths, like hallways between their lying-down spots, like a well-planned house made of different rooms. They might be theirs, the stray reindeer they hadn't managed to herd into the corral.

Now the game was over; now they were searching for the reindeer. They crossed the border of the clearing and headed back into the forest. Mattias took the lead, and they followed. Then both snowmobiles stopped, but were kept idling. Lasse quickly glanced back and told them to stay put. His voice sounded so stern that Elsa and Anna-Stina didn't even dare to look at each other.

Lasse sank into the snow as he trudged over to Mattias, who was standing in snow that was up to his knees. Elsa cautiously leaned over the side, over the edge of the sled, and saw antlers. And the snow wasn't white. Red spots were scattered across the snow. Anna-Stina slowly leaned out on her side.

"Intestines," she whispered. "Look!"

Elsa took a firm grip on the sled and sat up straight. Anna-Stina elbowed her.

"Come on, look!"

Elsa shook her head and squeezed her eyes shut. Anna-Stina got up on her knees to see over the snowmobiles.

"There's blood everywhere."

Elsa covered her ears.

"Sit down!" Lasse snapped.

Anna-Stina didn't listen. Instead she stood up to look. Her cheeks, which had recently been so red, went pale.

Mattias and Lasse conversed in low but agitated voices. Mattias got out his phone and Lasse took a few tentative steps into the snow, which held his weight in that particular spot. He picked up something that looked like hooves. He trudged back to the snowmobile and turned it off, pushing at Anna-Stina, who refused to sit down. Mattias too turned off his snowmobile. Then all was silent, as though the forest were holding its breath as well.

Mattias stomped around taking pictures on his phone. Not once did he look in the girls' direction.

Lasse's phone rang, and the trilling ringtone cut through the silence.

"At least two butchered reindeer." He spit out his snus. "No, no heads left. It's all gone except for the innards, antlers, and hooves."

Lasse cast a brief glance over at Elsa, who met his gaze. He hurried to start the snowmobile again and muttered something into the phone.

"You two are going home. Sit down, Anna-Stina! You stay here, Mattias, they're on their way."

Lasse tried to back up but couldn't turn around in the dense forest; instead he had to head into the snow alongside the trail and around the killing site. It was a tight circle, and Elsa looked at the blood that had flowed out and frozen into ice atop the snow. The intestines looked stiff, not shiny and soft as they were back home in the sink, when Mom rinsed them off to fill them with reindeer blood and make blood sausage. The antlers were the worst, because they had been cut off and part of the reindeer's head was still attached, a bloody scrap of stiffened meat. It was a majestic set of antlers, with long beams that must have arched over the reindeer's head. Elsa turned away and looked up at the sky and the tops of the pine trees. She gazed back at Mattias, who was on his snowmobile, slouching, his head down.

Anna-Stina's cheeks had recovered their flush and she sounded brash.

"I told you, they cut the reindeer open. Just like the time they took the calf."

Lasse drove slowly across the clear-cut, over the second lake, through the forest, and onto their own lake. There they met Dad and Ante. Dad listened attentively as Lasse described the spot and pointed the way, and she tried in vain to make eye contact with him. He looked only at Lasse before flipping down the visor on his helmet and accelerating across the lake. The two snowmobiles were quickly out of sight, but the sound of their engines lingered for a long time before fading away.

CHAPTER TWENTY

Guoktelogi

The police didn't show up this time either. It didn't take long for Elsa to realize that there was no point in waiting for them. Dad stood by the kitchen window, making faces as he drank coffee that hadn't had time to cool off yet. Mattias sat on the kitchen bench, tugging at the fringe of the tablecloth and picking up his phone over and over again. Mom kept her back to them, washing a big pot, her elbows jutted out like sharp shields.

Elsa opened the refrigerator door and looked for the piece of chocolate cake she'd been saving. It was gone; she wanted to shout at Mattias.

The room was uncomfortably silent. Elsa could tell that they wanted to get rid of her, that they wanted to talk about everything she wasn't allowed to know. She tiptoed over to the pantry and hung on the handle while she looked for some cookies. She moved the knäckebröd and the salt, picked up the box of macaroni, and finally found the oatmeal cookies with stripes of chocolate icing. She took out three and sat on the kitchen bench, just far enough from Mattias. Dad poured more coffee from the thermos. Mattias couldn't sit still any longer, and he left the kitchen with his heels hitting the floor hard. The coffee mug was delicate and strikingly small in Dad's hand. When he was finished, he set the mug on the counter and went to the front hall. He stomped his feet into his shoes. The door opened and closed.

Mom swiped the dishrag over the countertop and wrung it out thoroughly. Her footsteps on the kitchen floor could hardly be heard. She lifted the rug, grabbed the brass-colored handle, and pulled up the hatch. She unfolded the steps, went down to the root cellar, and soon came climbing back up again. Elsa had always loved that space, underground, but Áhkku had judged the root cellars at both their houses as the most dangerous place in the world. No hatch was to be opened if there was a child in the kitchen.

Mom tossed the rug back over the hatch, and it took a moment for the slightly stale, earthy cellar smell to fade from the kitchen. She put a jar of blueberry jam into the fridge and stood gazing at the shelves for a long time.

"I'm going to the store."

It was dark now, and as usual Elsa could only see a distorted version of herself in the window. But when Mom went out, the lights came on. The car started and backed out of the driveway.

From Mattias's room came the sound of volleying shots. He was playing a game online and was trying to sound older as he barked commands to the others.

Elsa got a stomachache from the cookies and lay down on the kitchen bench. It was made of wood, and the hollow storage area beneath the seat was full of old newspapers and fishing clothes. The lid was rock-hard, and she could feel her shoulder blades and spine pressing into her skin.

The plow went by at high speed, and its blinking orange light flashed rapidly over the kitchen walls. Soon after that, a truck thundered past.

Through the window she could see a shifting tone in the sky. The northern lights! She quickly threw on her coat, snow pants, hat, and mittens. This time she would listen closely and hear the guovssahasat.

She ran up the plowed rise next to the smoke goahti and lay down in the snow. How it danced above her—ribbons of green, yellow, purple, and icy blue wreathed across the sky. And soon she heard the crackling sound.

"Hi, guovssahasat!" she cried with all her might. "I hear you!"

The northern lights changed shape at breathtaking speed, from wide waves to narrow tendrils.

"Guovssahasat!" she called again.

Then she heard quick steps coming up the rise, and suddenly Áhkku stood before her, her eyes wide and a howl in her voice.

"What are you doing! You can't lie there shouting like that! Hasn't your father told you it's absolutely forbidden? It's one thing that your mother doesn't understand, but your father!"

She grabbed hold of Elsa and hauled her to her feet.

"But—"

Áhkku dragged her down the rise, staring fiercely at the ground. She couldn't speak the northern lights' name until they were inside.

"You didn't whistle or wave, did you?"

"What? No!"

"You have to understand that you must show respect to the northern lights. And you don't go around shouting like that. It could be dangerous!"

Elsa gazed at the floor. Dangerous, that was Áhkku's favorite word. There were so many things that were dangerous or sinful. She wasn't sure if God was the one who decided that the northern lights were dangerous.

"You must not tease the northern lights. Or even go out to look at them."

"I think they're pretty."

"Nothing good comes with the northern lights. Quite the opposite!"

"I want to go home."

"Then go home. But do not look up at the sky, do you hear me?"

Elsa nodded, opened the door, and dashed across the yards, her sobs burning in her chest.

CHAPTER TWENTY-ONE

Guoktelogiokta

Mattias put his headphones down on the desk. His ears were hot, his hairline sweaty. His heart was still pounding from the game. He took big gulps of soda until the bottle was empty. The killing helped, the shooting and winning. But it wouldn't last long. He reached for his phone and sent a text to Lasse. He needed to get out of the house, to have a smoke. His phone dinged and he exhaled, took off his sweaty T-shirt, and put on a long-sleeved black one.

In the kitchen he inhaled a couple of cold, leftover slices of Falu sausage. He could feel Elsa's eyes on his back. She was on the kitchen bench, braiding her own hair. He ought to ask how she was feeling, but he couldn't bring himself to. He just wanted to get out, get away from it all. It was like there was a pressure cooker inside him, as fucking angry as he was. Dad snuck off every single time, called the police and got sulky when they didn't show up, then took off without a word. Mattias didn't want to think of him as cowardly. He wanted Dad to put his foot down, say, *That's enough, dammit, you will send someone here.*

"Where are you going?"

"Out. With Lasse."

"Can't I ever come with?"

He shot her a tired look.

"No."

Lasse was his.

There was a honk from the yard and Elsa jumped up to wave out the window. Bright lights flashed back. She waved childishly, with both hands, until they skidded out of the yard.

Shit, maybe he shouldn't have left her on her own. Mom would be furious when she returned home and found her there alone.

"I need a smoke and a drink," he said, drumming his right hand on his knee.

Lasse kept his eyes on the road.

"Don't got nothing to drink."

He was lying, but Mattias knew not to push it.

"Where do you want to go?"

"Anywhere something is happening."

Lasse hit the gas and Mattias felt it in his stomach. Lasse didn't let up until they reached the gas station in the next village. The store part was dark, closed. They rolled down the windows and each lit a cigarette. Mattias held the smoke in his lungs, then blew it out slowly.

"It's Saturday, there's got to be a party somewhere."

He wanted to spur Lasse into action, do something, force himself to think about something else. And drink—just to dull a little of the irritation that made his body feel jittery. He turned the volume all the way up, making the whole car vibrate, and turned to Lasse, hoping for the right reaction.

Lasse shook his head, but he smiled and shouted, "I think you've been partying too much."

"What?" Mattias gestured exaggeratedly, his hand cupping his ear. "I can't hear you."

Lasse turned down the music, reclined his seat a notch, and blew smoke out the window.

"I'm worried about the girls," he said after a moment of silence.

"Which ones?" Mattias flicked the butt away.

"Elsa and Anna-Stina."

He sighed and leaned back against the headrest. Shit, he couldn't get away from it even with Lasse.

"They'll survive," he said acidly. "Gimme another ciggie."

When Lasse didn't immediately hand over the pack, he felt uncertain. He didn't mean to sound so angry; he was just hoping for a few hours of freedom from all that shit. He glanced at Lasse, trying to think of something funny to say, but there was only silence. Instead, both of them stared after a black Audi that blew through the village at high speed, leaving a cloud of snow in its wake.

"Shit! He must have been doing over one hundred miles! Who was it?"

Lasse shrugged, then held out the pack of cigarettes.

It was a big deal, hanging out with him, getting to ride in his Volvo and smoke with him. Or cracking open a beer by the river when they went fishing. Lasse had other friends, ones his own age, and Mattias did too, but they were drawn to one another. At least when Lasse was in the village. But what they did together was always on his terms. Then again he was the one with the car. Freedom. But in the summer, on their motorbikes, they were equals. Mattias liked to brag to his cousins whenever he'd spent time with Lasse. He frequently exaggerated the number of beers they'd drunk. Lasse never gave him more than one, maybe two, but Mattias would have to beg for the second one, swearing he wasn't drunk. The story changed when he told his friends about it later.

"You know I feel like a big brother to Elsa and Anna-Stina too. That was bad today, real bad."

"We could shoot him. After all, we know who's killing the reindeer," Mattias said.

He had that gleam in his eye. He didn't have the strength for this right now and he hoped Lasse would catch on. They'd had this discussion before, they joked about it, and Lasse sometimes made him laugh until his stomach hurt.

"Gotta pee."

Lasse headed for the nearest snowbank, completely unbothered by the houses nearby. Maybe he would leave his initials in the snow. "Me and the dogs, we mark our territory in this village," he liked to say with a laugh. But that was only when they'd been drinking.

Mattias checked his phone, wondering if he should call someone else after all. Obviously Lasse wasn't in the right mood tonight. He sent a text to Linus.

Lasse plopped back in the driver's seat, his walleye worse than before. Mattias's phone dinged.

"Hey, there's a party at Linus's. Want to go?"

"No way, you won't find me hanging out with little kids tonight or any other night."

Lasse put the car in gear and started doing donuts. Mattias felt nauseated but didn't stop him. It was nice that Lasse didn't consider him one of the "little kids." Or did he?

The spinning stopped and he gulped hard.

"Or the two of us could do something?"

"I'll drive you there."

Lasse chewed on his lip and didn't say a word, all the way to Linus's parents' house. Mattias unfastened his seatbelt. He wanted to go and he wanted to stay.

"How will you get home?" Lasse looked expectant. Now he was tired of him. Mattias could see it in his eyes.

"Oh, I'll probably just stay over. Or someone with a car will come along."

"So are you okay? I mean, given what happened today?"

Mattias threw out his arms and smiled. "We've seen it before."

Lasse looked at him in disappointment. Or was it irritation? It was hard to tell in the darkness.

"It's Saturday. I want to have fun, not think about all that."

"You don't always have to be so goddamn cocky."

Mattias recoiled. He forced himself to laugh.

"But I am. Not much I can do about that."

He curled a biceps under his coat and grinned.

"Okay," Lasse sighed. "Okay."

Mattias opened the car door and found himself standing there with it open. He wanted to say something Lasse would respect, but his brain was empty. So he raised his hand in a salute and closed the door.

Music blared from inside the house, and he hoped like hell there would be beer. Lasse honked three times as he headed down the hill toward the highway.

CHAPTER TWENTY-TWO

Guoktelogiguokte

They had all been waiting, sometimes gently asking if she was going to come with them to the corral. Not since Nástegallu was found dead had she gone to help feed the reindeer. So when Elsa strapped on her skis in the morning, after the previous day spent quietly waiting for the police who never showed up, Mom and Dad exchanged glances but said nothing.

"I might ski to the corral," she said.

"Don't you want to go with the rest of us later?" Mom asked.

Elsa looked at her, suddenly uncertain. She was trying to do everything a little better, make them happy, not think about what happened yesterday.

"It's fine. That's great, unna oabba," Mom continued, her voice shrill.

Her arms trembled as she picked up her poles and glided a few yards. She wouldn't make the same mistake as last time. This time she would whistle or maybe sing loudly as she approached the corral. If he was there and had killed yet another reindeer, he would hear her and go.

Mattias was looking under the hood of his snowmobile and his fingers were stained black. Elsa hoped he'd heard she was on her way to the corral. She recalled his smile when he beat Lasse in the race, before they found the butchering site. She wanted nothing more than to see him smile again. But she didn't dare say anything, because she would be so disappointed if he didn't care.

Elsa skied out of the yard, and through the long grasses and vegetation that pierced through the blanket of snow. When she came to the gentle slope that led to the lake, she had to tense her thighs to remain steady. The snowmobile trail was icy in spots, and she kept slipping, so she tried skiing outside of it. There was almost enough of a crust, but when she started falling through every other yard or so, it was just as well to get back to the trail. Her poles couldn't get much of a hold in the ice, but if she managed to thrust a few times she would glide ahead at a good speed. The mild overnight temperature had come as a surprise, and the snow was just beginning to loosen and melt when it quickly plunged back below freezing. Áhkku knew exactly what was going on; the Bible certainly made no bones about the storms, cold, heat, and fire that would destroy the earth. Dad shook his head and talked about the threats of climate change.

Now it was a good thing they had the reindeer in the enclosed corral. When the blanket of snow turned to ice, it was impossible for the animals to graze. So the herders had eventually decided to feed the reindeer for a certain amount of time, instead of letting them roam free. This decision had been made the year after they'd lost so many to starvation, and Dad couldn't stand to see it happen anymore. Anna-Stina had been happy to chatter on about the wolverines—they could run even faster on the icy snow and leap onto the reindeer's backs and bite their necks. Just for fun. Sometimes they weren't even hungry, just bloodthirsty from the hunt. And the herders would find half-dead reindeer, their necks torn, gasping their final breaths with panic in their eyes.

Elsa shook her head; she had to start thinking about something else. About summer, about the mountains, when it was calf-marking time. Summers that were sometimes so cold everyone wore two down coats, or summers when the heat came as a surprise and the reindeer hardly had the energy to move. And Áhkku, who said in an ominous voice that it had never been like this before. Anna-Stina's mother liked to say that you shouldn't pay too much mind to those Christians, and she should know because her aunt was a devout Laestadian Lutheran who had done her best to terrify her nieces and nephews with all her talk of hell and sin. On those occasions when Elsa repeated what Áhkku had said, Hanna told her it was nonsense and Elsa felt calmer. Sometimes, if Áhkku wouldn't give in, Hanna would send Elsa and Anna-Stina off to see if anyone needed their help with the calves. And that sort of trust was precious to them, so they would scamper off right away.

It was at one of these times that Dad called out to say he had a calf for Elsa. Nástegallu. Dad knew which calf he wanted to give her, and they searched for the cow among hundreds of reindeer. She would never forget the feeling and the sounds that day. The reindeer's grunts, ruovgat, antlers knocking together, bells around their necks, and the low drum of hooves against their grounds that vibrated up into her legs. A sound that never faded as long as they stood there with the suohpa, the lasso, in hand. Large reindeer tramping by right next to her, a circle going around and around, always counterclockwise because the earth's gravitation made it so. Dad saw the cow and pointed; it came closer, brushing along the edge of the temporary yellow plastic fence. Next to her, the calf with that distinctive white spot on its forehead.

As soon as she saw the calf, she knew she would never forget how it looked. It had unusually long legs, which helped it keep up with its mother effortlessly. They missed with the lasso the first time, but now they had the calf in their sights. The second time, she was caught. The line went taut and Dad helped her pull. The little one leapt, veering this way and that. Elsa knew she had to calm her down, say that she would soon be back with her mother.

The cow called for her calf. The little one answered. They lay her down gently and Elsa whispered in her ear, calming her and stroking her soft fur. What she saw in the calf's eyes brought her to a standstill. Dad urged her on. It was time to take the knife from her belt. The ear was so small and soft and wanted to yield beneath the blade. Dad covered her hand with his and together they made her mark, which was an extension of his. Warm blood trickled over Elsa's hand, and she wiped it on the grass, but it was already caught beneath her thumbnail. Her calf. Nástegallu. They loosened their grip and set her free. She called out, and her mother answered. Elsa watched their search and reunion. They were alike now, they belonged together, but of course they knew that already.

"In oamas du, leat du iežat. Leat beare luoikkašin munnje," she whispered. "I do not own you, you belong to yourself. You are only mine on loan." She'd once heard Mattias say this to a calf, and she'd repeated the words quietly to herself each night before she fell asleep to make sure she wouldn't forget them when it was her turn to release a calf.

She made a wrong stride and found herself sitting in the trail, her skis crossed, before she got up again. She'd come all the way across the lake. It was time to start making noise. She thought of a special joik, but the idea of singing it made her feel so dark and sad inside.

No one knew that she practiced in secret, trying to find her sound. She'd heard people say that Áddjá always joiked in the mountains when he was young, but she'd never gotten to hear him. Áhkku had strict Christian opinions about the sin of joiking, but Elsa didn't want to believe that she'd silenced Áddjá. She hoped he still joiked his grounds.

She was in the forest now, and she started softly. A magpie flew up from a branch, frightened. She joiked louder, and now they must be able to hear it all the way in the village, and definitely in the corral. She was out of breath from skiing at the same time. Suddenly her throat constricted, as if someone were squeezing their hands tight around her neck. The panic grew and she had to toss her poles down to feel if his hands were there, if he'd snuck up behind her. She whirled around, fell to the ground, and yanked down the zipper of her coat. She could breathe again.

"Hey! Princess! What are you doing?"

Lasse stood about twenty yards away, his arms crossed.

"I was just wondering who was joiking so beautifully that even the reindeer stopped to listen."

Elsa untangled her legs and poles until she was standing steady again.

"I fell."

"I can imagine, with all that effort. Well, come here."

She poled onward and skied the last little bit straight into Lasse, who laughed and pretended to lose his balance.

He made no remark about how she was back, or that they'd all been worried. He said nothing at all, and she loved him for it. She blushed when that thought came to her. Love was a big word, one you shouldn't just throw around.

She took off her skis. Lasse tugged her hat down over her eyes and she pulled it up again with a laugh.

"You're just in time to fill the sled and head out with the pellets. We're starting to run low, but tomorrow the feed truck is coming with twenty tons."

They worked side by side, hauling heavy sacks to the sled. Lasse chugged slowly into the corral, and she made sure to close the gate properly before hopping up on the sled behind the snowmobile. The reindeer were used to this; they knew what was coming. The empty feed troughs had to be filled, and she worked quickly and methodically to pour in the pellets. They hardly had time to drive off before there was a crowd. Not just anyone could eat first; there were some who butted and shoved. Elsa couldn't pick out Nástegallu's mother, and she wanted to ask if Lasse could. Did the cow search for her calf, call for her? Had she seen the knife go into Nástegallu? Elsa filled the next trough and fended off the reindeer who got too close with their antlers.

Reindeer were quiet. They didn't scream if someone cut them with a knife; they didn't scream when the wolverine bit into their necks and paralyzed their bodies. They didn't have screaming in them.

She held out a handful of reindeer lichen to one animal who had been brusquely shoved aside by a large havier, a castrated male. It seemed to say thanks, gazing right into her eyes, and she almost felt shy. Once you had gazed into a reindeer's eyes and understood, you realized you had no choice but to be right there. So Hanna liked to say, and Elsa knew it to be true as well. She had known since Nástegallu; she would never forget that gaze. And she had said so to Hanna, who pulled her close and pressed her lips to the top of Elsa's head.

Elsa looked at Lasse, saw how he smiled and whistled when he was with the reindeer, talking to them and prodding them with a firm but kind hand when he needed to, as though they were his children. Elsa hoped Lasse would never have kids of his own. She wanted to stay his little princess forever. He'd promised her that there wouldn't be any children, hadn't explained why, just said he'd made up his mind not to become a father. That was a secret he'd told her last summer, when they were sitting on the big rock outside the corral during calf marking, each with a lukewarm juice box. Elsa had been on the verge of tears over the cow who'd run around calling for her calf, which had died in the night, and without thinking she had said it would be better if the mother had died rather than the sweet, new calf.

"The calf wouldn't survive without its mother, you know that," Lasse had said. "It's worse when mothers die."

"Like when your mother died, even though you weren't grown up yet?" This hadn't made Lasse angry. He let her say anything she liked. This time, he even thanked her and squeezed her with his free arm.

"It's lucky you have Hanna, because she's like your mother. She's the nicest mom I know." As soon as she'd said it, her chest felt heavy. What if Mom heard her say that? She didn't mean it that way. But not even then did Lasse look at her oddly.

"You can have more than one mom. Extra moms are a good thing, and Hanna is one of those. You know that too, don't you?"

She couldn't remember what she'd said in response.

"And us oops babies often end up with extra moms."

"What does it mean, anyway, 'oops baby'?"

At that he laughed, and his laughter blew away the black cloud that had been looming over her.

"You know, váhkar, the littlest, someone who has big brothers and sisters maybe years older. The last baby, a happy surprise for their parents. You and me, we're happy surprises."

Elsa had bit her tongue to keep from saying what she absolutely must not tell him.

"But the problem with being the youngest is that sometimes they can end up feeling left out, like they don't count. But Elsa, I want you to know that you count, I promise. I will make sure of that if I do nothing else!"

In retrospect, she sometimes felt like that conversation had never really happened. She got mixed up about what had been said, but the most important part, about moms, she never forgot. Still, she oftentimes felt a little sick to her stomach when she recalled how she'd said that Hanna was the best mother. It was just that Hanna never cried. Elsa didn't think grown-ups should cry.

Lasse hit the throttle and the jump-start interrupted her thoughts. He drove them out of the corral and she closed the gate carefully behind them. A calm had settled.

He lit a cigarette and leaned against the handlebars. She gathered scattered bits of lichen into a small pile, which she scooped into her hands so she could toss it into the corral. None of it must go to waste. It was expensive to feed the reindeer, she knew.

Lasse's left eye was wandering today, and Elsa looked at his nose instead.

"Good work. I almost can't believe you're a princess, with how hard you work."

The cigarette dangled from his lip and bobbed as he spoke; some ash floated down.

Elsa smiled and did a cartwheel, just because her body felt like it.

"And you're a little gymnast too."

"Do you think the cow who lost her calf last summer will have another one this year?"

"I'm sure she will. She's a good cow."

He stubbed out his cigarette on his hard boots and returned what was left to a pack he kept in his breast pocket. He went over to the feed and seemed to be counting sacks, tugging at them to arrange them a little better.

"So, should we head home now?"

Elsa's eyes narrowed and he sighed.

"Aw, what am I saying? Of course we can head home. I'm sure no one is fighting over food by now."

He turned away and counted the sacks again.

"Are the police going to come look at what we found?"

Lasse stopped mid-motion, then turned around and walked briskly toward the snowmobile.

"I don't think so," he said, his back to her.

"Why not?"

"They think they've got more important things to do."

"Like what?"

Lasse laughed and scoffed all at once.

"You're right about that. Like what? You're a smart one."

Elsa fiddled with the zipper of her snow pants pocket. She had taken off her mitten. There, in her pocket, was the ear she had retrieved from the storage shed early that morning. She wouldn't have been able to ski without it.

"Did someone kill the reindeer and take the bodies with them?"

Lasse raised the hood of the snowmobile and poked at some random part.

"What did your dad say about it?"

Elsa slipped her hand in her pocket and squeezed the soft ear. She didn't respond.

"I followed the trail last night, and I guess I'll call the police and let them know in which direction it was going. Then maybe they'll show up after all."

He didn't look at her while he spoke. Instead, he lowered the hood and took out his cigarette again. His eye drifted to the side.

"Did the trail go to the next village?" she asked quietly.

Lasse nodded and sucked hard on the cigarette, then blew out rings of smoke. Puff, puff, puff.

She let go of the ear and slowly pulled her zipper up again.

"Why does he keep killing our reindeer?"

"Who? What do you know about it?"

"You know . . . that guy Robert, who . . ."

She snuffled up her snot.

Lasse smoked the cigarette down to the filter.

"Don't think about that stuff. Let the grown-ups handle it."

Her disappointment made her turn away.

A crow flew overhead with heavy wingbeats, cawing loudly.

"He'll go down for it someday, that whole gang will. I promise. No one can attack reindeer and get away with it. Sooner or later, that's all I'll say."

She peered over her shoulder and they smiled at each other.

"So! Do you want to ski home, or do you want a lift?"

"Maybe you can tow me?"

"Excellent idea!"

He unhooked the sled and tied a bright blue line to the snowmobile. He made a loop at the end of the line and she put her left hand through and held on tight.

"How fast can I go?"

"As fast as you want!"

She tensed her legs and belly and bent her knees slightly, gliding slowly forward on her skis to prepare for the jerk. Although Lasse started slowly, the line snapped taut and it felt like her arm would be pulled clear off. They drove through the forest. Now the lake was in sight and she had settled in, found her balance and the perfect angle. Then she realized she'd forgotten her poles and called out to Lasse, but he was wearing earplugs and squeezing the throttle. Oh well, what was a pair of poles when you could fly? The snowmobile roared across the ice and she followed behind, the world's fastest princess with her hair streaming in the wind. And now she could joik clearly; the sound of the snowmobile drowned it out and guarded her secret. It was just her, the ice, and her lands.

CHAPTER TWENTY-THREE

Guoktelogigolbma

T he old white Sámi school and the recently renovated gray village school stood beside each other in the next village. The schools shared a cafeteria and gym. Neither had enough students, and over the years the Sámi school had needed to combine some grades. Elsa had heard the politicians were planning to close the village school and bus those kids to town instead. She often wished it would happen, especially when she ran over to the cafeteria, which was in the village school.

The lunch ladies wore white aprons, and with their strong, stout arms they offered up big serving trays full of steaming hot potatoes and Falu sausages that hardly had a crisp on their casings. But since hitting the reindeer, Astrid Johansson could only set out the smaller aluminum containers of shredded carrots, cucumbers, kidney beans, and limp lettuce leaves. And she made a big deal of it. Around her neck she wore her brace, tightly strapped so that everyone would notice her suffering.

When Elsa came into the cafeteria, Astrid's eyes followed her. She often placed a hand pointedly on her brace and moaned about the pain. Everyone in the whole school was aware of exactly where the Johanssons had hit a reindeer, and how badly hurt Astrid was. She had even had to take sick leave from work for the first time in her whole life. Now she was back on the job, but she made sure everyone knew that without naproxen, she wouldn't be there at all. Everyone also knew that the car had been totaled, because she had to take the bus while she waited for her husband to pick out a new car. It was important they buy one where you sat higher up, preferably an SUV; they would need to see properly because "Next time we'll hit the goddamn reindeer without injuring ourselves too."

Lunch lady Astrid's tongue had slipped more than once when she complained about the Lapps' reindeer, letting out that slur. According to rumors, it had happened often enough that she'd been called to the principal's office to discuss her choice of words. After that, she mostly refused to open her mouth at all while at work.

Elsa helped herself to very little food; she had to eat every bite. The sausage was so pale that it made her stomach turn just to look at it. But she mashed up the potato and added a little butter, until it was almost like actual mashed potatoes. Then, into her mouth went the sausage and she chewed fast. She managed to swallow it and took a few sips of milk, shudders running all the way down her back.

She was alone. The rest of her class was sitting at a table near the window. Sure enough, even if that table was full, the other kids would rather crowd their way in than sit with her. But on Wednesdays and Thursdays, Anna-Stina had lunch at the same time and they would typically eat together. They never talked about the fact that Elsa usually sat on her own. Not even the teachers raised their eyebrows anymore; they said Elsa must prefer it that way. But when a student teacher came to the village school, he practically pulled the fire alarm, he was so upset.

"How is it possible that none of you says a word when a student is so clearly sitting alone?"

At the moment the handicraft teacher was also squeezed in at the round table, and her mouth made a plump little "o" when she was confronted. But if this southerner thought he could just show up and give the village teachers a talking-to, he had another think coming. And anyway, it wasn't as if Elsa was being bullied, right, Elsa? And that's how the student teacher ended up sitting with her for a few weeks, which was almost worse than sitting by herself. Because now it was really obvious what was going on. Previously she had developed a strategy of arriving last to the cafeteria and walking past the round table, exclaiming at a decent volume, "Whoa, it's so crowded at your table, guess I'll sit over here." Then it didn't feel as much like being left out.

No, it's not as if anyone was bullying Elsa, exactly, but for some reason there just wasn't room for her. Maybe it was because some of the kids in her class belonged to the family Dad didn't want to talk about. Or maybe it was because Mom was considered a rivgu, something that wasn't forgotten among cruel tongues. Elsa had heard whispers that you were only half-Sámi if you didn't have two Sámi parents. When that happened, she wanted to stand up and shout out loud that Mom was too in a Sámi family book.

But Elsa managed; eating alone three days a week wasn't so bad. Except for *him*. Markus. On Mondays, he sauntered in with his loud friends. His pale wolf eyes seemed to search for her. She had exactly fifteen minutes to eat before he appeared, but the rule was you had to sit for at least twenty minutes of your lunch period. So she ate fast and then sat staring at the second hand of the big clock by the door, waiting to be allowed to put away her tray.

Now the round table was full of raucous laughter because someone had a milk mustache. Soon a bunch of kids had them, and the laughter grew. But did Astrid go over and tell them to quiet down? No, she mostly seemed to be staring at Elsa. And Elsa was staring at the clock. When the wolf came in, he had his eyes on her too. But there was a line to get food, and he wasn't able to cut this time. Elsa gazed out at the schoolyard, looking for Anna-Stina. The wolf was getting closer to the food while the second hand moved forward, slow as a snail. Elsa's knuckles were white, she was holding on to her tray so hard. Twenty seconds left. Then she could finally get up, push in her chair, and stumble over to the kitchen without looking his way. Astrid stood in the humid air by the dishwashers; sweaty strands of hair had escaped her hairnet. She tapped her watch with her index finger.

"One more minute before you're allowed to get up."

"But the clock out there . . ."

"It's wrong."

She shooed Elsa off with a limp, chapped hand. Elsa couldn't move, because now the wolf had his food. He was wearing his cap, even though it wasn't allowed inside, but no one told him to take it off. His jeans hung low on his hips. He was laughing and roughhousing with another boy.

Astrid stared at her as she loosened her collar to reveal a sweaty, red neck. She scratched at it with her fingernails.

By now Elsa's classmates were done eating too, and they came and lined up ahead of her. She was last even though she'd been first. Astrid turned her back on her and the dishwasher hissed as she closed it.

Elsa kept her eyes on the floor as she hurried off. In the coatroom she ran into the substitute teacher, Anette.

"Aren't you in a hurry!" she said with a laugh, catching Elsa in a hug.

Elsa inhaled the faint scent of her perfume and Anette's hair tickled her cheek.

Anette scrutinized her. "Is everything okay?"

Elsa gave a stiff smile but assured her everything was fine.

"I just wanted to get outside. There's a race to see who can get to the top of the hill first."

She had never, ever run up that pile of snow, even though she knew she was faster than anybody else. But they would only push her off if she tried to go up.

"Well, you'd better hurry then. Hope you win!"

She ran for the classroom, fighting hard not to sob.

CHAPTER TWENTY-FOUR

Guokteloginjeallje

There was nothing to complain about. The beds were made, all the surfaces dusted, the rugs had spent some time in the snow and now lay stiff and ice-cold on freshly mopped floors. The grout in the bathroom had been scrubbed down, the sink was sparkling clean, and the mirror spotless. *I deserve a few minutes' rest*, Hanna thought, but she didn't actually sit down. She adjusted the blanket on the sofa, rearranged the photos of Anna-Stina, and, with a smile, stroked her first-grade class picture. She remembered her daughter feeling more pride about the gap in her bottom teeth than about her gákti. How Hanna had struggled, the evening before, to get that new shawl fringed, and then it was hardly even visible because the photographer had cropped the photo just a couple of inches below her chin. Yet her little sweetheart only cared about the loss of her tooth anyway.

The picture of Lasse in his confirmation gákti had ended up at the very back of the bookcase, and she found herself standing there holding it. His bangs had been long, an attempt to cover the eye that liked to wander to the left. He was pale and skinny, but, as always, sported a huge smile. He'd loved confirmation camp, had so thoroughly been in his element, a star, a fixed point, the one everyone wanted to get close to. The gákti made him look broader. Hanna had sewn it. He was more like her son than her little brother. When Enná died, and then Isá, it went without saying that she would be there for him. Enná had been ashamed of her unexpected pregnancy, saying that she was far too old. She'd been a young mother to Hanna, but an old one for Lasse. And then she died, suddenly and way too young, of an aortic aneurysm, and Dad, who was almost fourteen years older, died too, just months later. Hanna still found herself paralyzed with grief when she thought about that spring. Lasse had become an orphan. So had she, but there was a difference between being a grown woman with a family and being an eighteen-year-old who was still attending high school in town. Somehow they had managed to move on. After the funerals, Lasse stopped coming to the village on weekends, and he never moved in with them. She would have liked him to, but they both knew it wouldn't happen. It wasn't up to her, and he would never ask. She was so ashamed that she could hardly look him in the eye when he said he would get his own place in the village after graduation. One of their brothers had taken over their parents' house. She had argued with him, saying that Lasse needed the house.

The front door opened and she could tell by the footsteps that it was him. He came into the living room and laughed out loud at the photo, that he'd been such a little scarecrow of a kid.

He typically came by when Ante was out with the reindeer. Those two just didn't mesh. In her darker moments, she thought there was some envy on the part of her husband. He sometimes sounded scornful, saying that a grown man ought to be able to take care of himself. But Lasse was still in high school, far from grown up. He would turn twenty-two this year, but that didn't matter to her.

"There any coffee?"

Lasse was already in the kitchen, and she took a deep breath and followed him.

When the coffee was in the cups, and the cubes of gáffevuostá, bread cheese, was bobbing in it, he began to drum his fingers. The gáffevuostá was squeaking between their teeth, as he reached over and turned on the radio.

"You must be the last person in the world who still has a radio with a tape deck."

He knew it had belonged to their isa, the one he'd used to record the music crossword show because he couldn't follow every clue and needed to listen again. She would never get rid of it.

Lasse refilled the coffee and the drumming stopped.

"I might have to take that job at the mine after all."

He didn't look up, and she turned to gaze at the yard. Snow had fallen, and she ought to plow again because Ante wouldn't have time.

"So? There's nothing wrong with that."

She formulated each syllable in her mind before she said it out loud, but it still sounded forced.

"Or else I'll have to set my sights on Linda after all."

With her he would end up with more reindeer, enough to be profitable.

He laughed and rapped his knuckles hard on the tabletop. "If she still wants me."

Hanna dropped a few more cubes of gáffevuostá in her coffee and stirred.

"But who the hell knows if it's even a good plan? Between the predators and the poachers, her whole herd will be gone soon."

When she didn't respond, he made a face and then grinned.

"Right, sis?"

She got a rag and lifted his cup to wipe its underside, and the table where it had left a ring.

He took a sip.

"So, the mine."

When his left eye drifted to the side, she wanted to hold it still. Reassure him.

"You need the money. It's only during the PS, right?"

PS—a planned shutdown at the mine. Some parts of production would be temporarily halted to conduct maintenance. She knew Lasse was sought after because he was good with machines.

"Yeah, as usual, a big group of us from the villages will go." He flicked finger after finger against his palm, making a loud snapping sound. "But it'll probably last longer this time, might be more of a permanent thing."

She could tell, from the corner of her eye, that he was waiting to see how she would react.

"If anyone's going to sell their soul to the devil, it's me," he said, grinning again.

"Stop it."

"You look so grumpy, but I'm actually happy. It's a lot of money. I'll be able to travel again."

"Is there really nothing else available?"

She regretted the words as soon as they left her mouth. Ante's voice echoed in her ears. "He's a grown man, not your responsibility. Stop interfering all the time." Easy for him to say.

"I just mean, I'm sure Nils Johan could use your help."

"Don't worry, I'll come out once the spring sunshine is warm enough."

Happy hollering came from the yard. Elsa was chasing Anna-Stina. Hanna knew the little one could tag Anna-Stina whenever she liked, catch up and even run past her, but she held back.

"I feel so sorry for them," Lasse said.

"What do you mean?"

"I shouldn't have driven them past the moose stand. They shouldn't have to see—"

"How can we protect them from it? Are we supposed to walk ahead and look for dead reindeer before we let them out? Clean up the blood? What kind of life would that be?"

"The police never called back."

"Are you still hoping for justice?"

Hanna heard the sharpness in her voice, but he was smiling at the girls tumbling around in the snow.

"Now's the right time to start working at the mine, when it's dark day and night," he said.

"And where will you live?"

"I'll commute."

"How long can you rent the house in the village?"

He shrugged, took out a pack of cigarettes, and twirled one between his fingers.

"Now, don't you be smoking in front of the girls."

He threw up his hands and gave her a crooked smile.

"No, God, no. Why should they have to see dangerous things like cigarettes?"

The dishwasher beeped and she got up to open it; steam rose to the ceiling.

"She's terrified," he said.

"Who is?"

"Elsa. I think she saw Robert Isaksson."

Hanna sighed and took out a dishtowel, picked up the cheese slicers, and polished them dry.

Just then, there was thundering from the front steps and the door flew open. Giggles came from the front hall, someone fell over, and both girls burst into peals of laughter.

"Hot chocolate and buns!" Anna-Stina called. "We're freezing!"

Their cheeks and noses were rosy, and their eyelashes sparkled with melted snow. They curled up next to each other on the kitchen bench, whispering and tittering.

Lasse threw out his arms and approached them.

"The village princesses!"

"No hugs!" Anna-Stina said firmly, sticking out a foot. The girls giggled.

Lasse lowered his arms and stood there for a moment; then he grabbed Anna-Stina's foot and voilà, she was hanging upside down and screeching. Elsa laughed until tears came to her eyes.

"Stop that right now, you fool! You'll drop her!" Hanna exclaimed.

"You can always trust me."

He lowered Anna-Stina until her hands could touch the floor, and she smoothly rolled onto her back. She lay there gasping, her face even redder now.

"Do Elsa now!"

Lasse aimed a sly look at Elsa, and Hanna could see how badly she wanted to dangle upside down too.

"It's almost like Gröna Lund," he coaxed her. The amusement park in Stockholm.

"You've never been there!" Anna-Stina protested.

"You don't know everything about me."

"Mom?"

"They took a field trip there when he was in middle school."

Lasse reached a hand out to Elsa.

"Do you trust me?"

Hanna watched the little girl's cheeks grow red even as she nodded solemnly. Lasse would be an amazing father someday, that much was clear. He had a real soft spot for the small and defenseless. When their parents died, he'd kept an eye on Anna-Stina even in the midst of his own grief; he had comforted and entertained her, had been perfectly attentive to the needs of a seven-year-old.

Elsa hooted as Lasse swung her around. She finally grabbed his legs and he carefully put her down.

CHAPTER TWENTY-FIVE

Guoktelogivihtta

H anna wasn't the first to arrive at the mailboxes in the village. As usual, a green Mazda was there. She waved at the old man, who lifted his hand. He didn't get out, and his radio was blaring. She was using her mitten to sweep snow off the ten mailboxes when the mail truck rolled up.

The mail carrier offered a cheerful greeting and placed Hanna's mail right in her hands. After she thanked him, she dumped it all into a bag. She took off, the bag hanging from the handle of the kicksled, but hadn't made it more than a few yards before she went back to Marika and Nils Johan's mailbox. She took out a few white envelopes and some flyers for stores that only existed in the cities on the coast.

She didn't actually have time to collect the mail; she needed to do Lasse's laundry. He had waited until the last minute to tell her, which meant she had only two days to prepare everything he would need.

The doorbell was broken, so Hanna opened the door and called out that she was too snowy to come in. She shook off her hat, slapped the snow off her shoulders, and held out the stack of mail to Marika.

"Thought I'd grab yours too."

"Oh, thanks! Come in. There's coffee."

"I don't have time, I need to get going on Lasse's laundry. He's headed to town today."

But she took a step into the front hall and closed the door behind her.

"I don't know how Nils Johan is going to manage without him," Marika said.

"Mattias is basically a grown man. I'm sure it'll work out."

Marika flipped through the pile of mail and showed Hanna the envelope with the police logo before slitting it open.

"Closed. Again. Straightaway this time. Usually it takes a little while to receive notice. Usually they at least pretend they're planning to do something, investigate something."

She stuffed the document back into the envelope and tossed it up onto the hat rack.

"I won't show it to Nils Johan tonight. Things'll be calmer that way."

Hanna nodded and said she understood. Her hair was dripping and she wiped her hand across her damp cheek.

"Hey, I was thinking. How is Elsa doing? Have you talked to her about what happened?"

"She didn't see much of the butchering site, I don't think."

"No, not that, I mean out at the corral, when she was alone. I was talking to Lasse, and he said she seems awfully scared."

Marika turned her back to Hanna and hung up a scarf that had fallen from its hook.

"I don't think so. She'll forget about it soon enough."

"But she's too big to forget. Maybe the school nurse . . ."

"What would she have to say?" Marika shook her head. "Elsa will let it go, or else she'll have to get used to the fact that this is just the way things are."

Hanna stuffed her fists into her coat pockets.

"But we can't simply let the children deal with it on their own. We don't have to tell them more than necessary, but when such disturbing things happen they need our support."

This came out more harshly than she'd intended, and Marika looked at the floor.

"We talk to Anna-Stina and explain a lot," Hanna said, trying to make her voice gentler.

Marika looked up and opened her mouth to say something, but then she pursed her lips.

"It's unfortunate, but, you know, this stuff was going on back when we were little too."

"It's happened to *you* before. Yeah, I know."

Marika had emphasized that "you" and Hanna felt annoyed again. What was with her? Without realizing it, she was clenching her damp hat hard and it dripped on the hall rug.

"If you want, I could talk to Elsa. Sometimes it's easier to talk to someone other than your own parents."

"That won't be necessary."

Hanna pulled on her hat and gloves.

"Well, I guess I'll be heading home. The laundry. He could do it himself, but it's easier now that we've got that new dryer."

"Right."

"He might get a permanent job at the mine. But I don't know if that's such a good thing."

"They make good money, at least."

"Sure, that's true. But he wants to be with the reindeer. You know, when you've grown up that way."

Marika's gaze went black again.

"Thanks for the mail."

Hanna's cheeks blazed as she stood on the stoop. That was the last time she'd do them a favor.

She whipped the kicksled around and headed for the main road. It was snowing even harder now, and she hunched down. She'd always had a hard time understanding Marika. Not talking to your kids? How ridiculous was that? Sometimes it was so obvious that she hadn't grown up around reindeer. She might wear a gákti and speak Sámi, but there were some things she would never fully understand. Hanna waited for a car to pass before she crossed the road. On the uphill stretch, she walked between the runners of the kicksled, the bag of mail swinging back and forth.

Lasse's Volvo was in the yard, idling. She hurried to kick the last few yards home.

ELSA CLIMBED OFF THE school bus and immediately glanced up the hill toward Anna-Stina's house, looking for Lasse's Volvo. She had been wringing her hands on the way home, twisting her fingers tightly around one another in the hope of making it in time to wave goodbye to him. When Anna-Stina said today was the day he was leaving, Elsa couldn't get home to the village fast enough.

But the yard was empty. She turned around, her shoulders slumping, and hung her head. She dragged her feet through the newly fallen snow and made herself a path from the main road to their house. Gazing back, she liked what she saw—being first, making her own pathway. Then it struck her, what she ought to do. Today was the day. It had stopped snowing, but the plow hadn't come by yet. She hesitated another moment, but when she didn't see anyone through the kitchen window, she made up her mind. She opened the door and tossed her bag inside, then ran back to the road. It wouldn't be long now. She had to listen carefully, to tell which direction the plow was coming from. She tucked her reflective badge into her coat pocket to be as invisible as possible, pulled her hat down over her ears, her coat sleeves covering her gloves.

There! She heard the plow's engine. Definitely coming from the next village. She dashed across to the other side of the road. Maybe she should crouch down, or should she get into the ditch and run back up when the plow was close? Anna-Stina would have known what to do. But this time Elsa would impress Anna-Stina, do something all by herself.

The lamp in the living room came on and Elsa threw herself onto her belly. Mom was walking around with a dust rag, picking up potted plants and wiping down the windowsill. It looked like she was talking to herself, or maybe singing. Mom actually had a really nice singing voice.

Now the plow was close. She wanted the snow to come flying at her whole body; if she was crouching down it wouldn't be the same. The blinking light was visible way on the other end of the curve; it was only a matter of seconds.

She stood up and looked at the living-room window, had time to see Mom startle and lean closer to the glass. The truck was thundering her way and the giant arc of the plow cast up a wave of snow. She smiled, but then she couldn't breathe anymore. The snow hit her with such force that she was thrown backwards. She fell but landed in a soft bank and was, for a few seconds, lost in a massive cloud of snow. There was snow everywhere. Her eyelashes stuck together, her hat had fallen off, and her hair was white. She did it!

Mom's roar echoed across the yard, and Elsa tried to collect herself and find her way up.

"Elsa!"

Mom threw herself down and grabbed her shoulders.

"Are you hurt? What are you doing?"

Elsa smiled and reached out her arms.

"I did it!"

"Do you have a death wish, child?"

Then Elsa saw her tears. And her snot. Mom was sobbing hysterically and hugging her so hard it hurt.

"How could you do something so stupid? Didn't you see the plow?"

She suddenly had superstrength and picked Elsa up. This wasn't quite as fun now that Mom was sobbing, but at the same time Elsa's whole body was vibrating as though she were invincible, and that made her smile.

In the front hall, Mom rolled off her coat, snow pants, and scarf, and put her on her lap while she took off her boots. There was snow everywhere and her clothes were in a pile. Mom stood up with Elsa in her arms, and Elsa threw her legs around her waist and let her head rest against Mom's shoulder.

CHAPTER TWENTY-SIX

Guoktelogiguhtta

Elsa ran up the hill to Anna-Stina's house, and could hardly breathe by the time she flung open the door. Hanna met her with a look of amusement.

"Early as usual, but clearly something big is afoot. I can tell."

"Is Lasse coming to the village today?"

"No, he found an apartment, so he probably won't be coming back every night. Did you want to talk to him?"

Elsa nodded so violently that her hair whipped about her face.

"Did you sleep at all, child? You've got circles under your eyes."

"I woke up at six."

She wanted to dash past Hanna and up to Anna-Stina's room, but Hanna, teasing, was blocking the door to the kitchen.

"Can't you tell me too?"

"Only Lasse. And Anna-Stina. Is she awake?"

Hanna nodded and moved aside with a smile. Elsa took the stairs two at a time and threw herself onto the bed. Anna-Stina was warm from sleep and lifted the blanket. Elsa had been planning to ask her "guess what," but her whole body was fidgety and she had to get it out.

"Yesterday I stood in the ditch when the plow went by and the snow sprayed all over me!"

Anna-Stina's eyes went wide.

"I flew backwards and there was snow everywhere. It was like flying! With snow!"

"I've totally stood in the ditch and gotten snow all over me when Dad was plowing with the tractor," Anna-Stina said with a yawn.

But Elsa wasn't discouraged. Nothing could stop her now. She slapped her hands on the blanket, exhilarated.

"But this was *the* plow! That must have been two yards of snow that knocked me over!"

Anna-Stina bit her lip and then it happened.

"My mom's going to have a baby. But it's a secret and no one can know."

"The plow is a secret too."

But Elsa cast her eyes down. Anna-Stina always won. A baby. A little warm baby. She pictured Hanna, how she'd just been standing in the doorway in front of her, the plant mister in hand. There hadn't been any bump on her belly, had there?

Elsa wanted to go home. She rolled the blanket off her, but Anna-Stina pulled it back.

"What do you think my little sister's name should be?"

And a girl, to boot. She shrugged.

"I think Melanie is pretty."

Anna-Stina looked at her. Elsa glared back.

"Are you sure it's a girl?"

"You can't pick, of course, but I hope it is. She'll be my best friend."

Elsa clenched her teeth so hard that pain shot through her temples. She wasn't allowed to tell. She wasn't allowed to tell.

"I wasn't a normal baby."

"What?"

"I came from a star egg."

Anna-Stina raised her eyebrows.

"Star eggs are more valuable than regular ones. Because they cost money. And before I was inside my mom I was made outside her."

Elsa had seen the pictures of sperm swimming into an egg. They looked a lot like the sticklebacks they would catch in nets at the beach in the summer.

"Wait, what? How?"

Her stomach hurt. She'd said too much.

"It's just true. But it's seriously a secret no one is allowed to know."

"If my little sister isn't Melanie, she can be Minou instead."

THAT EVENING, WHEN MOM AND ELSA were sitting on the sofa on their own, watching a movie, she couldn't keep the secret in any longer.

"Can't I have a little brother or sister?"

Mom looked surprised.

"What made you think of that? You've never talked about wanting more siblings."

Elsa crunched the potato chips between her teeth for a long time.

"Well, now I do."

"But you remember how I told you that you came from a star egg and . . ."

". . . that it was expensive and difficult, I know."

Mom snorted in surprise.

"Elsa, I never said that! And it makes absolutely no difference how much it cost. Goodness, you're so precious to us."

Elsa bit her tongue, wanting to say that she'd heard Mom and Siessá talking about that IVF stuff that cost so much, and how it's expensive to keep reindeer fed so they couldn't afford to make more star eggs.

Mom scratched Elsa's back. "Besides, I'm too old now."

Elsa had also heard Mom and Siessá talking about how Hanna really wanted to have more children. Siessá was always saying they needed a boy and that made Mom laugh, and none of this sounded very nice at all. But if Anna-Stina was going to have a little sister like she said, maybe this baby wasn't a good thing after all. Elsa had to stuff her mouth with candy to keep from telling the secret.

She wriggled her way off the couch and went to the bathroom. The hall lamp flickered and she looked up. On the hat rack was a letter that looked like it had something crumpled inside. She used the shoehorn to knock it to the floor and carefully smoothed out the paper.

"Should I pause the movie?" Mom called.

Elsa went back to the living room and held out the letter.

"The police aren't coming this time either?"

CHAPTER TWENTY-SEVEN

Guoktelogičieža

R obert tossed a big scoop of water on the rocks, and there was an angry hiss as the flames shot in all directions. He wiped the sweat from his forehead and rested his elbows on his knees with a groan.

The heat prickled his face, his back, his chest. Sweat trickled down his neck and under his arms, and the rolls of his belly were wet. He had the towel wrapped around his waist, but Pop sat naked on his blue towel on the bench below him. In past years, it was the other way around. Pop would sit on the highest bench, tossing scoop after scoop of water on the rocks until Robert leapt outside to get some air. It was always humiliating to open the door and come back in afterwards. Pop would be sitting up there with a beer in his fist, dully gazing at him. If he was in a really bad mood, he would toss more water on as soon as Robert sat back down. Then he had no choice but to force himself to stay even though it burned like fire all over his body and in his lungs.

But it had toughened him up, and there was no one else in the village who would stay when Robert doused the rocks in the public sauna next to the communal laundry facility. He would sit on the top bench and watch the other villagers surrender one by one. So, he supposed Pop hadn't been totally useless after all; he had made Robert tough.

But now the old man was sitting across from him on the lower bench, all frail and feeble. He was nearly tipping forward, and it was evident that his breathing was torture. His beer had grown warm beside him.

Pop had come to the forest with him to take the reindeer. He wasn't that old, really, nearing sixty-eight, but it was his body—it was worn out. He grasped his chest and complained of pain, coughing so hard that he shook with spasms. COPD, the doctors said. Today, in the forest, Robert had had reason to think that soon enough he might not have company anymore. He would have to do everything on his own.

"Ready to give in yet?"

It was Robert asking, and he ran his hands down his sweaty arms, longing to go out into the snow. But he wasn't going to be the first.

"Giving up already?" The voice was raspy, and his chest wheezed and whistled when he spoke.

"No, but you seem to be having trouble breathing."

"Bah!" Pop had a coughing fit and gasped for breath. "The sauna is for being quiet," he managed to say.

That man talked so much bullshit, but Robert let him be. An uncomfortably sharp whiff of sweat rose from the old man. He always refused to shower before the sauna, and his pores unleashed hell all over them. Sweat and old hangover.

For his part, Robert was starting to relax. That familiar hum in his head and his body, which thawed out after his third or fourth can.

Things had gone fine after all. The steaks were packaged and ready.

He moved his shoulder carefully, lifting it up and down. In the sauna everything softened, joints and muscles. The heat prickled like red-hot needles on his skin, but his muscle cramps were easing up.

CHAPTER TWENTY-EIGHT

Guoktelogigávcci

Áhkku had said that liars go to hell. It was the first thing Elsa thought of when she woke up. She lay still, stretching out her toes and relaxing them. She splayed her toes so they looked like a fan. No one else in her family could do that. Everything that was different about her must be because she came from a star egg.

Elsa had made a big mistake. She had revealed Mom's secret about the star egg, which was something she'd promised never to do. But the biggest secret, she had kept to herself. The one she should have told, so that maybe everything would be different now. So maybe they wouldn't keep getting those white envelopes with the police logo on them, the ones that made Mom and Dad so sad and angry. So maybe Henriksson would sit at their kitchen table, nodding and writing down everything she said. But what if Robert didn't go to prison? He would kill them all. Or at least Elsa, who had told, who had said it was him.

She looked for the reindeer ear under her jeans on the floor beneath her bed. She sniffed it cautiously. She had taken a chance, bringing it inside yesterday. Soon it should be fine to have the ear in the house all the time without Mom complaining that something stank.

She sniffled and let the tears run down her face and into her ears. It tickled inside her ear, and when she rubbed it, it felt sticky and wet. Once Lasse couldn't fly home from Majorca because he had too much water in his ears. He had told her about it, and Elsa laughed and said he was making things up. She herself had never had salty Mediterranean water in her ear, but cold river water had nearly frozen her brain.

Lasse might come home today, Hanna had said. If anyone could manage to listen to what she had to say, it was him. She wiped her cheeks with her palm and tried to think of the plow and the snow that had taken her. Then, at least, she got a few butterflies in her belly. Lasse would like that story, and she could actually tell him about the plow first and the other stuff later, once he was happy and impressed with her for being so brave. Hopefully he would understand that she had been protecting them all.

There sure were high expectations for a kid who came from such an expensive star egg; Elsa had figured out that much. Maybe that was why Mom didn't want anyone to know that this is what she came from. Because she hadn't turned out like they'd hoped. How was she supposed to be, then? There must be something special about her, something more than just being able to fan out her toes.

She pulled up the blinds and gazed into the darkness. It had snowed overnight and the window was half-covered in snow. She would keep an eye out for Lasse's Volvo and run up to Anna-Stina's house as soon as she saw it skid into the driveway.

Áhkku was out shoveling the yard. Elsa saw her come speeding by with the shovel, heaving snow up onto the embankment. She was breathing hard, taking frequent breaks. Áddjá was sick. He hardly ever went outside anymore. He sat at home in his easy chair by the woodstove, adding more dry birch logs. He wasn't all that talkative anymore, not that he ever had been. And his clothes had gotten too big and his cheeks were sunken in.

Elsa suddenly felt like she was in a hurry to talk to him. She hid the ear in the little box on her bookshelf and pulled on her jeans and a white sweater. She dashed past Áhkku, who called after her, but she pretended not to hear and stomped the snow off her shoes and stepped inside. Sure enough, Áddjá was in his easy chair in the living room.

"Oh, look who it is."

He blinked slowly, and his wrists, which had once been sturdy, were now bony and swam in his sleeves. He had on the checked dress shirt that he only wore when he went to the doctor.

"Are you coming to the market next week? I'm singing in the choir."

She sniffed the air; the house smelled like Áhkku.

"I think I'll probably stay home."

Áddjá closed his eyes. She wondered if he had suddenly fallen asleep, as he often did these days.

It was stiflingly warm and she glanced up at the ceiling fan. Only Áhkku dared to turn it on without asking. But now Elsa stood on tiptoes and pulled the gold chain. The fan started turning, and Áddjá's thin gray hair fluttered on his scalp. He looked displeased, but she ignored him.

"Yesterday I stood in the ditch when the plow went by, and I got totally bowled over by snow. Two yards of snow!"

Áddjá looked at her for a long time and then smiled.

"Well, I never."

She knelt on the sofa and bounced up and down. Finally! Someone who appreciated what she'd done. Just like Lasse would.

"I must have flown three yards backwards!"

When Áddjá laughed, she almost bounced off the sofa and into his arms.

"I can do it again, I'll show you."

Big flames licked at the glass in the woodstove. Elsa pulled on the fan's gold chain again, turning it on high, and Áddjá's hair stood up like a pointy hat.

She cupped her hand around his big ear and whispered that it was a secret. He nodded and turned her head so he could whisper back. Shivers went down her spine.

"I'd be happy to watch you fly in the snow, but turn off that fan right now before we get an ear infection."

She obeyed him, sat down, and thought for a while. She picked at the button on the sofa pillow, sighed aloud.

"If I did get an ear infection," she began.

"Yes?"

"Well, if I did get one, it wouldn't matter because you can take it away."

There, it was said. What you weren't supposed to talk about. She gazed nervously toward the yard, where Áhkku was dashing back and forth. Just as long as she didn't come inside right now. Áddjá didn't say anything. Another log went into the stove.

"I was just wondering how you do it?"

Her anxiety made her voice hoarse.

"Come here," he said, reaching out his hand.

She scooched to the corner of the sofa, and Áddjá lay his warm hand over hers.

"Could you have saved Nástegallu?" she whispered.

He shook his head. When, after a while, he let go of her, he smiled. Elsa didn't understand why, but she smiled back.

"It was good that you came here today, unna oabba."

"Don't tell Áhkku I asked."

"I won't."

"But can I know how you do it?"

"You'll know when you get older."

She wrinkled her nose. She didn't like that kind of grown-up answer. Áddjá closed his eyes again, and a quiet snore rattled in his throat. Now there was no doubt that he had fallen asleep.

CHAPTER TWENTY-NINE

Guoktelogiovcci

Mattias huddled down in the car, tugged his hood over his head, and held his phone in front of his face. They had parked right next to the entrance to the store in the next village. It was general knowledge that you had to shop there as much as possible, or it might go bankrupt. There was a handwritten note taped to the door; on it the owner pointed out, in a nearly illegible hand, how crucial it was to support them. The old lady was nearly eighty, but she had no plans of leaving her spot at the cash register, although these days the store was usually staffed by her son, who lived with her. He would soon be sixty and had never moved out. Mattias didn't want to be reminded of the risk of becoming a weird bachelor who had never left his parents' home.

Dad started the car, letting it idle as they waited for Mom. It was cold again. The weather patterns were shifting more and more often. Mattias hoped he would be allowed to get a practice drive in on the way home, but above all he just wanted to get out of there before anyone spotted him with his family.

Elsa was beside him in the backseat, humming some song or another. They noticed the old, dark brown Jeep at the same time and she fell silent. It was parked at a careless angle. A big set of reindeer antlers was fastened to the spare tire on the back hatch.

"Sargeoaivi," Dad muttered grimly.

Mattias too recognized the shape of the two long, narrow horns. He grabbed the driver's seat and heaved himself forward.

"Hey! What the hell?"

Robert left the car idling and, with two long strides, went up the stairs to the store. That bastard walked like he owned the whole world, Mattias thought.

"Is the axe in the back? I'll cut the antlers loose!"

Spittle flew from his mouth as he spoke, and he had already opened the car door.

"Take it easy!" Dad growled.

"That could be our reindeer. It definitely came from one of ours!"

"Shut the door!"

Mattias was breathing hard and Elsa looked frightened. That made him even angrier.

"But it could be evidence!"

He got out of the car, but he didn't grab the axe. Instead he took pictures of the antlers from various angles. He lingered, hoping that asshole would come back out. He was ready for a fight.

"Get back in, Mattias," Elsa said, her voice pitiful.

If only she weren't with them. He reluctantly sat down beside her and handed his phone to Dad.

"Do you see his fucking bumper sticker? 'Don't ratify ILO 169.'" The Indigenous and Tribal Peoples Convention.

It was impossible to sit still. His pulse was sky-high and he punched the seat, startling Elsa.

Mom came out of the store with two full bags. She opened the trunk and stuffed them inside, then got into the front passenger seat. Dad nodded at the Jeep. She paused, then slowly pulled out the seatbelt.

"Dad won't let me cut the antlers down."

She cast a quick glance into the backseat.

"What is wrong with you? Let's get out of here."

Dad put the car in reverse but didn't let out the clutch. He stared at the antlers.

"Please, Dad, let's go," Elsa whispered.

Robert came out with the day's issue of *Aftonbladet* in hand. He slowly walked past their car, smirking but not looking at them. Mattias punched the driver's seat.

"Stop that!" Mom said, her voice tense.

Dad put the car in first gear and hit the gas but didn't let out the clutch. Mom looked terrified.

"What are you doing? Back out of here this instant. Do you hear me?"

Mattias thrust his head between the front seats.

"Hit him, Dad!"

"Absolutely not!" Mom said, hissing close to Dad's ear. "Elsa is in the car."

The Jeep lurched backwards and came very close to their bumper. The tires skidded as Robert hit the gas too hard. Then he was gone.

It was silent in the car. Mattias collapsed back into his seat. Dad backed up and Mom gazed out the window.

CHAPTER THIRTY

Golbmalogi

Sometimes Hanna had the feeling that something was too late. The feeling of having lost something. She walked silently through her house. Ante was at the corral doing one last check. Anna-Stina had fallen asleep long ago.

There was nothing to straighten, nothing to dust; she'd done it all. So she walked around in the silence, gazing out across the village. Lasse had called. He was supposed to have come home yesterday, but had taken an extra shift. Good money, he said.

Was there something she'd forgotten to tell him? She straightened the fringe of the kitchen rug with her toes, placed a hand on her slightly rounded belly, and smiled to herself. It was just her hormones making trouble again. She kept having terrible nightmares and waking with a sore throat. She wasn't thinking clearly; the hormones were messing with her. She calmed herself, took a seat at the kitchen table. She had to remember to switch to an LED bulb that was easier on the eyes.

She leaned back in the white chair to let her eyes rest, but quickly sat up again. She ran her hands across the smooth tablecloth with its green floral pattern, rearranged the candle holders.

When her phone rang, the blocked number gave her pause. It wasn't the hormones.

After she had answered, she dropped the phone to the floor. Her field of vision narrowed and her legs swayed. There was no more air. She staggered outside so she could breathe.

She stood in the snow on the front steps, barefoot.

Screaming.

CHAPTER THIRTY-ONE

Golbmalogiokta

L asse was dead.

It had been two weeks, and she still couldn't talk about it. Hanna had a hard time saying the word "suicide." But in front of the pastor she had formulated the sentence for the first time: he took himself away.

He was in the hearse that drove ahead of their car. In the coffin. It was inconceivable. Sometimes it felt like she was going numb there in the front seat. Ante was driving, but he was looking more at her than at the road. In the backseat was Anna-Stina, mute and red-eyed. She should reach back to squeeze her hand, but she couldn't do it.

They had picked him up in town and were on their way to the funeral. They would drive behind him, home to the village. She caught a glimpse of the pastor's blond hair in the passenger seat of the hearse. Hanna had specifically requested Carin Gustavsson. She didn't care about any indignant Christians who didn't want to see a woman pastor in their church. Carin had known Lasse, and he had talked about her after Sámi confirmation camp, saying that she was different from the other pastors, that she listened and was even funny. So Hanna had chosen her and hoped she would be able to say something about Lasse, something that could explain what had happened. That there had been something there back when he was fifteen, something Hanna had overlooked.

Carin had been forthright, saying that her husband worked at the mine so she had heard about the suicide right away. He had been found dead in one of the underground areas. Carin said that his coworkers were shocked, because he was always so cheerful, and indeed, that was how she remembered him from confirmation camp.

Back then she had been a relatively new pastor. Lasse had made a big impression on her, and she too would describe him as a positive person. The one who cheered everyone up and who believed in looking past difficulties. She had had private conversations with the teens. But, she told Hanna, it was impossible to get into deep topics with him. He just wanted to have fun.

"And I believed him."

Hanna had listened, looking into her warm eyes and recognizing herself in them. She too had believed him.

"But that was just who he was. Surely it wasn't all pretend, was it?" she had asked.

Carin had taken her hands and held them between her own.

"You must not blame yourself."

It was a beautiful day, with pink streaks of light across the sky. In town, Hanna, Ante, and Anna-Stina had gathered with her brothers and their families. Many cars would join the procession as they approached the next village and the church. Lots of families would be coming from Norway as well. They would gather from all across Sápmi. To say goodbye to her Lasse.

The caravan would grow into a long, winding line before they reached the church. Oncoming cars stopped out of respect for the final journey of the deceased. Those who were coming to the funeral waited in their idling cars outside their houses, or along the road, ready to take their place in the procession of grief. Never would Hanna have imagined that she would be at the head of a caravan to bury her little brother.

The tears began to flow again, and her throat ached as she tried to keep her sobs inside. Ante placed a hand on her thigh and squeezed gently.

"Breathe," he said.

He hadn't left a letter, there was no explanation, and he had sounded so happy when he called her the day before. Her thoughts ran in loops, always returning to the same question. *Why?*

She glanced in the rearview mirror; there were so many cars she couldn't see the end of the line. How would she get through this day? She didn't want to watch his casket lowered into the ground. The thought made her panic, and she grabbed Ante's hand. The whimpering in her throat was back.

"Breathe in." He demonstratively took a deep breath, made her follow his lead. "And out, slowly."

They breathed together. Long, deep breaths.

In the backseat, Anna-Stina started to cry again, and Ante wriggled his hand loose so he could pat her leg.

"It'll be okay, it'll all be okay," he repeated.

CHAPTER THIRTY-TWO

Golbmalogiguokte

The casket sat heavy on the spruce needles in the yard of Hanna and Ante's house. Simple and white, no garlands on top. Mattias could hardly look at it. He didn't know where to fix his gaze. Ante held Hanna up. Her face was twisted with grief. Mattias didn't know how he looked but his face felt stiff.

Lasse's sisters-in-law and a few elderly relatives were rustling paper; there would be psalms sung in Sámi. But most of them knew the words by heart; after all, the old ones couldn't read their own language.

Mattias observed the pastor, who was standing in silence. Later, in the church, she would take over. But this was the family's ceremony, a chance for the dead to come home one last time. But this wasn't even Lasse's home!

Elsa hid behind Siessá. Her bright blue gákti fluttered in the breeze, though her down coat covered her shawl and freshly polished risku. She wore no mittens, and her right hand kept digging in her coat pocket. Unna oabba was white as the snow; even her lips were pale, almost bluish.

Only a few of the men were singing; otherwise it was the women who combined their bright, trembling voices.

Mattias noticed that Áhkku wasn't singing. She had pinched her lips tight and was staring straight ahead to the road. Her brooches were fastened carelessly. Mom had wanted to help, but Áhkku had only waved her off, annoyed. Everyone else looked perfect, their brooches in a straight line across their chests, their shawls unwrinkled. Their shoe bands were neat and exact, and everyone's silver buttons, clasps, and brooches were freshly polished. Mattias hated all of it. But there he stood, back straight and proud as he always was when he wore his gákti.

THE CHURCH WAS FILLED to bursting. Gákti shone bright in all their colors, and brooches reflected the light. It was warm and stuffy, and the snow from their shoes had quickly melted into puddles on the floor.

Mattias couldn't look his friends in the eye. The girls were sobbing and leaning on each other in the pews. The women were crying an unbearable lament. He wanted to hold his ears like Elsa was doing. The men's tears were silent, if they cried at all. Dad hastily wiped a hand across his cheek. Ante held Hanna, and her shoulders shook.

Elsa didn't want to take off her coat, and Mom whispered in irritation. Mattias wanted to rip it off her. She gave in eventually, but kept her hand in her coat pocket. The warmth inside the church had brought the color back to her face. The wooden pews with their curved backs weren't comfortable for the little ones, and she tucked her legs up beneath her. Mom sighed, but didn't have the energy to say anything.

He forced himself to look at Lasse's smiling picture next to the casket. It had been impossible to find a different picture, because this was how he always looked. He probably wanted to be remembered this way. But no one trusted that smile anymore.

Mattias tried to control his breathing and ran his hands up and down the leather pants Áhkku had sewn. Couldn't someone open a window? For Christ's sake, it was boiling in here!

The flowers on the casket and next to the altar gave off a stifling scent. The pastor held her Bible in a firm grip. She looked right at Mattias with a gentle smile, and he fixed his eyes on her. *Don't fucking smile! What are you smiling for?* The pastor seemed to lose her train of thought for a moment, as if she had heard his thoughts.

The organ began to play and Mattias hated that too; it only made the crying start up again. Elsa went still beside him; her eyes grew shiny.

When the last note faded away, the pastor took a deep breath and began to speak. About his Lasse.

IT HAD BEEN DECIDED that Lasse's friends would serve as pallbearers, and Mattias wasn't one of them. He had wanted to protest, say that obviously he should take part, shove aside that one who was at the front and had tears streaming down his cheeks. Mattias would have carried Lasse on a strong shoulder without crying like that.

It was cold outside, and people shivered next to him. Mattias wasn't freezing in the least. Mom rested a hand on his shoulder but he pulled away. They watched the casket as it slowly disappeared below the surface of the earth. Elsa took a few steps forward, and then a quick step back.

There was muttering among the women who were supposed to choose a Sámi psalm. Their voices were brittle, as before, but the song gradually grew.

Hanna hung like a ragdoll between Ante and Mom. Exhausted and blank. Mom patted her cheek and whispered in her ear. Elsa must have spotted her chance to flee, because suddenly she was gone. He saw her by the wall, with her back to them and her shoulders raised. He should take care of her, but he didn't have the strength.

CHAPTER THIRTY-THREE

Golbmalogigolbma

The smörgåstårta had three layers; the salmon was fresh, the shrimp large, the cucumbers cut into spirals, and the sprigs of dill had not yet wilted. Efficient women moved quickly between tables bearing carafes of coffee, pitchers of milk, and freshly mixed fruit drink.

Elsa looked around the room in surprise each time she heard laughter. She impatiently brushed away strands of hair that had fallen out of her braid. Mom had braided her hair too tight and now her scalp hurt. But tomorrow when she woke up, she would have angelic curls.

She picked the salmon out of her piece of smörgåstårta. The fish was salty and soft on her tongue. She didn't want to talk to anyone, but kept her eyes on the pastor, who was sitting at the end of the table. She was talking to an older man who seemed to be hard of hearing.

Elsa waited patiently, and when the pastor finally stood up she hurriedly followed suit. The pastor put on her black coat and Elsa got into hers, which Mom had let her keep on the back of her chair after she stubbornly insisted.

It had gotten dark outside, and laughter came from a massive snow-bank, where Elsa saw her cousins climbing up and down to wrestle at the top. She stood there, swinging her gákti around her legs. She wanted to climb up there and play too. But when she saw the pastor heading briskly around the side of the building, she had to follow.

Elsa peered around the corner, and there she was, taking a drag from a cigarette. The cherry flared up. Elsa approached her slowly; she was quite close before the pastor noticed her and stubbed her cigarette out against a snow-covered windowsill.

"Hi!" she said, smiling with her mouth closed.

Elsa said hi back but gazed down at the upturned toes of her beak boots.

"What a lovely gákti you have."

She nodded but didn't look up.

"Did your mama make it?"

"I helped."

Her voice was weak but now she looked up, feeling braver.

"Wow, what a clever girl. Was it hard?"

She shook her head. Squinted.

"Are pastors allowed to smoke?"

"Yes, as a matter of fact, we are."

"I don't think pastors should smoke. And I don't think people should laugh at a funeral."

There, she said it. Her heart beat faster. Pastors could fly into a terrible rage; Elsa knew from accompanying Áhkku to her Laestadian services. Áhkku had told her they weren't angry, that she wasn't listening properly.

"Well, you know, it's a good thing to laugh and remember all the fun things about Lasse. It's okay to cry and laugh."

"No."

"Okay."

The pastor rubbed her palms together and waited. Elsa looked down at the ground, then straight into her eyes, and then down again. She chewed at her upper lip, which was already red and chapped.

"Will Lasse not get into heaven because he killed himself?"

The pastor grew serious and spoke slowly. "Of course he will get into heaven."

"But my áhkku says it's a sin to kill yourself."

The pastor placed a hand on Elsa's upper arm and squeezed it lightly.

"But I'm a pastor, and I know. And I say he'll go to heaven. You know, people used to say that kind of thing in the past, before they knew better. And old folks sometimes believe that."

"But I've heard kids say the same thing. They said so at school."

"That's because they've been listening to old folks who shouldn't say such things."

"Are you sure?"

"One hundred percent."

Elsa's eyes roved. Her cousins were on the snowbank, laughing loudly.

"Anything else on your mind?"

Elsa slipped her hand into her pocket, felt Nástegallu's ear, let her finger-tips follow its softness.

"Um."

The pastor crouched down. She cocked her head.

Elsa took a deep breath and whispered, "If you tell a lie, will you go to hell?"

"Did you tell a lie?"

"Maybe."

"Sometimes you have to, and everyone does it. It doesn't mean you'll go to hell."

Anna-Stina called out to her.

"I have to go."

"So your name is Elsa. What a lovely name."

Elsa slowly pulled the zipper of her pocket closed.

"Do you promise I'm not going to hell?"

The pastor nodded and took Elsa's cold hands in hers. She gently pressed them together.

"I promise."

PART II

CÄKČADÁLVI

AUTUMN–WINTER 2018

CHAPTER THIRTY-FOUR

Golbmaloginjeallje

The green metal can stood open in the snow, and the smell of gasoline tickled his nose. Robert stuck the funnel he'd made out of a plastic bottle into the engine of the snowmobile and picked up the can. He groaned through the first few glugs but then it went faster and was easier. He had to put in oil too, he reminded himself.

He'd had the Ski-Doo, a Formula 500, for more than twenty years, but what use would he have for one of those new ones, which he couldn't fix himself. The finish on the front left-hand side was scratched, but it wasn't all that visible. He'd been planning to repair it, just in case someone checked up on him. But time passed and no one came. The can was empty now and he dropped it, grabbing his bad right shoulder. He was out of tramadol and the doctor wouldn't prescribe more. Take Tylenol and ibuprofen, she said, but they were like air. They had absolutely no effect.

Robert screwed the cap onto the can and wiped the gasoline from his fingers on his pants. The tough yellow fabric was soiled with black stains; he never realized how strong the smell was until he got inside and hung the pants up in the entryway. He pulled up the zipper of his blue fleece, which had only cost fifty kronor on sale at Intersport. He should have bought more. He pulled on the black coat hanging on the handlebars of the snowmobile. It was Pop's old one; the lining was coming out of a tear just above the pocket, and the cuff of one sleeve was ripped. But it was warmer than any other coat he'd ever had. It shielded him from wind and water. And it was a Helly Hansen, even if, by now, the two letters of the logo were visible only as two shadows on the chest.

The snow crunched beneath his Graninge boots, which had also belonged to Pop. They were a size too big, but with an extra pair of ragg socks they fit perfectly. He lifted the garage door with his left hand. The gun safe was open and he took out the hunting rifle. Pop's old Mauser was still in the safe. He'd left it behind when he died, just like everything else. Robert had no siblings. It had always only been him and Pop.

Ma had left them back when he was in elementary school. Pop always said she'd had weak nerves, that she needed to get help at the hospital. But Robert had seen her in town. The time his whole class took a field trip to the swimming pool and the bus stopped outside and everyone piled out. He hung back because there, between the birches, on the path, stood Ma, laughing with another woman. Ma had been wearing a short yellow dress, and her hair was cut short, with straight bangs.

He hadn't said a word to Pop. He'd climbed off the bus, walked into the pool complex, and then jumped off the thirty-foot diving board, landing partway on his back, which stung something awful.

Pop drank a lot, and Ma had said she was fed up. Apparently she was fed up with Robert too, because he was left behind in the village. He had vague memories of Ma sweeping him into her arms, and Pop holding his Mauser. Maybe she'd meant to take him, her little boy, with her after all. But when she got to town, she probably discovered that life was better without the both of them.

His fingers trembled as he searched for the ammunition in the metal box under the workbench. In past years it had smelled of curly wood shavings from when Pop used the planer. That smell had long faded by now, and the workbench was covered in dust and screws and nails that needed sorting into smaller boxes.

He smacked his hand against his thigh twice, hard, but the trembling wouldn't stop. He dropped a shell on the floor but left it there, grabbing the rifle and closing the garage door behind him. But it wouldn't fully close, and snow would blow in through the half-inch gap overnight. These were the sorts of little things Pop had been so good at fixing. Robert could fix them too. Pop had made sure he knew how to do everything, but he'd never been totally satisfied with Robert's work. Pop would've fixed that gap in fifteen minutes.

Robert took out his phone and found it was almost impossible to hit the right spots with his shaking index finger. No one called these days; it was all texts, and he didn't like it. He typed out the time and place. Received a thumbs-up in return. Like stupid little babies, sending all these cartoon thumbs.

The cough tore at his throat, and he pulled the zipper up all the way to his chin. It was beautiful out, so much so you could stand there staring like an idiot. The sky was violet, with pale rays of sun so low they almost didn't make it over the mountain. November was nearing its end, and in December the sun would abandon them to the season of blue light. He snorted; he didn't give a shit about the colors. It took some effort to throw his leg over the black seat. He turned the key. The starter cord had gotten awfully hard to pull recently, and he should fix it. The way it was now, he wouldn't be able to pull hard enough, with that shoulder hurting like the devil all the time.

He'd left the window light on in the kitchen, and from the outside it actually looked cozy, with the curtain and the glass lamp. Raija barked un-happily from inside when she heard the snowmobile. Soon he could see her in the window; she'd gotten up on the kitchen table, despite her limp. He brandished a fist at her.

"Down, Raija!"

She didn't pay any attention, and her barking turned to a loud whine. He wanted nothing more than to have her sitting behind him on the snow-mobile, the way they'd ridden together for the past seven years, but he couldn't. Her limp had gotten worse.

He accelerated slowly across the yard and rounded the fir trees he'd planted three years ago, which were finally coming into their own and blocking the view to the neighbor's house a few hundred yards away. Pop would have probably said he'd planted them too close together and three trees weren't enough; it should have been five.

He followed his old snowmobile tracks to the stream where he always fished and approached the lake, where in past years he'd netted whitefish from the old plastic rowboat. You used to be able to sell whitefish for a good price, but not anymore; the lake was probably totally dead. He'd had trouble recovering this loss of income.

He stopped and listened for Petri's snowmobile, then turned off at the widest path, which would take you all the way to town, faster than by car. He looked behind him, no one there. A regular old day. Most people were working, and it was too cold to spend time outside. There probably wasn't much of a risk, but it still set his heart to pounding; his pulse was galloping too fast.

Petri was waiting for him at the old whitefish lake, his snowmobile idling, and he grinned.

"A small flock, less than two miles that way."

He waved one big beige leather mitten, indicating the direction. That was good. They could easily split the flock and take one, maybe two.

Petri had finally gotten his hands on a cabin, and it was even down by the river. He'd overpaid by an incredible sum, but he'd told Robert time and again that it was worth it. Especially around Midsummer, when the salmon were heading upstream. Or in the spring, when he brought the auger down to the river to go ice fishing, morning to night.

Not long after Pop died, Robert had taken the snowmobile and gone to visit Petri and the ice-fishing holes. He put some feelers out, dropped it for a month or so, and then came by the rapids with his fishing rod and was offered coffee by the fire. Finally, in the sauna back home, after a few beers, he'd asked if Petri would like to help him out with something.

And here they were, a few years later, and it had gone better than Robert had expected. They rode calmly, didn't want to scare the reindeer. But who the fuck would believe those Lapps when they said snowmobiles scared the reindeer, considering the way *they* rode around.

The wind stung and chilled his ears. When he pulled down his hat, he felt a jolt in his shoulder that made him groan. He squeezed the throttle harder and grimaced. Petri sped up too.

Sure enough, there was a flock of six reindeer trying to move through thick snow. Some had their heads deep under the snow cover, kicking their hooves to try to get at the pasturage. One or two looked up and spotted them. They stopped, and Petri pointed at one reindeer that had ended up slightly farther away from the rest. Robert nodded, climbed off the snowmobile, unhitched the old wooden sled, and took the rifle from under the tarp.

"Should we have some fun first?" he said, getting back on the snowmobile again.

Petri lit up. "For sure!"

The flock sensed danger in their movements and retreated toward the pines on a nearby hill. The lone reindeer looked up in surprise and heaved itself sideways. Its skinny legs sank deep into the snow. It wouldn't be able to go anywhere fast enough. Robert was disappointed; he didn't want it to be too easy. He wanted a good chase.

"Get out your phone! Record this!" Petri called, driving right up beside the reindeer.

Robert turned on his camera and Petri threw himself from the snowmobile onto the reindeer. He grabbed its antlers and managed to cling to the animal's back. The reindeer began to run, and Robert laughed so hard he couldn't hold the phone steady. Petri was heavy, and the reindeer was panting as it struggled to get onto the snowmobile path. Suddenly it slipped, and Petri fell off. He lay in the snow, giving a thumbs-up.

"You got it all, right?"

Robert nodded and the phone went back in the inner pocket of his coat.

Enough messing around. His adrenaline was pumping, but his hands didn't shake when he grabbed the handlebars and squeezed the throttle. The reindeer ran on nimbler legs along the snowmobile track, probably thinking it was all over, but this was only the start. Robert didn't wait for Petri; he accelerated, first slowly, then faster. He followed the animal as it turned off into the snow, and the snowmobile brushed its hind legs. Not enough for them to break. Good. He didn't want it to be over too soon. Now Petri had caught up and cut off the reindeer's escape route from the other side, and it got tangled up in itself, jumping this way and that. Robert raised a hand to warn Petri back. He waited for the reindeer to get on the snowmobile path again, and then he drove behind it, letting the roaring engine do its job. He hit it from behind, so it tipped over on its side and the skis of the snowmobile rested on its neck. Perfect. The reindeer's eyes looked like they were popping from their sockets, and it panted with its tongue hanging out. Not dead yet. No broken bones. He got out his phone again and took a picture. Then he backed up, letting the reindeer go free. But it lay there like it was paralyzed. Maybe he'd crushed some vital part after all? He circled it once on the snowmobile, and Petri did the same.

"Let's just kill this one," he said.

"No, what?" Petri dragged his wrist under his runny nose.

The reindeer had gotten up on unsteady legs.

"It's too stressed already. I'm not about to deliver bad meat."

"What the hell."

Petri gazed over at the pines, where the other reindeer had fled. No sight of them. They could be far away by now.

"You go on and take one of the others," said Robert.

Petri looked at him in surprise but nodded, then took off in a tight turn, leaving Robert behind with a reindeer that had started to limp along the snowmobile track. Its fur was grayish-brown, and it was a well-fed creature. The Lapps were always going on about how their reindeer were starving, demanding subsidies to feed them, but here, right in front of him, was proof that they were lying.

He stuck his finger under his upper lip and the wet snus flew out of his mouth and landed in the snow. He ran his tongue across his front teeth and up into the gap where there were always leftover bits of tobacco. He spit on the snow.

Now.

He hit the throttle hard and accelerated over the path. The reindeer tried again to leap aside, to run in the deep snow. It sank down and whirled around, kicking, struggling. He liked that. He hit its hind legs with decent force and—*crack*. There was no way he could have heard it over the engine, but he knew. The reindeer lay still with its eyes turned to the sky. Robert stopped but let the engine idle. He went over and inspected its legs, which were broken and pointed in the wrong direction. He got out his phone and took video, panning from the broken legs to the trembling muzzle. Its gaze was no longer full of terror, just resignation. Maybe he should cut off its antlers while it was still alive. Just because.

A sudden shot echoed through the darkness and a magpie flushed out of a pine. Petri. That settled it. He had to hurry. He kicked the reindeer in the head with his Graninge boot, while he considered his options. He knew it would be a while before Petri was finished. He'd trained him well—there were important measures to take, to keep from ruining the meat.

As the reindeer closed its eyes, Robert got down on his knees and watched it closely. Warm air gusted from its nostrils. Its fur was shimmery. He grabbed it around the muzzle, hard, with his whole hand, even as he gazed over at the sled. Should he get the axe? Yes. He stood up, walked over with some effort, lifted the green tarp, which was stiff with cold, and found the axe. Butterflies in his stomach. Chop off one hoof at a time, maybe? Last time he did that, Petri just about threw up and Robert had laughed at him. Petri always wanted to kill them too fast. He had no patience.

He let the blade of the axe slide about four inches above its front hooves. There was no point in doing its back hooves; the hind legs were already broken. Reindeer don't scream in pain. Too bad, really.

Petri's snowmobile was approaching, and Robert gazed toward the rise. He lifted the axe, swung, and brought the blade down on the reindeer's head, splitting its skull. The smell of warm blood rose like steam in the cold air.

Petri pulled up beside him and tilted his head back in a nod, pleased. He'd tied the reindeer to the snowmobile by the antlers, dragging it behind him. There was a trail of blood the whole way, and Robert wanted to scream at his dumbass friend that he should have come to get the sled. Petri saw his axe and made a face.

"Nasty."

He untied the reindeer from his snowmobile and together they shoved it onto the tarp. Robert took special care to make sure there was tarp both beneath and on top of the animal.

"We better hurry the fuck up, since you fired off that shot."

"I had to. No good way to use the knife. Plus I couldn't hear any cars or snowmobiles around."

"Still."

"Taking it to your place?"

"You think I'm going to cut it up at home?" Robert snorted. "We'll go to the usual butchering spot and take care of it, then I'll take it all to the freezer."

"I don't get why we can't butcher them here."

"Well, I suppose we might as well since you left a trail of blood that whole way. But we're not going to."

Looking sullen, Petri pressed each nostril down with his index finger, one at a time, as he rocketed out the snot.

CHAPTER THIRTY-FIVE

Golbmalogivihtta

There was unusually little snow for this time of year. The E45 highway was bare in spots. The painted white lines on the asphalt had nearly eroded away. The road was cracked, and in the spring the little blades of grass would push their way through once more, as if the ground were trying to heal itself, return to what it had once been, make everything green and forested again. The cracks in the concrete were deep, and one pothole in particular, on the road between the villages, had wrecked the undercarriage of a number of cars.

Elsa was driving slowly in her dad's new red Nissan Qashqai, looking for signs in the ditch. She slowed down well before the pit. The Transport Administration hadn't put up any warning signs—really, there should be signs along large stretches of the road between the villages. Sometimes the Finnish asphalters came by and for a while there was smooth, black asphalt, but everyone knew that it wouldn't be long before the road was barely passable again. As a little girl, Elsa had loved all the bumps, and Dad knew just how to accelerate to put a tickle in your stomach. But they could only do that in the old car.

If there had been snow on the road, they could have followed Áhkku's little footprints. Dad had headed the other way in the old car and Elsa drove toward the next village. It seemed most likely that Áhkku had gone that way but turned off onto the gravel path that led to what had once been their meeting place. Back when Áhkku was a little girl. Elsa wanted to drive faster, but she had to search the road along the way. Sometimes

Áhkku didn't have the strength to go far, and they might find her in a snowbank, red in the face with effort or blue in the lips because she was chilled through.

Áhkku was no longer able to live on her own, so Mattias was going to take her house. Maybe that was what had set off her anxiety today. Something had woken her legs, made her go searching. For what had once been.

Áhkku had been living with them for the past few weeks now. After she nearly burned down her own house by leaving a forgotten candle lit on the kitchen table, Dad had had enough and took her key away, carried over her necessities, and installed her in the bedroom. Mom hadn't complained, just made up a bed for herself in the living room each night. And eventually Mattias was told that it was time for him to move into Áhkku and Áddjá's house, as had long been the plan. Áddjá had died years ago. He had slowly faded away until he was almost transparent at the end. Elsa had held his hand as he lay in his bed with its freshly washed and mangled sheets. Mom and Áhkku had needed to work together to get him up so they could change the bedding. This was when death was approaching, and Áhkku said that no pastor would find her husband in filthy sheets.

Áhkku had grieved in silence and stillness, had let no one embrace her. Then it was as if her mind couldn't take it anymore. It had happened gradually. A pot left on the stove. A forgotten name. A vacant look at Elsa. The recognition was no longer there.

Dad resisted for a long time, didn't want to see it. Mom minded her tongue but watched over Áhkku. It was easier now that she was living with them. But sometimes even Mom needed to attend to other things, and these were always the times when they found the front door open and the little footprints heading for the road.

On occasion a neighbor would call and say, "She's taking off again." The ones who knew her well would stop and try to offer her a ride, but most of the time she just looked at them with a darkness in her eyes. Maybe she would say that she was going home to her mom and dad. But the one she was looking for was her little sister, who had died before her eighth birthday. She'd caught pneumonia up in the mountains. There had been six siblings, until the youngest didn't make it through the winter. Áhkku had been eleven, had been closest to her little sister and felt responsible for her.

Elsa often sat with Áhkku on the living room sofa, listening once more to the same description of her little sister, who had looked alive but felt ice cold. Her eyelashes had rested on the blue circles under her eyes. Áhkku would cry, speaking like a child, like the grieving eleven-year-old she had been.

And now she was out searching again.

The thermometer said it was ten below. Not terribly cold, but who knew how warmly dressed she was this time. And it was strange that no one had called. Maybe she had trudged straight off into the forest; maybe she had taken one of the snowmobile trails. It would be impossible to find her if she had. She was so slight that she hardly left any footprints when she walked on those trails.

A car approached Elsa from behind and passed her at high speeds. Honking. Annoyed that she was doing hardly thirty miles per hour in a zone marked fifty-five. Norwegian plates. She honked back.

She turned off onto the gravel road, which was covered in even more snow. The car bounced heavily over the potholes, which typically filled with water in the summer. She gazed out on either side; no footprints in the snow and few snowmobile tracks. Her phone rang, and she put it on speaker.

Dad's voice was tired.

"Did you find her?"

"No, I'm on the gravel road now."

"Call me the minute . . ."

"Yup."

He hung up. They should have come here together and split up on the trails. Elsa rolled the window down a crack and the cold air whined around her head. She stopped the car and turned off the engine to hear better, then opened the door and climbed out.

"Áhkku!"

Her call flew across snow-covered forests and bogs, then faded into silence. That thick silence threatened to burst her eardrums with its pressure. Elsa walked to the closest snowmobile trail and had to lie down on the ground to look for indentations. Nothing. She decided to drive up the hill; it would give her a better vantage point to gaze out across the bogs.

Just as she reached the crest of the hill, she caught a glimpse of a shadow to her right, in the forest. She hit the brakes and focused her gaze, then turned off the engine and got out. Yes, there was movement near the birches that had never recovered from the invasion of the peppered moth caterpillars. Only their trunks remained, and they were turning black from the top down, dying slowly. She headed down the snowmobile trail; she didn't leave much of a trace herself. People said they were alike, she and Áhkku. Small and quick. Elsa could see that, their noses and lips and smiles, but her eyes were just like Mom's.

Áhkku was propping herself against a birch with her hands. It looked like she was stretching. Elsa almost wanted to laugh, but she knew it would only turn into tears.

"I think she's hiding," Áhkku said, her lower lip trembling in the cold.

She wasn't wearing mittens and her hands were red. Her hat had been tossed on the ground. Elsa picked it up, shook off the snow, and gently pulled it over Áhkku's gray hair. Her braid had come loose and her long hair hung down over a spine one could easily feel with the gentlest touch of the fingertips. At least she was wearing a coat, but her pants were far too thin. When the wind picked up, the fluttering fabric revealed her skinny legs.

"We have to go home now, Áhkku."

Elsa texted her father: "Found her." He wouldn't reply.

"But we're playing," Áhkku said with a cheerful smile.

"Yeah, but it's almost dark and we need to go home."

"I peed my pants."

Áhkku looked down at her legs and Elsa saw the dark spots on the blue fabric. She sighed and hoped the blanket was still in the backseat of the car.

"All the more reason to go home, so you don't get too chilly and catch a cold."

"But I can't leave my little sister in the forest."

Elsa took out her phone and held it to her ear.

"Oh, so she's at your place. All right then. Yeah, then we'll head home too. Glad to hear little sister is inside."

She spoke clearly and nodded resolutely at Áhkku, who squinted with suspicion.

"You heard that, right? Little sister is inside already."

Áhkku looked around in concern, even as Elsa gently took her by the shoulders and guided her toward the car. She was a head taller than her áhkku. She'd been overjoyed when it happened, the first family member she'd surpassed in height. Mattias had laughed, saying that this was no great feat. He himself had shot up and was almost six feet tall. Towered above Dad's short, stooping body. Mom had remarked, rather thoughtlessly, that it was lucky Mattias had gotten her genes.

Elsa spread the blanket over the passenger seat and helped Áhkku up and onto it. She buckled her seatbelt, got behind the wheel, and locked the doors. Áhkku had tried on previous occasions to jump out of a moving vehicle. There was nowhere to turn around, so she backed up and onto the main road again.

"Where are we going, Elsa?"

She was back, almost herself again. Brief moments of her real áhkku, sometimes it happened.

"Oh, we're just going home for dinner now."

The strong stench of urine wafted through the warm car, and Elsa gagged. She pulled her wool scarf over her nose and leaned on the gas.

CHAPTER THIRTY-SIX

Golbmalogiguhtta

The TV was on low and Áhkku was sitting still under the blanket. She shivered every time a cold gust of wind found its way in from the front hall. Mattias and Mom were hurrying in and out, carrying clothing, a lamp, a boot warmer, and a box of ladles and bowls. When Áhkku's head fell back and she dozed off with her mouth open, like a hungry baby bird, Elsa slipped gingerly off the sofa.

She pulled on her down jacket and stuck her feet in Dad's big boots, just because they were the closest ones. Mattias was standing in the shed with his arms crossed, watching as Mom cleaned it out. She was talking to herself, as usual; they knew not to answer her or ask questions, just let her be. Her chatter was the way she created structure, and she didn't want anyone to butt in. Now she was leaning into one of the old white wardrobes, which was full of snowmobile suits, work pants, hats, and mittens.

Elsa raised her eyebrows in Mattias's direction, but his expression didn't change.

"Might as well get rid of some stuff while we're moving you," Mom muttered. "No one has used these snow pants for years. Toss 'em!"

Elsa's old black Peak snow pants flew through the air and landed at her feet. They were still in fine shape, but she left them where they were.

"Isa should have tossed these old waders ages ago. Why are they still here?"

They were black too and came flying out, landing in the "toss" pile.

"Weren't we going to bring in some old dishes and a bedside table?" Elsa asked.

Mom looked over her shoulder and nodded at the pile of boxes to the left of the door as she threw a blue down vest.

Elsa grabbed the box; it was heavy. She turned to Mattias.

"I need your help with this."

"Get the bedside table first. You can manage that yourself."

He had a deep voice, but he often spoke so softly that you had to strain to hear him. He was twenty-six. Subdued. A mutterer. And he never held anyone's gaze longer than necessary.

"Well, what are you waiting for? You grab something too, so we might actually be done at some point," she said, picking up the blue bedside table, which Mattias had ordered from IKEA a long time ago.

That was when he had been planning to move out of the house for the first time, but in the end it never came to pass. The house he was supposed to rent was sold instead. He'd taken the news without much of a reaction, and put the table in the storage shed. That was how he ended up at home for another year.

It was strange to be living in the house with four adults. Elsa had graduated from high school in June and returned from town, back to her room with the pale green wallpaper, which she'd picked out when she was fourteen.

At first she had been thinking of applying to other places, of going to the Samernas Education Center in Jokkmokk, but she ended up changing her mind. She was too homesick after her years in town, and it went without saying that she would return to the reindeer.

Mattias bent down and thoughtfully rolled up the old waders, then tucked them into the box that held the set of dishes. He squeezed past her. Elsa followed him, staggering, searching for the right words. They climbed over the piles of snow that separated the two houses. Mattias pushed the handle down with one elbow and the door opened with a creak. He didn't take off his shoes, just headed straight into the kitchen and gently placed the box of dishes on the table. It was covered in a red-checked tablecloth, which was quite the eyesore with its tiny holes and burn marks left by a hot pan. He was going to replace everything, he said. Elsa kicked off her shoes, went into the bedroom, and set down the table. He'd brought in his own bed. Áhkku's bed was in Mattias's room now, and with it came the sharp odor of urine. Mom thought it should be burned, and Dad said nothing at all.

Elsa went back to the kitchen.

"Should I put the dishes in the cupboards?" She lifted a flap of the box. "Weren't we going to toss these waders?"

Mattias whipped around to face her; he'd been drinking directly from the tap. The water was so cold it was probably turning to ice on the enamel.

"Yeah."

"Okay, well . . ."

"I'll take care of it, Elsa."

She missed the days when he called her unna oabba. She didn't know why he stopped, and by the time she noticed it was too late to ask him to go back to doing it. She must have been about ten. It wasn't long after Lasse died. But by then everything was so confusing and weird, and words had lost their meaning. For a long time, she hardly heard what anyone said to her. It was like her ears were blocked. She still shuddered, sometimes, at the memory of that sensation. And somewhere along the way, her existence as unna oabba had come to an end. To Mattias, she became Elsa.

"You can't fish in those anymore."

They were Áddjá's old waders. His initials were neatly inscribed in black marker on the white lining, near the seam in back. They all had memories of times when he needed to guide the reindeer through a stream and had to pull on his waders. He'd also fished in them, in the calmer parts of the river; no one went in too deep. It was easy to slip on the wet rocks.

"I know."

Mattias's voice vibrated in his chest. He draped the waders over a kitchen chair and then picked up six plates, placing them in the pine cupboard above the sink. The porcelain clinked when he placed six shallow bowls next to them.

Elsa sighed and left the house. Mom was standing in the shed, inspecting an old Monopoly box.

"Do you want to keep your games?"

"Come on, Enná, are you really going to sort through all this stuff right now?"

"It's driving me nuts that it never gets cleaned out. Soon I won't even be able to get to the freezer, and when I have to start moving things out of the way just to get to the meat, it's time to get rid of it."

The freezer was white and rumbled quietly in its corner. But the many power outages of the autumn made it anxious. The 150-gallon freezer was full of months', if not years', worth of food. Reindeer and moose steaks, salmon, char, the grayling that needed to be eaten soon, gáhkku, cinnamon rolls, cloudberries, lingonberries, and blueberries. If Elsa needed something from the bottom, she had to boost herself up and tip the top half of her body over the edge to fish it out. There was another freezer in the kitchen, an upright one, next to a fridge that was just as full. Mom and Elsa always made sure they had meat sauce, lasagna, and meatballs on hand. Elsa could cook. She could sew. And she could care for the reindeer. So why would she be anywhere but here?

Elsa patted Mom on the shoulder and told her to calm down.

"Just tell me what to carry in next, okay?"

Into her arms Mom shoved curtains: long, gray pelmets they'd once had in the living room, simple white lace curtains that had been in her bedroom, and a heavy, over-patterned green pelmet that had been in the kitchen window. Mom had ordered new curtains for all the windows.

Elsa could hardly see over the pile as she wandered back through the cold, across the yards, and into her brother's house. He had a house now. He was a grown man with a place of his own. Sure, it was next door to theirs, but he was his own person now. Then again, he really wasn't *that* alone. Or maybe he was *too* alone. No girlfriend since Inga-Lill dumped him four years ago. And that kind of thing didn't go unpunished, it was like, *That was that.* If he wasn't good enough for one person, no one was good enough for him. Inga-Lill moved on, met someone from town, was expecting her second kid, and posted pictures on Instagram, always the same flattering angle with a Mona Lisa smile. Elsa couldn't help but look. Maybe Mattias did the same, and thought about what might have been. A family of his own, it probably would have been good for him.

Elsa placed the curtains on the living room sofa. It was one of those deep, chocolate-brown leather sofas with a high back and big, round arms that everyone had in the early nineties. Mom and Hanna had replaced their sofas ages ago, but the old monstrosities were still in the homes of the old folks. Easy-to-clean genuine leather sofas were not the sort of thing you sent to recycling, according to Áhkku.

"You're going to get rid of the sofa, right?"

"Yeah."

"Are you going to look for a new one in town?"

Mattias let out a snort. "Sure, like I have the time for that."

His shoulders were raised in irritation; he was banging silverware around in the drawers. The top one was sticking, and he shoved it in, hard.

"Want me to hang up the curtains?"

She didn't wait for his reply, just dragged over Áhkku's old stool with its foldout footrest.

"You can't toss this stool. If you don't want it, I do."

She took down the white curtain rod and blew off the dust, slipped the gray curtains on, and hung it back up. She tugged and fiddled with the fabric until the folds looked just right. Through the window she could see Áhkku, who was still asleep on the sofa.

CHAPTER THIRTY-SEVEN

Golbmalogičieža

The gravestone was covered in white from the recent snowfall and last night's storm winds. Only the top of it was visible. The siblings hadn't chosen a smooth stone with a polished, gleaming surface. They'd picked one that had a rough texture and some sharp edges, so you could feel it beneath your fingertips. No straight lines. An untamed stone for a man who had never let himself be tamed. Elsa couldn't help but think that it was exactly what he had wanted—to be tamed, to belong, to be like everyone else—but it was never possible, for reasons she had been way too young to understand. His promises had left her in the wind. And the answers she had waited for, that were supposed to return on the wind, never came.

She leaned against the wooden shaft of the shovel. Anna-Stina was rustling the plastic bag, counting the gravesite candles; as usual, she didn't want to look at the gravestone.

"I forgot the matches," she muttered, turning back toward the plowed path between the graves.

It was always something she'd forgotten and Elsa left behind. In the summer, with mosquitos stubbornly whining around her face, as she tried to plant the flowers they'd bought at the gas station in the next village. And in the winter, like today, with snow shovel in hand.

She tensed her arms and abs and drove the shovel hard into the ground, but it didn't go more than halfway down. She heaved and groaned, throwing snow behind her. Moving faster, scooping and tossing. Soon her back was hot. As she got closer to the stone, she moved the shovel cautiously forward until it stopped. A dull clunk.

She made a tiny path leading up to his name and the dates. It was still unbelievable. She scraped at the stone with her gloved hand to loosen the snow. In the spring it sometimes looked like the stone was crying, as the snow melted and trickled down its rugged surface.

Anna-Stina returned and fumbled with the candles, placing them close together near the gravestone. She lit a match. The flame flared up and she cupped her hand around it.

Over the past few years, this was their ritual. When they were little, they came along with Hanna and watched her plant flowers or light candles. When they got old enough to do it on their own, Hanna didn't come as often. She didn't believe he was there anyway. And forgiveness seemed far off. But it was seldom to anyone's advantage to be angry at the dead.

Elsa and Anna-Stina never cried at the gravesite, but then again typically no one cried in the company of another except at funerals. The tears she didn't have time for on that freezing winter day would have to find some other occasion. Neither of them said much either. Musing aloud over who he might have become was pointless. The ball was in Anna-Stina's court, then as now. Elsa would have gladly cried and reflected with Anna-Stina, especially when they were firmly in their teenage years and crying came easily. But Anna-Stina had rejected all such attempts.

"He's dead, and we're still here," she said.

Today he would have turned thirty-two. He probably would have sent pictures from another country. A big smile. With that wandering eye. Everyone would have believed his happy grin; no one would have questioned his decision to celebrate his birthday on a different continent.

It was easy to forget people who had died, especially if you were only nine when it happened. For a while Elsa had circled the grown-ups, trying to hear, to find an explanation for why he no longer existed. She lay under the kitchen table, lingered in the laundry room, followed Mom around as she talked on the phone, and pressed her ear to the door when it was closed in her face. Áhkku only talked about sin, and Elsa didn't want to hear any of that. Mom shut herself in a room to cry, but it wasn't easy to understand why. Elsa wasn't sure it had to do with his death.

And Mattias.

She didn't even want to think about him. She didn't know whether their parents had tried to reach out to her brother. Presumably they had all just fled in different directions, in the hope that they would soon be able to move on, to forget.

Elsa looked at Anna-Stina, who was awkwardly trying to brush the remaining snow from the gravestone.

Elsa had asked if she knew why, but Anna-Stina had been quiet and sullen and eventually shoved Elsa backwards into the snow, shrieking that it was none of her business. So they went their separate ways, sitting far apart on the school bus and eating at different tables in the lunchroom. That winter, she had hated him.

The snow melted, spring arrived, and when the birches leafed out in June, Anna-Stina turned eleven. Mom and Hanna had run into each other at the store in the next village, and Mom came home with more than milk. It was an invitation to a birthday party. Elsa had been ready and dressed for hours before it was time to leave, and she had wrapped up the book she'd actually bought for herself a week or so earlier. She had tried to control herself and walk slowly along the main road and up the hill to the house no one in the family had visited in months. When Anna-Stina hugged her and took the present, everything instantly changed. They were friends again.

"Shall we go?" Anna-Stina asked, without waiting for a response.

Elsa bent down and rearranged the candles into the shape of a heart before following slowly.

The seatbelt was stiff and reluctant to buckle. Anna-Stina's car, an old Renault, was not made for the cold.

"When are you going to get a new car? Don't you remember what Lasse said about the worthless French?"

Anna-Stina laughed and Elsa wanted to reach out a hand and squeeze her shoulder, but she didn't. Some people said their friendship was unequal, that Anna-Stina was always in charge and that Elsa was too submissive to her. But it wasn't true, not now. There was no way she would live in Anna-Stina's shadow anymore.

Death had left them more or less alone, to solve the problem that was life. And sure, there were times when she and Anna-Stina had grown apart, like when she started using makeup and her body developed in ways that embarrassed Elsa. Childish, Anna-Stina's friends called Elsa. But that hadn't stopped Anna-Stina from coming to visit her in the evenings. And when Elsa started seventh grade things evened out again. When Mom let her wear mascara.

Siessá sometimes asked why she didn't have any friends, but Elsa would just laugh and say she had Anna-Stina. And it didn't hurt. It was true. And it didn't matter that she was only good enough when no one else felt like driving Anna-Stina to the next village.

In between the times they spent together, she became her own person.

"Do you want to go home or are you coming over?" Anna-Stina asked.

Elsa smiled and said she obviously wanted to come over. Anna-Stina had her own place, a small apartment in the only building in the next village that had six units.

Elsa had kept her apartment in town, the one she'd rented during high school. Sometimes she went to town just to be there. She often brought her skis and went downhill skiing or saw a movie with some of her friends who'd stayed, electing not to continue their schooling somewhere else.

These days, the apartment was a place of refuge, a far cry from when she first moved there at the age of sixteen. Back then, she had been completely unprepared for the overwhelming sense of loneliness. Coming home to the village on weekends and breaks only reminded her of everything she missed—life with the reindeer. An absolutely vital part of her life went on without her. It wasn't that Dad and Mattias needed her; she needed them, or rather she needed what held them together. Mattias never went to high school, because he knew he'd always stay in the village and keep reindeer. Elsa knew this about herself too, but it was inconceivable that she wouldn't continue her education. And Anna-Stina got after her, telling her how fun it was. They had one year together in town, Elsa's first year and Anna-Stina's third. Once Anna-Stina had thrown her student cap in the air, she packed up her car and returned to the village. And Elsa was left behind. For two long years. But it wasn't as if all she did was miss Anna-Stina; for the first time she made friends who weren't her cousins. She began going downhill skiing, working out at a gym, and partying. She could have elected to leave reindeer herding behind then and there. Girls weren't subject to the same expectations; it wasn't a given that they would choose the reindeer, especially if there were brothers in the family. But Elsa would have chosen the reindeer with or without siblings.

The windshield wipers were a blur; the snowflakes were heavy. It was quiet in the car. As usual, Anna-Stina was driving too fast and too close to the ditch. It was almost as if she was hoping the car would skid, just so she could correct, turn the wheel like it was nothing, and steer her way out of disaster.

Big semi-trucks thundered past them, creating a white wall of snow. They were practically blind and held their breath until they could see clearly again.

"I'm heading up to Per-Jonas's tomorrow," said Anna-Stina.

Per-Jonas and Anna-Stina had been a couple for almost a year. He came from the reindeer collective whose lands bordered on their own. Per-Jonas was four years older than Anna-Stina. He was talkative, almost to a tiresome extent. And he made Anna-Stina a different person. But Elsa left that unsaid.

Anna-Stina downshifted and hit the blinker to turn off at her place.

"His dad's going to be away overnight and I promised to help out."

The hand brake whined as she pulled it.

"Want to come with?"

Elsa recognized her tone. It was about Niko. He was sure to be there. She knew he was interested in her, but even so, she didn't feel the same.

The snow swirled around them and they hurried into the house. Anna-Stina turned on the hall light and hung up her coat. The kitchen was a mess, with dishes out and letters from the county administrative board on the table and clothes hung from the backs of chairs. Anna-Stina put a filter and grounds in the coffeemaker, then set out two white mugs. Soon the smell of coffee filled the kitchen.

"Please, come with me," she said as she took the milk from the fridge.

"Did Lasse ever have a girlfriend? I don't remember."

"Why do you ask?"

Anna-Stina poured the coffee and Elsa reached for the milk.

"Sometimes I think about how he might have been really lonely. He always traveled by himself."

"He had time to travel, no one else did."

"But going alone . . . I don't know . . ."

"You, though, you need a boyfriend. It would be so great if you and Niko . . ." She poked Elsa in the leg with her toes. "We would have so much fun together, the four of us."

Elsa shook her head and made a face at Anna-Stina, who giggled.

Needing a boyfriend. As if it was as simple as picking one. Or taking the one who wanted her. Just because.

CHAPTER THIRTY-EIGHT

Golbmalogigávcci

T he letter from the Social Insurance Office sat all alone in the mail-box, and Robert weighed the heft of the envelope in his hand. It was too light, wouldn't be notifying him of any changes. He gazed out at the village, the houses in a neat row along Inland Road and the smaller gravel roads. Smoke rose from the chimneys. Crows flapped their wings, heavy above the old telephone poles that hadn't been in use for many years. He went back to the car, which was idling, its exhaust creating a thick cloud around it.

He sat down heavily and grimaced when his shoulder protested; as usual, the pain had begun to radiate through his shoulder blades and then down his back. He fumbled to get an index finger in to open the envelope but gave up and ripped off one corner. He took out the one page of paper with just a few sentences and, as always, a series of paragraphs about how to appeal. They were well aware that no one could phrase an argument well enough to be granted an appeal. There was always some clause he failed to adhere to. The Social Insurance Office's physician had pronounced him perfectly capable of working, in no uncertain terms. They didn't want to actually see him in person. And that goddamn Jeanette at the clinic just sat there pursing her lips every time he came by to get more painkillers. It was time to go somewhere else and hope no one would look at his records. Maybe take a trip to Luleå. Or just say fuck it.

He slammed his palms onto the wheel and put the car in gear, hitting the gas until the wheels spun in the snow.

Things weren't looking good. Soon the electricity bill from Vattenfall would come, and he should really take Raija to the vet to get her hips checked out. He scratched the back of his head and tossed his cap into the backseat. Raija sniffed it and lost her footing as he turned. She whined in pain and Robert glanced back at her.

"Sorry, Raija, didn't mean to."

He reached out his hand and the elkhound pressed her nose to his palm and snuffled. She'd been four months old when he got her, payment for a job he'd done. It had actually been his idea. He'd seen the litter of puppies in the yard and asked if he could have one. There hadn't been a dog in the house since Robert was a teenager, since that autumn day when Pop took Onni out and came back without a dog. Pop's eyes had been red, but when Robert asked, his mood took a turn, as it had so many times before.

"Don't you know it's cruel to keep a sick dog alive? He was in pain."

Robert was shocked into silence. He hadn't even gotten the chance to say goodbye. He could have killed Pop in that moment. They didn't get another dog after that. Onni had been an Irish setter, the best bird dog in the village, if you asked Pop. He had mostly stuck close to Robert, and Pop had probably tried to beat that habit out of him sometimes. So the old man made sure to get the last word. He shot Onni and never said what he did with the body.

He got another dog on a whim; he'd seen Raija tumbling around, the bravest pup in the yard. He needed a reliable moose-hunting dog. He'd long been having issues with his hunting party; some people didn't want him there, said he was untrustworthy, that he drank. Then he got Raija and made himself useful. Raija was the best, just like Onni had been the best. Pop didn't say a word when the puppy padded into the house. And Robert made it clear to him whose dog she was.

Raija lay down in the backseat and whimpered. Robert turned up the radio.

At the gas station he saw a new gray Audi he didn't recognize, pulling a trailer with the shape of a snowmobile visible under the black tarp. He turned his head and passed slowly. Well, he could sure as hell guess. Another fucking reindeer herder with a new car and probably a new snowmobile too. How many cars did they have now? Three? Their son must have two. That would be a good job for the Tax Authority, checking up on those deductions.

He drove on, out of the village, aimlessly but with his foot pressing harder and harder on the gas pedal. He passed a car frantically flashing its high beams. Reindeer on the road, probably. Yep, sure enough, he saw them after the bend. Four big reindeer licking salt off the road. It would be so easy to knock them down like bowling pins. They stared at him with their vacant eyes and didn't move a muscle. He laid on the horn and they jumped, then slowly headed for the ditch. He began to roll forward, only to brake again as one of the reindeer came back onto the road. He honked repeatedly, and it leapt back and to the side.

Sometimes there was no time to think. A parking pull-off, a sudden braking, open the car door, open the trunk, and out with the rifle.

Raija was on full alert; he heard a gurgling growl come from her throat but that was all. She never barked at the wrong moment and all he had to do was lift a warning finger for her to fall completely silent.

The reindeer had moved up toward the spruce forest and he raised his weapon. Aimed. Fired. A hit. The animal fell. He fired again. Another hit. The two others sank into the deep snow, trying to flee. Shot number three missed.

He collapsed, his hands suddenly shaking and his pulse pounding in his ears. Way too close to the village. Three shots. Breathing heavily, he glanced down the road, listening for cars. He staggered to the trunk of the car and tossed his rifle in. He took his phone from his coat pocket and dialed Petri's number. Brief and harsh: I need a trailer and bags. Now.

He took out a cigarette and almost dropped it as he brought it to his lips. He shouldn't stay there with the car. He looked for the shells, found two; the third was missing, maybe under the car. He heard an engine and threw himself into the backseat, accidentally hitting Raija, who yelped. It was a truck thundering by. He peered through the rear window as it passed. Norwegian. No one who would recognize his car.

He stayed where he was, lying with his knees tucked almost to his chin, and the pain in his back shot down into his hip and up into his upper back. He tried to roll onto his back but got stuck in a crooked position. He punched the seat back, listened for more cars, and was passed again, the car vibrating gently. A small pickup. This time he didn't get up to check the license plate.

IT WAS SLOPPY AND messy, but they managed to carve out steaks and shoulders. They dragged the reindeer farther into the woods, chopped parts off with the axe, and gathered innards, hooves, antlers, heads, and tufts of fur in the blue plastic bags. They kicked snow over the blood. Sweat was trickling down his temples. He was in so much pain that his vision was flashing. Petri swore at regular intervals. They were doomed to fail at getting the bodies onto the trailer before another car came by. It was Friday, and the usual weekend stampede would soon be starting. Townies who had long since abandoned the villages where they grew up came back every weekend to light fires in their cabins and enjoy the sauna.

Petri heaved the last garbage bag onto the trailer.

"We're splitting the meat, right?" he asked in a low voice, covering it all with the tarp.

Robert just lifted a hand, waving as if this went without saying.

"Just make sure the bags disappear."

Petri nodded and hopped in the car. Robert lingered for a moment, rubbing his lower back. The wind whistled through the treetops. He tried to bend over to see if the shell was under the car, but halfway down he had to stop. As he lifted his right leg into the car he gasped and bit the inside of his cheek, hard, until the taste of blood filled his mouth.

A car approached and he instinctively turned his face away. But it was no use since everyone in the villages knew each other's license plate numbers. A new red Qashqai whizzed by, and he recognized it. Nils Johan's.

His breathing had gone back to normal. There was nothing to worry about. He'd call the restaurant in Piteå and say there was more meat to pick up. Or maybe the company in Finland that paid even better. He would also burn the letter from the Social Insurance Office when he got home. He didn't need them. Everything always worked itself out, one way or another.

CHAPTER THIRTY-NINE

Golbmalogiovcci

Elsa peered into Mattias's house. She'd grown used to calling it his house. It was harder for Áhkku—a few times a week they had to go get her and lead her back. She would stand on the steps, upset, wondering how the door could be locked. And why hadn't someone left a broom there to show that no one was home instead of locking it? Mattias locked it so she couldn't come in. He was tired of explaining.

Elsa went over and knocked on the door, heard footsteps before she was let in.

"I have to show you something."

There always had to be a reason to knock on his door. He'd started keeping the blinds down too. They pretended not to notice, but Mom often stood at the kitchen window, quiet, her gaze fixed on his house.

The video of a man riding a reindeer had shocked Elsa. Anna-Stina, who'd gotten it from Per-Jonas, had forwarded it to her. The clip was short and there was no sound, but the abuse hit her like a punch to the gut. To think they were so bold and unafraid that they would film their attacks on the animals. It was almost impossible to take in.

There were no dirty dishes around and the kitchen smelled like pine soap. The wax tablecloth was gone, and in its place was a long, gray runner with a deep brown bowl on top. Mom wasn't the one who cleaned; he did it himself.

Elsa sat on a kitchen chair and took out her phone. Mattias poured himself some coffee and offered her the thermos, but she shook her head.

He looked relaxed; he seemed more at ease, lighter on his feet. The move down to the winter grazing lands had gone smoothly, and the herd appeared to be large and healthy.

She met his gaze, even smiling a bit. Rátkin, the separation, was only a few days away. Entire herds had been brought down from the mountains to the winter grazing grounds near the village, where they were grouped together in a large corral. From there, each herder would count their reindeer, which they recognized by the unique marking on their ear. Thereafter, the herders would capture and then separate their reindeer into a smaller corral, where they would be counted again. When the counting was complete, some let their reindeer roam free with other herders' reindeer, while others kept them in a corral to be fed. During the separation season, they would receive confirmation that what Mattias had seen during the move was accurate—that it was the best year they'd had in a long time. There were lots of reindeer and above all lots of calves that had survived the sometimes harsh conditions and the threat of predators during the migration.

Elsa let her phone fall to her lap. She could wait. Until after the separation, maybe. But at the same time she wanted to know what he thought, whether they should file a police report. Before she came over, she had paged through the stack of police reports. She and Dad were the ones who made sure they ended up in a binder, and it was often her handwriting at the bottom of the page: *preliminary investigation closed.* She was the one who called the station to ask for an update on their reports. Dad had been happy to let her take over that part, and she was a better writer too. He'd been awfully impressed when she wrote a letter to the leadership of Police District North about the local police's unwillingness to investigate crimes against their reindeer.

"Or more accurately, against our way of life," she had pointed out in the letter.

Mattias seldom wanted to look at the reports, but he ought to see this video. Maybe he would recognize the man riding the reindeer.

"What did you want to show me?"

"I think I'll have some coffee after all."

He gave her a cup and they drank in silence.

"Well?"

She flashed a cautious smile. Swallowed. But no, she couldn't do it. She thought fast.

"The snowmobile you wanted to trade in for is ready. Per-Jonas told Anna-Stina."

He rubbed his jaw and nodded. "It's a damn good one."

"Can you afford it?"

"The company can always afford it," he said with a grin.

"Don't say that."

"What? That's what everyone says. Might as well let them believe it. Someone's always jealous."

"Aren't you ever going to open these blinds?"

"Don't feel like it."

She half-stood and slanted them open. Mom was standing in the kitchen window and took a quick step backwards.

"Have you noticed she never comes over here?"

Yeah, Elsa sure had.

"Sometimes it's hard to know what you want, brother."

"Eh!"

"But Áhkku comes, anyway."

She wanted to get him to smile again, and he whacked her gently on the head before getting up and going to the bathroom. She paged absently through the pile of magazines in the old wooden box on the floor. Between *Big Game* and *Fishing Journal* was a photograph. She turned it over. Lasse. The portrait that had stood next to the coffin.

He hadn't left a note, but in recent years she had suspected that maybe Mattias knew. The two of them had been close friends. To be so close to another person and to still not be enough, that must have felt terrible.

But it was what it was. Maybe she had missed the explanatory conversations after his death. Maybe everyone knew more than she did. They'd long heard that Sámi were overrepresented when it came to suicide, but apparently recent findings said that wasn't true. She'd been half-listening to the news on Oddasat and turned it off when Mom came into the kitchen. This was something she'd learned—to avoid the topic of how and why Lasse died. Soon after the funeral she'd heard Mom trying to comfort Hanna by saying he was in a better place now. Elsa had kicked Mom in the shin and run all the way home. How could anyone say it was better to be dead! She'd heard other fuzzy declarations, people saying he wasn't meant for this life. But who got to decide that?

Psychologists and counselors had tried to reach out to his grieving next of kin, but both immediate and extended family had closed ranks. Don't let anyone get too close. Don't talk about it. Just let it be. Anyway, none of the psychologists spoke Sámi, so obviously it wouldn't work.

How Mattias had grieved, she didn't know. She only remembered that he refused to hold her hand at the funeral and that he didn't cry.

Lasse wasn't the first person in Sápmi to take his own life; more had followed him. Little Elsa had thought it was no wonder, when people like Mom said they were better off wherever they ended up after death. It was like giving permission.

She shuddered and placed her palm over Lasse's smiling face. What if it was the ones who took their own lives that were doing the right thing? The ones who said they couldn't take it anymore and left behind everything that hurt. The ones who made a statement to the whole world. See what you drive us to do? We can't take it anymore. We would rather kill ourselves than watch our reindeer be tortured and killed while we listen to how much you hate us. We would rather kill ourselves than watch you take our land for a mine that won't give you more than a decade's work, tops.

Anxious parents kept watchful eyes on their teenagers and adult children, limited them, held them back, didn't let them move farther away than across a snowbank to the next lot over. But nothing could help if you didn't take away the reason they wanted to leave this life.

Her thoughts made her roil with anxiety. The toilet flushed and the tap ran soon after. Elsa slipped the photo back between the magazines.

"I have to go now," she said when he came out. "I have an appointment at the salon."

CHAPTER FORTY

Njealljelogi

There was talk about the shots that had been heard just outside the village the day before. Someone claimed to have heard two; another said three. In broad daylight. Elsa didn't mention to anyone that she'd seen Robert's Jeep in a pull-off. She'd meant to discuss it with Mattias but ended up avoiding that topic too. It could have been someone shooting the mangy fox, went the line of reasoning at the store. Or else it was someone shooting reindeer. No one said that quite so loud.

It was separation time soon. Things would calm down again. Elsa was counting down the days; everyone was. The forecast called for cold weather, but it had been mild over the past several days.

Down south in Jämtland, the reindeer collectives were tired of running the separation in rain, snow, and harsh winds, and had built a roundup enclosure with a roof. "With a roof?" exclaimed the elders in Elsa's reindeer collective. It was unnatural and wrong.

Dad hadn't said a word when it came up, just went out to the shed. They all knew something was seriously wrong. Rain in the middle of winter. It frightened Elsa. How they had raised the alarm, trying to get people outside the reindeer grazing grounds to understand—can't you see what's happening? We've known for a long time! For years we've been warning you that the climate is changing. But as always, their voices were too weak, and the wind hadn't been strong enough to carry them where they needed to go. So there were reindeer collectives that built roofs and they thought, well, at least it's warm. But if they looked at their grandchildren, their legs gave a little. Eventually, a roof wouldn't provide enough protection from the increasingly volatile elements.

Elsa got in the car, the first one that was really hers, a bright blue Škoda
Octavia she'd bought from a cousin for cheap. She drove slowly toward the
parking pull-off just outside the village, and sat there for a while. Sometimes
it was better not to know. But she climbed out and inspected the ground. The
plow had come by a few times, so anything that had been there would be in the
snowbanks by now. She stepped carefully and gazed out at the snow. White and
untouched. But in the distance there were clear tracks left by reindeer. She took
big steps through the deep snow. At least a couple or several reindeer, many
tracks leading to the forest. She tried to walk in their prints, kicking at the snow,
but didn't find anything. When she was up among the spruce trees, she saw that
the tracks led farther into the forest. These reindeer had made it. No tufts of fur,
no blood, just snow. It must have been a mangy fox after all. She walked back in
the same tracks and wiped the snow off her jeans, then got in the car.

When she got to the stream, she could see them in the distance, ravens
alternately flapping in the air and landing. It didn't necessarily mean anything,
but it could be a reindeer that had been run over. She drove by slowly, watching
the excited birds. Another two hundred yards on, she pulled off the road into a
parking area, arguing with herself and her timeline. She was supposed to be at
the salon in just over an hour. It might be the mangy fox, tossed in the ditch by
the shooter. She just needed to find out, and then she would be back on her way.

She made a tight U-turn to go back to the stream. It wasn't visible from
the road, so Elsa drove as close to the ditch as she could before turning on
her hazard lights and getting out.

The ravens flew off. Left behind were two blue plastic bags with a min-
ing company's name on them. One was half ripped open and the other was
still intact. A loop of intestine was coming out of the hole. She went back
to the car and found the thick gloves in the trunk.

The ravens were perched in the treetops, watching her with their coal-
black eyes. The beginnings of a hole were visible in the ice, as if someone
had tried to chop through it with an axe. Maybe they'd wanted to dump the
bags in the stream, in the hopes that they'd sink to the bottom? She cautiously
lifted one bag and a bit more of the intestine slipped out. It didn't appear to
be frozen solid; the bags might have been stored in a warmer spot before they
were discarded in the forest, she figured. The contents were heavy, and she

steeled herself to look at what was inside. The ravens had managed to make a pretty big hole with their sharp beaks. She took hold of its edges and tore the plastic. The reindeer head made her stagger backwards. Her stomach turned and she cleared her throat. The mark on the ears. It was Mattias's reindeer. Its head was soiled with blood and beneath it lay intestines, organs, and hooves. She lifted the second bag, just as heavy, and ran her hand along the plastic, feeling the shape of another reindeer head.

A sound escaped her, a wail. After a few breaths she got hold of herself and looked around before moving, on shaky legs, to the closest birch, where she stood on tiptoe to break off a branch. The branch was tenacious, and she shouted in anger as she hung on it with all her weight until it cracked and gave way. She used it to dig around in the bag. There were slippery, thin plastic gloves inside. DNA. His car in the pull-off. She forced herself to look at the head again. The bullet had gone in right below the eye.

She wouldn't call Dad or Mattias. Not now. Not when everyone was getting ready for one of the high points of the year. She could handle this on her own.

A few months ago, she had managed to get her hands on the number to Officer Henriksson's direct line, but she had never used it. She had always gone through the proper channels, by way of the station command or the regional command post. But now she was truly furious.

Henriksson answered on the sixth ring, his voice harried and out of breath. She introduced herself and thought she heard a sigh.

"I found two bags full of butchering waste from at least two reindeer. Yesterday shots were heard outside the village, and I see a bullet hole in one of the heads. I have only opened one of the bags, to keep from destroying evidence."

She wondered if he ever thought about her visit to his office a decade ago. They hadn't seen each other since, but Elsa had spoken to him on the phone a couple of times.

"Well, I'm not really the one you should be calling. But I know we are unable to come out right now, unfortunately. The patrol is full up."

"So am I supposed to just leave these bags here? The ravens have already torn one open and are eating the contents. The evidence is disappearing. There are even gloves in one of the bags. I was thinking DNA—"

"Could you please take care of the bags and file a report? We'll come when we can, but right now it's not possible."

"I think there might be tracks here in the snow that you should take a look at."

"Like I said, it's not possible." He sounded annoyed. "File a report and we'll be in touch."

"Can't you take my report now?"

"We're just about to have our wrap-up meeting before we're done for the day. Call 114 14."

She hung up without saying goodbye.

THE TRAILER WAS IN the driveway and she hitched it to the car. Mom came out on the steps; Elsa could see her in the rearview mirror before she drove off again. She sped back to the site and drove into the ditch, facing oncoming traffic, and put her hazards on again.

The ravens flew up as she trudged to the bags. They'd managed to peck at the head, had taken one eye. She dragged the bag along the ground to the trailer and went back to get the other one. When everything was in place, she tightened the straps. The bags probably would have fit in the trunk, but she couldn't bring herself to have them so close. It was probably an unfounded fear, but she was afraid they would start to thaw and smell, and if the odor didn't go away she would have to get rid of the car. Not because she was sensitive to the smell, but because it would always be there to remind her.

The trailer kept her from driving as fast as she would have liked. She had no choice but to forget about the hair salon.

WHEN SHE GOT TO the police station, she backed in and took up two parking spots. She'd been capable of backing up with a trailer since she was sixteen, better and faster than Mattias.

The door was locked and the lights were out in the lobby. She took out her phone and dialed 114 14, and asked to be transferred to the regional command post. Minutes passed before anyone picked up. She introduced herself once more and added the name of her reindeer collective.

"I'm standing outside the police station with evidence of a poaching."

"Oh, okay . . . have you filed a report?"

"That's what I'm doing right now. Can someone come take care of this?"

"I mean, the patrol unit isn't in town right now. What is it you have with you?"

"The remains of two reindeer that were shot."

"So, a theft." He took a patronizing tone as he corrected her. "Reindeer are on par with domesticated animals like dogs or sheep, so it's not a matter of poaching. Moose, however—"

"I'm well aware of the law," Elsa said, "but I'm standing here with proof that someone shot and butchered two reindeer."

"I'm sorry, but like I said, there's no patrol available to deal with this matter at the moment."

"So what should I do?"

"I think the unit might be back in about two hours."

"Are you saying that there is not a single officer at the station who could come take this off my hands?"

"No, the investigators have gone home for the day and the command post you're speaking with is in Umeå, and, you know, there's only one patrol unit up there on weekdays. I'm sorry, but . . ."

Elsa hung up. She loosened the straps, which were ice-cold on her fingertips, and dragged the bags to the doorstep of the police station. She took a picture and sent it to the local paper's tip line.

She scrolled through her phone and found the video she should have shown Mattias. The journalist, if one actually got in touch, was going to see it. It was a brief sequence, the focus was sometimes blurry, filmed by an unsteady hand. There was no sound. A man riding on a reindeer like it was a horse. He was holding onto its antlers and kicking its sides. The man was only visible for a brief moment, from behind. He was short and pretty fat and wearing black clothing. She recognized the forest, just a few miles from their place, a familiar moose-hunting stand flashed by quickly.

The video hadn't started to circulate widely yet, but it was only a matter of time.

Fifteen minutes later, an older white Toyota pulled into the parking lot. A young woman in a black hat, a heavy parka, and black boots climbed out of the car. She raised her hand in a wave and headed straight for Elsa and the bags.

"Hi! Are you the tipster? My name is Lovisa Wikberg."

She took off her mitten and held out a warm hand for Elsa to shake.

"There are two dead reindeer, or mostly butchering leftovers and the heads of two reindeer."

"I have to say, you have chosen a very dramatic way to report a crime. It's not common for someone to dump bags full of reindeer cadavers outside the police station."

Lovisa had fished out a small notepad and a pencil.

"I got sick of always hearing the same answer. That there aren't any police who can come when we find poached and tortured reindeer."

Lovisa quickly scribbled down what Elsa said, looking up at her at the same time.

"The police won't take it seriously," Elsa went on. "We lose so many animals every year and the people who do it walk free."

"Why do you think that is?"

"Because it's classified as theft or property damage, and they're not interested in devoting resources to that. But to us, it's not theft. It's murder, it's a deliberate killing."

Elsa's voice went hoarse. She took out her phone.

"I think you should look up this video too. It's a man torturing and riding a terrified reindeer."

Lovisa looked genuinely horrified as she watched.

"Jesus, that's awful! How does it make you feel to watch this?"

She turned the page and held the pencil at the ready for a new blank line.

"I don't think anyone who doesn't have reindeer can really understand. It hurts." Her voice cracked and she cleared her throat. "We don't just work with the reindeer, they're part of our way of life. And when no one cares when our reindeer are killed, it . . ."

"I understand, it must be horrible."

Lovisa lowered her eyes.

"I'm going to take a few pictures. Is that okay?"

Elsa nodded and watched as she fiddled with a flash on the camera. Lovisa muttered to herself that it was hard to get a good shot when it was so dark. Elsa realized that she should be taking pictures too. It wouldn't be the first time evidence simply vanished. She held back the edge of the hole in the bag and photographed the head, with the bullet hole and missing eye.

"Do you know whose reindeer it is?"

"Yes." She hesitated. "It's from our collective."

"And hey." Lovisa looked up. "How could they be so stupid and upload a video of themselves? I'm sorry, but that is just incredibly dumb."

"Simple. They don't have to worry about being caught. The case will be closed."

"But someone could recognize this man, don't you think? In which case the video is solid evidence."

Elsa had watched the brief sequence so many times. Sure, maybe someone would recognize him. She didn't. It was too fast and too blurry.

"Even if someone did recognize him, no one would help the police by sharing what they knew. Plus we have no idea whose reindeer it is, so there's no injured party. But maybe you could put some pressure on the police, ask these critical questions?"

Lovisa smiled suddenly.

"I'm actually a culture writer, on loan from Luleå for a few months, so I'm not exactly a crime reporter. But of course I'll ask about it." She glanced at her wristwatch. "I was just on my way to a concert at the church, so unfortunately I have to go now. But if you give me your cell number we can be in touch later, after I've talked to the police. And listen—can I take a picture of you?"

"I don't know."

"Well, can I include your name and which reindeer collective we're talking about, at least?"

"Sure, I guess that's fine."

Lovisa lingered, smiling a little, then took out her car keys and fingered the camera hanging against her chest.

"Maybe I could take a picture just to be on the safe side, and you can decide later?"

Elsa nodded. It was always harder to keep going once her anger had drained away. When hopelessness took over. When the feeling that nothing mattered struck her full force. No one in the family had ever been in the paper before. It was usually the chairman of their reindeer collective, Olle, who acted as their spokesperson. Most of the time the journalists weren't interested in writing more than a short notice about dead reindeer. Maybe this journalist was different. Or maybe it was the image of the slaughtered reindeer on the police's doorstep that had caught her attention. Elsa didn't want to appear whiny; she just wanted people to understand. Far too often it was the most outspoken Sámi that took up all the space in the media, because journalists liked to provoke conflict. Some Sámi folks liked to test the limits and give sharp, scornful, and almost threatening statements about the wider society. They painted an "us versus them" picture. Elsa didn't have much patience for that kind of rhetoric. And it made it far too easy for the haters to lump them all together and call the Sámi whiny or troublesome. Now maybe she was the one taking things too far, standing there with her arms crossed in front of her dead animals.

"You can take a portrait. I don't want to be photographed with the bags."

Lovisa nodded, appearing far too eager to help Elsa feel at ease. Elsa wore a grim expression as the flash lit up her face.

"It's important for this to be right, for people to understand," she said.

"Definitely. I think this is super-important. I'll call you after the concert, and you can tell me in greater detail where you found the bags and so on."

Lovisa looked at her watch again and thanked Elsa for the interview, then walked briskly toward her car.

Elsa felt exposed; she had the uneasy feeling that she had opened herself up to someone who had no intention of hearing her out.

CHAPTER FORTY-ONE

Njealljelogiokta

It had snowed overnight, but not so much that the road up to the mountains wasn't passable. Anna-Stina kept it under thirty miles an hour and braked before the crest of the hill. The road was only wide enough for one car, but there were frequent pull-offs. Elsa yawned, sleepy, slightly annoyed at her inability to say no. But this time, she had welcomed Anna-Stina's nagging her to come along to Per-Jonas's. She didn't want to be home when the newspaper arrived, or when anyone in the family read the article online.

The higher they got, the sparser the birch trees. Here and there, the old, weather-beaten wooden fence, there to keep the reindeer on the right side of the collective's land, was leaning. There was a brisk wind blowing snowdrifts onto the road. Soon they would need to plow. Elsa felt a shiver down her spine, recalling the time when she stood in the ditch and waited for the plow to come by. So incredibly stupid.

Per-Jonas's reindeer collective had already done their separation, and now feeding was in full swing and you better believe Anna-Stina was going to head up and prove herself useful. They spent much of the ride in silence. Anna-Stina was focused on the road and Elsa was thinking about what she'd said in the interview.

The first houses came into sight.

"Did you hear there was another fight about a cabin up here?" Anna-Stina asked.

"What is wrong with people?"

Envious villagers liked to appeal new construction, but the reindeer herders were well within their rights; the cabins were necessary to run husbandry operations in the area. Elsa was so sick of the angry comments about how new cabins wouldn't be necessary if the reindeer roamed free and weren't fed. Non-herders thought reindeer husbandry should be done as it was a hundred years ago, on skis, with no motorized vehicles.

"We should all live in goahtis, don't you know." Anna-Stina rolled her eyes. "Everything else in society can be modernized and improved, but not reindeer herding, that would be too fucking weird."

They passed some cabins. Anna-Stina looked at her reflection in the mirror and tucked her long bangs behind her ear before they turned off the road.

"Finally made it!"

She parked, and Per-Jonas's black herding dog came bounding for the car, barking but wagging its tail in the air. It dashed in circles, excited and joyful, and jumped on Anna-Stina when she got out. Then it ran around the car to give Elsa's outstretched hands a cursory sniff.

The sky had cleared, but the clouds beyond the mountains were already closing in quickly.

In the yard were two tame reindeer tethered on long ropes. The large havier stood still, his eyes following the dog. In a few months they would lead the herd to higher ground, to the summer grazing grounds in the Norwegian mountains. The eternal circle of life.

"We'll mark the calves here before we head on to Norway in June," Anna-Stina said.

She had already started saying "we" even though her own reindeer were in their collective, not Per-Jonas's. If they got married, she'd probably do what was expected of her and move her reindeer to his collective.

In past years, Per-Jonas's collective had done the calf marking in Norway, just as Elsa's did, but now they said it was no longer possible. Predators took far too many animals before they even reached their destination. Now, with the herd gathered and fed, and with calving and marking done in the same place, the collective could save almost all the calves. Per-Jonas always said it was a matter of economics, but for Elsa it was even more about not wanting to see the reindeer mutilated.

"We should do our calf marking down here too," she said.

"Well, we are." Anna-Stina looked at her. "At least that's what Dad says."

Elsa's own father was hesitant; it meant more work, feeding for a longer time. But there was another reason for concern too—the risk that the reindeer would fall victim to poachers or abusers. Letting the reindeer walk their familiar route northward also meant rescuing them from the men who wanted to kill them. Nothing had improved on that front. Reindeer still disappeared. But it wasn't so easy for Robert Isaksson to come up to these grounds, and he certainly couldn't do it unseen. Here above the timberline you could see a snowmobiler from miles away. No one could kill under the cover of dense forest.

Per-Jonas had put an addition on his cabin, and it was freshly painted a pale green with white window frames. As soon as that was done, he had hammered six thick nails on either side of the door, where he hung full bags, ropes, a frying pan, and a saw. Skis were leaning against the outer wall, as well as a shovel.

The warmth hit them as soon as they stepped into the house. On the faded rag rug stood heavy boots of various sizes, and on the hooks were snowmobile suits, gaiters, goggles, and hats made of hide with white fur lining the earflaps.

Per-Jonas was sitting at the kitchen table. He nodded in their direction, then brought binoculars to his eyes and aimed them out the big window. A practiced eye could see the reindeer as black dots against the white snow on the bare mountain, even without binoculars.

He joked that they were late and Anna-Stina threw her arms around him from behind, kissing him on the neck.

Elsa peered into the bedroom, where the beds were made. She usually slept in the loft; the ceiling was high and there was room enough for three.

She sat down on the sofa; the cabin's largest room was both kitchen and living room. Per-Jonas had mounted a big new TV on one wall.

"Niko's coming too," he said, grinning in her direction, but she pretended not to notice. She shouldn't have come.

Anna-Stina moved here and there, picking up cereal boxes and mugs that had been left out, running her palm across the table to collect crumbs. Elsa found this demonstration annoying. Anna-Stina tied her long hair into a bun on top of her head and rolled up the sleeves of her wool base layer. She stood there with her hands on her hips, looking around.

"We have to make it cozier in here."

Elsa dug her nails into the sofa cushion and closed her eyes for a moment. Anna-Stina had no ambitions when it came to being with the reindeer; instead she wanted to show off the skills that would make her a most competent wife.

Per-Jonas stood up, stretched his arms up in the air, which lifted his shirt and exposed his abs. He let out a grunt. Elsa took the binoculars and aimed them at the mountain. The reindeer were moving slowly, a few of them digging listlessly in the snow. The snow situation had been hopeless this winter. There were frequent and surprising changes in the weather patterns. It might rapidly go from thirty below to above freezing. Snow, rain, cold, and springlike temperatures, one after the next. The ground couldn't absorb the moisture and turned to ice. And that meant the reindeer wouldn't be able to paw through the hard-packed snow and ice to reach their pasturage. All the reindeer collectives in the municipality had been forced to apply for disaster relief from the Sámi Parliament to feed their reindeer.

Per-Jonas had pulled on his thick brown leather trousers, and now he let his gákti fall over his head. Bright blue with yellow and red bands. He put on his hat with the white fur and tugged heavy-duty overshoes on over his regular shoes. Then he left the house. Anna-Stina got dressed quickly. Elsa was considerably slower.

He had started the snowmobile, a brand-new Polaris Indy 600, and was ready with one knee on the seat. He nodded at the older snowmobile, an Arctic Cat, indicating to Elsa that she was supposed to take that one. He had hitched a sled to his snowmobile, a homemade one with a wooden box and an opening that made it possible to scatter pellets while driving around. They went through actual tons of pellets each week during the feeding period.

Anna-Stina settled in behind him, putting her arms around his waist and pulling herself close. He hit the gas hard and she squealed. Elsa gritted her teeth and squeezed the gas hard too. The trails were packed firm, easy to drive but bumpy in spots.

Niko was on his way. She could hear his snowmobile approaching from the west, and sure enough, there he was, driving fast and in a crouch. He headed out into the deep snow and circled past Elsa before pulling up in front of her. She saw him smile but didn't smile back, fixing her eyes in the distance.

After a few miles in the sparse woods, they emerged above the timber-line higher up. The reindeer heard them. They recognized the sound of snowmobiles and moved toward them. They welled forth, hundreds of them, from all directions; they moved in unison, all with the same goal.

The three snowmobiles rode slowly in among the animals. The rein-deer's sounds were like a melody, a joik, Elsa always thought. They stopped, and the reindeer came close, one of them nosing her glove. Fed reindeer weren't as shy as free-range ones. She stayed put and watched one of the calves. So much like her Nástegallu.

She reached for the sack of reindeer lichen that was strapped behind her on the seat, untied it, and held some out. The trust in the calf's eyes made her gasp.

Per-Jonas drove slowly, and Anna-Stina opened the hatch so the pel-lets fell out in a stream. He drove back and forth and the reindeer lowered their heads to eat. This was better than the feed troughs Elsa's family used. Around a trough there might be a fight to reach the food, the animals butt-ing heads and making clear who had the right to eat first, or even eat every-thing. Her Nástegallu had been brave, dared to crowd in, hadn't let herself be scared off. Maybe that was why Robert managed to get her too. Elsa shook out her shoulders, exhaled, thought of something else.

Niko and Per-Jonas circled around the bare mountain, and the pellets lay like long, winding snakes in the snow. They gestured at one another. There really wasn't anything wrong with Niko. He was a stable guy with a bull neck and eyes that seemed to change color like the northern lights when he was in the mood. Sure, they'd made out once or twice, mostly because there wasn't much else to do. His hands had been damp with sweat, and she'd felt it through her shirt when he pressed one hand to the small of her back.

But he was like his father and the other old men in the reindeer corrals who side-eyed any woman who wanted to assert herself. Men who had opinions about where womenfolk belonged, who wouldn't willingly share space or knowledge. She didn't need them; Dad and Mattias had taught her everything. Niko, though, he was looking for a woman who would be a good homemaker, someone who would never complain about the weeks and months alone, who would keep the freezer full and the babies' noses wiped. But this much was okay—she was allowed to pretend to participate, drive a snowmobile and rope the occasional calf.

Certainly they were impressed; they'd seen her rope reindeer. They would raise their eyebrows and smile. But that was only for now. It wasn't that girls weren't allowed to take part at all—everyone in the family had to lend a hand during separation, calf-marking time, and slaughtering time—but if it was up to the men, everyone would stick to their clearly assigned roles. And what Elsa wanted was the prescribed male role. Entirely by herself. She had an earmark of her own, and she was a member of the collective, but Dad was head-of-household, the only one in the family with the right to vote in the collective. The one who spoke for her and Mattias, and Mom of course. Mattias would become head-of-household down the road, but Elsa could not expect the same. The old men in the collective would put a stop to that, she was sure of it. But there was no way she would take her reindeer and join up with Niko, if that's what they were thinking. She didn't want to be handed from one head-of-household to another. She'd rather remain under Dad, who at least muttered on occasion that the system needed modernizing. Not that he would ever lift a finger to change anything. He had enough to deal with just living, surviving yet another winter without sleep and full of constant worry.

Elsa looked at Niko and Per-Jonas, who didn't seem to live with that worry in quite the same way. Or maybe they were like the wood grouse cocks, with their ostentatious leaps in the air. They showed off their reindeer herds, which were larger than many others'. But what about at night? Maybe they too lay awake, worrying about predators, mines, and what social media would be saying about the goddamn Lapps the next day. But for now, they laughed at the whole world, kings of their own grounds.

Niko pulled up alongside Elsa. His face was red and his lips moved stiffly in the cold.

"How is Nils Johan's Elsa doing, then?"

He always did that. Pointed out whose kid you were. He was also happy to rattle off his own whole name. Great-grandfather, grandfather, and father. Clearly proud of the long line of names that culminated in his own. The old men liked to do that too, recite the names to know whose kid you were and, in the long run, figure out whether you were related. Or whether there might be some lapses in there somewhere. There were considerable lapses on Mom's side, even if her name was written down in that much sought-after Sámi family book. But in Dad's stable family line, there was no fault to be found.

"I'm good. You?"

He winked.

"Primo! As always."

She noted that he talked like the old men. He was an only child, and although he'd had plenty of cousins around him when he was young, he was steeped in adult words and wisdom. Or lack thereof. Maybe it was that he'd never had to fight, never had to assert himself. What's more, his father brought an annoyingly arrogant attitude to the collective meetings, thanks to his high share of voting power. His herd was known far and wide for its size, and Niko knew his worth. Humility, though, was lacking.

"So what are you doing here? Doesn't your pop need you?"

"I was forced to come."

He laughed, hoarsely and for too long. "So you don't like being with the reindeer."

"I have zero problems with the reindeer."

"Oh, so it's the people then. Me!"

"If that's what you think, then . . ."

He cut off his own laughter, but was still smiling. "I heard you dropped off some dead reindeer with the police."

She tried to look unbothered. "Yes, I did."

"Well done. I haven't read the article myself, but there's a lot of talk about it," he said. "So you're not afraid?"

"Afraid of what?"

"Those aren't exactly nice guys."

"I'm not all that nice either."

She turned the key and hit the throttle before he could respond.

Anna-Stina shot her a displeased look. Elsa slowly drove up to her.

"I'm heading back to the house. I'm not needed here."

"But they're not finished. We're going to check on a few reindeer who are having trouble adjusting to the feed."

"Per-Jonas has Niko. They don't need either of us. There was never any reason for me to come, and you know it."

Anna-Stina gazed after Per-Jonas, who was walking among the reindeer, as though she were hypnotized.

Elsa grabbed her arm. "Can I take your car and go home?"

"What? No! How would I get home? And Niko's going to stay and have dinner with us."

"That's great for him."

Anna-Stina's eyes went black. Elsa didn't know where this feeling was coming from. She normally didn't mess with the balance in their relationship, but there, among the reindeer and the alpha males on snowmobiles, it was all just too much.

"We'll head back tomorrow, okay?" Anna-Stina said.

Elsa pulled her hood up over her hat and nodded. "I'm going back to the house now. See you there."

CHAPTER FORTY-TWO

Njealljelogiguokte

The packing list was tidy and divided into categories: food, clothing, and the equipment needed to count the reindeer during the separation. Plastic bins were on the kitchen floor, and Hanna had already filled them with thermoses of coffee, bread, butter, Bullens tinned sausages, hot dog buns, ketchup, the cinnamon rolls she'd baked last week, the last of the dried reindeer meat—gurpi—and five plastic bottles of soda.

She watched from the kitchen window as Jon-Isak followed on the heels of his father. Ante pointed, and the boy lifted, pulled, fastened, unhitched, all like a little man. He came up to his father's shoulder and always stood up extra straight to get that extra inch. Their bond was stronger than hers and his.

They had so wished for another baby, and Ante had been overjoyed when she finally tested positive. They could hardly believe their luck. Then Lasse died, and Hanna shut down. Sure, in a purely physical way she had felt the flutter just above her pubic bone, which later turned into tumbling somersaults, and a net of bluish-purple stretch marks spread over her growing belly. But the baby—she couldn't quite accept it. There could not be a God who broke her so completely only to give her the son they'd been waiting for all those years. How was she supposed to be happy when it felt like she'd paid one life to gain another? A comfort, said those who didn't understand, a comfort amid the sorrow. It wasn't like that. Lasse had been like her son, not like a brother; he had been her child.

And the old women in the village, who stared so intently at her growing belly and tried to make their own religious calculations following a suicide. They had knocked on her door to share condolences like everyone else, but she hadn't answered. For the first time, she had locked her door. She wasn't afraid of hearing them talk about sin, but she was afraid she might beat them to death. Never had she judged anyone, never had she joined in the gossip when one of the village's young people chose to leave this life, so she could hold her head high. She could lock the door and sit up straight at the kitchen table as they went back and forth, trying to peer inside. Startled when they spotted her with a coffee cup at her lips. Without opening the door. Without hiding. No, she didn't want to talk to any old women who pretended to wish her well only to add that her brother had committed the gravest of sins. A suicide could not be forgiven. The jaws of hell had opened up and swallowed him. And there he burned. Still.

No, she hadn't been able to accept him, that little baby, even though he lay on her breast in the delivery room with his breathing so shallow and quick. Ante had been a sobbing mess. This was the son he had been waiting for. He would never say so out loud, and there was no question he loved Anna-Stina, but it was a son he had been missing. She had hated him for it but said he could take the little fellow because she needed to sleep. Some part of her had been hoping that she would look into Lasse's eyes when the newborn was laid on her chest. That he would come back in the form of a little boy who was well suited for life in a way Lasse hadn't been. But no, that gaze was its very own. He was a robust little guy who lifted his head to root for her breast right away. It hurt, and she cried, and Ante misunderstood and thought they were happy tears. But she would never be happy again. Anna-Stina could see it even before her little brother was born. She slipped furtively around the room, gave her long looks, didn't dare to get close as she had before. But Hanna didn't feel guilty about that either. She had lost her brother, her child, and she should have been able to stop it. This kept her awake at night. That, and later Jon-Isak, who tried to nurse the life out of her. She got skinnier week by week.

But she had done what was expected of her; she had borne a son. She had secured the future. Sure, a girl could have been enough, but they both knew early on that Anna-Stina didn't have what it would take. She had neither the eye nor the hand. But it would all work out; Hanna had never been worried. Her daughter had confidence, and in a few years she'd be turning heads in the village.

Never had she said this out loud, that the children were valued differently. She hardly had time to form the thought before she was filled with
the deepest loathing because she was no better than anyone else. But there
and then, it didn't matter. She could have said flat out that they needed a
son, and she could have opened the kitchen window to shout at the old
women that there was no God.

People went out of their way to avoid her. She would go to the store in the
next village, hugely pregnant and red-eyed after yet another morning of un-
controllable tears, without caring in the least. But it made the old women flee
in all directions with their baskets. She sometimes ended up leaning against
the mailboxes and sobbing when a letter showed up for him. And she had
seen the cars heading for the mailboxes drive past when they saw her there.

Jon-Isak's bright little-boy voice called across the yard and her husband
turned around with a smile. Certainly she was grateful, he was all the boy
needed. Their bond was so strong that they could hardly stand to be apart.
Jon-Isak cried each Sunday when he knew he had to go to school again. He
wanted to hang on his father's heels and be with the reindeer. There was
some suspicion that the tears had to do with more than just Dad, but she
didn't have the energy to deal with that. She breathed, packed bins of food,
chatted and laughed as though everything was fine, and even if there were
those who could tell that she wasn't fine, it was easier just to let her be.

This was the only kind of mom Jon-Isak knew, and he let himself be
satisfied with that. Sometimes he wriggled in close to her on the sofa and
she would put an arm around him. But Anna-Stina was the one with a mom
who had a before and an after, and Hanna should have felt guilty. But she
didn't. And so it came to pass, just as she'd predicted. Her daughter drew
increasingly away from home, went to high school in town, spent time with
her friends and the boys in the villages. And when she finally moved into
her little studio apartment in the next village, Hanna could breathe easy.

Yesterday's paper was on the kitchen table. She had studied the photo of
Elsa, her arms crossed and her gaze steady on the person who had taken her
picture. They'd published an enlarged shot of the sacks; there was a glimpse
of a reindeer head and intestines, and it was very hard to look at.

The police brushed off Elsa's accusation that they didn't care about

investigating stolen reindeer and animal torture. They claimed it was difficult to conduct an investigation without any suspects or relevant evidence.
Besides, they had to prioritize calls, and one patrol in a vast geographical
area couldn't perform miracles. Ante had clutched the newspaper in tight
fists. This hadn't been discussed in the collective—had the girl made up her
own mind to act? he asked aloud.

"It's great she had the guts to do it," Hanna said.

And she meant it. She'd always known that Elsa was made of different
stuff than Anna-Stina. Although her daughter had spent all those years trying to subjugate Elsa by virtue of being older, she'd known there would
be a shift in power sooner or later. She'd followed their games when they
were little, watched them go through their teen years and become young
women, and it was clear that Elsa would get herself where she wanted to
go. It didn't take a son to carry reindeer husbandry into the next generation.
It only took a child who wanted to and was able to shoulder that burden.
But they weren't there yet; sons were still in favor. Elsa, though, she could
show them all. Hanna was sure of it.

She had occasionally wished that Elsa were her daughter; she could have
given her a better foundation than Marika had been able to. To be sure,
Marika hadn't had it easy; it was hard to come to the village as an outsider.
You had to be a certain type of person to manage. It wasn't just about learning the language and being able to sew a gákti. She was too sensitive and
didn't understand their history.

Hanna and Lasse had shared their concern for Elsa, but once he was gone
she let go of that too. And the girl seemed to have made it through. She saw it
in her gaze in the newspaper. Hanna would tell her she'd done the right thing
in going to the police, that it was about time they flushed those killers out.

Jon-Isak came bouncing into the kitchen, breathless and rosy. She felt
tenderness for the little guy, their reaŋga, their little farmhand. She ruffled
his sweat-dampened hair and pinched his ear gently. He was a little bundle
of muscle just waiting to show off everything he could do, like Dad and
the other men. He had the green lasso tightly wound and hanging from his
right shoulder, then looped around his waist and back.

He picked up a bin of food, thrust his back out as far as he could, and staggered to the front door. She pulled his hat down over his head before he went back into the cold. Reaŋga and his father—they would always have each other. For him, the reindeer were nothing but a joy. Hanna and Ante weren't in agreement about which difficult discussions they should involve him in. Before Lasse's death, Hanna had felt that kids should be included in all their serious talks. But now, she sometimes wondered if everything that had happened to them, all the killed reindeer and all the hate, had driven her brother to suicide. It must not happen again. Sooner or later, some older friend would say too much to Jon-Isak. They would never be able to protect him, and she was sure he'd already heard plenty at school. She was grateful for her husband, though; no matter how tough life was, he always managed to fill both kids with hope and love for their life with the reindeer. Well, their son, anyway. Sometimes she thought it would have been different for her husband too, to have an Elsa in the house, a girl who wanted to be a reindeer herder full-time. It would have been good for him. It wasn't just that Anna-Stina was a girl and Jon-Isak a boy; they simply wanted different things.

Being Sámi meant carrying your history with you, to stand before that heavy burden as a child and choose to bear it or not. But how could you choose not to bear your family's history and carry on your inheritance? She felt a jolt of pain in her midsection. Lasse had tried, he wavered and he bore it, but in the end he couldn't manage any longer. But it wasn't acceptable, to say you wanted a different life. And she hadn't listened, that was the truth. She had been impressed by him, by his desire for the other possibilities life had to offer; she had believed that he was the one who would dare to do what no one else did. But she had misunderstood, and it was all her fault. No matter which way she looked at those last days with him, she always came to the same conclusion. She should have noticed, and she should have helped. She would not fail with Jon-Isak, because she had removed her guiding hand from his life. Passed the newborn to her husband, absolutely certain that he would know what the little one needed.

She put on her black snow pants, tied a blue woolen shawl in a triangle over her red down jacket, and pulled her hat down almost to her eyes. Juovlamánnu. December. Soon she would have made it through yet another year.

CHAPTER FORTY-THREE

Njealljelogigolbma

The herd surged back and forth in the rátkagárddis, the separation corral. They always ran counterclockwise; a few would take the lead and the others followed. Then they calmed down, once they realized there was no way out. The tendons in their hind legs clicked, and the steam of their rapid breaths lay over them like a cloud. A few owners walked inside the corral, prompting the herd to get moving again. The big spotlights shone over the girdnu, the circular middle point, setting the stage for the final sorting, each owner roping their reindeer into their own section. The children had climbed up on the fence, cheeks red, eyes tearing in the biting wind. They pointed and gestured, cheerfully calling out any reindeer they recognized as their own. Elsa saw Jon-Isak, most eager of them all. He made the others laugh out loud.

She would be pulling reindeer along with Anna-Stina. It had surprised her to learn that Anna-Stina wanted to help; she probably wouldn't last long. It took both strength and skill to haul around a reluctant animal that weighed almost twice as much as you did. Elsa was used to it; she pulled with strong, sinewy arms, tensed her core muscles, and hauled back with firm thighs. She hadn't turned out tall, but she wasn't so skinny anymore.

Mattias was already in place with his friends. Someone was smoking; they all talked over each other, and his laughter warmed her. When she got home that morning, she had put off going near him.

"You should have called," he'd said, sounding cross. "And you should have mentioned that you were going to be in the paper."

Dad had chimed in with an equally sullen mutter. "This could put you in danger."

They weren't afraid of clashing with the police; that ship had sailed. But the other reactions could be worse, like the flood of comments on social media.

The journalist had found the video Elsa had tipped her off about, and subscribers could see it on the newspaper's website. They'd blurred out quite a bit of the man's body, which made it impossible to recognize him.

Folks stood around the enclosure in groups, chatting and laughing. Elsa smiled and said hi right and left. The chairman of the collective, Olle, tried to make eye contact with her through the sea of people, but she avoided his gaze. He made a beeline for her, and she wished she could hide.

"So, you took reindeer to the police."

She nodded and stared at a spot beyond his right ear.

"The first call from someone threatening to shoot me came at 8:28 yesterday morning."

His voice was dry as kindling, but there was no mistaking its angry tremor.

"And from an unknown number, of course. My phone has been ringing off the hook ever since, but I haven't picked up."

"I just got so freaking sick of it all," Elsa said. "I found the reindeer and called the police and no one would give me the time of day so I went in."

"Bad timing. Right in the middle of separation."

"Or good timing, because they probably won't do anything while we're all gathered together."

"Those bastards aren't afraid of anything, least of all the police. They all know each other."

Yes, there had been talk that Henriksson and Robert were acquaintances, that they had done their compulsory military service together.

"But there were gloves in the bag, so there's DNA this time."

"DNA! They'll never send the gloves off for some pricey test for our sake. I imagine those gloves will vanish. They probably already have."

"I took photos."

"Sure, sure." Olle nodded at someone farther off and left her.

Her armpits were damp with sweat. He never would have gone after Dad or Mattias like that. A man probably would have gotten a clap on the shoulder. But not her.

She felt an arm slip around her waist. There stood Hanna, but as usual her smile wasn't reflected in her eyes.

"Forget those old men. You did the right thing."

"There's no such thing as doing the right thing here, you know that."

"They're just jealous because you're young and have your whole future ahead of you. Soon they'll be dead, the whole lot of them."

Elsa couldn't help but laugh.

"I'd put money on your becoming the collective's first female chairperson," Hanna said, nudging her with her hip.

"That day will never come."

"Don't say that."

"Olle received death threats because of me."

"It's not the first time someone has threatened him. And it's not your fault, as he well knows, that stubborn cuss. Now is when we need to stick together, put up a united front, and say enough is enough. He's just mad that he didn't get to be in the spotlight."

Anna-Stina was heading their way slowly, her face stiff. She stopped a few yards away, standing with her arms straight down by her sides, eyes darting around as if she were looking for someone else.

"Wasn't it a good thing, what she did? The article."

Hanna squeezed Elsa's shoulder firmly before letting go.

"Yeah, Elsa always does the right thing." She sounded snide.

Elsa had told Anna-Stina about the article as they drove home from Per-Jonas's, and she had been less than impressed. She felt that Elsa ought to think before she acted rather than make impulsive decisions.

"We need a woman who speaks her mind. It's about time," said Hanna.

Anna-Stina shrugged; then her face lit up. Per-Jonas had arrived. They could hear him all the way over there. She hurried off. Elsa didn't turn around. She clapped her gloves together with a dull smack and nodded at the enclosure.

"It's fun to watch Jon-Isak. He's a little bruiser."

Hanna nodded. "Yeah, he's tough. Well, shall we go show them what a woman can do?"

Elsa glanced back. Hanna elbowed her in the side.

"Or would you rather wait for Per-Jonas's little snookums?"

"Snookums!" Elsa grinned.

"Oh, who can bear to look at her when she's strutting around like that. Come on."

ELSA STOOD ON TIPTOE and lifted the string that secured the gate to the girdnu. Soon they would let in the reindeer. Now there were spotlights on the snow and voices in the darkness beyond. She could hear the reindeer in the distance. Jon-Isak was at her side. He snuffled and wiped his nose.

"I got to help drive them again this year. None of them dared to turn back. The reindeer are where they should be."

She knew the exact feeling you got when, as a child, you made an entire herd of reindeer turn and hurry in the direction you wanted them to go. The herders all spread out in a long line, occasionally holding something between them, plastic or a tarp, to appear wider. Someone hollered, someone clapped, and the reindeer moved forward, toward the center.

"Well done, you!"

"And now I'm going to catch my own reindeer."

"Of course you will. You catch it, and maybe I can help you pull it in?"

He looked her up and down and nodded. Yep, she would do.

The reindeer were let into the girdnu in waves. Elsa, her family, close cousins, distant relatives, and friends all took their places. First they stood along the fence and watched, keeping a lookout for ear marks, recognizing LED collars and the occasional pelt marking, like a tattoo carved into fur. It was crowded, which made it possible to grab an antler and pull the animal out. Most of the time a lasso wasn't necessary. Now and then someone might use a stávrá, a rod with a loop on one end, but usually it was enough to go in among the animals and get a firm grip with your hands.

Elsa was one of the first to start moving. She had spotted her earmark, but this particular reindeer was special and she would know it without the mark. The cow was long-legged, one of the best, had given them many calves. It made her smile to see her again.

Anna-Stina was on the inside now too.

"Let's go," said Elsa.

She snuck up and clasped her hands around the antlers, and the cow dug her heels in right away. Anna-Stina grabbed the antlers from the other side and together they pulled her out without much trouble, although Anna-Stina was grimacing. Elsa's mother stood at the ready with a syringe of dewormer to protect against botflies and to mark down in their papers that the first cow had been sorted into their family's pen. They opened the gate, and Elsa gave her reindeer a pat on the haunches before it rushed into the darkness, where it soon grew calm again.

Anna-Stina tugged at her arm, had her eyes on the next reindeer. If she wanted to, she could do this work just as well as anyone else.

IT WAS LONG PAST midnight when they pulled into the yard. Mom said they could leave the bins in the car. It was a starry night with a full moon. Elsa exhaled and rotated her sore wrists. Mom unlocked the door and vanished inside while Dad unhitched the trailer and drove the snowmobile down the ramp. Mattias had stayed at the corral, so his house was dark.

Dad began carrying the reindeer skins to the storage shed, but then he stopped suddenly and turned to look out at the lake. Elsa heard it too. Snowmobiles. They exchanged glances; he raised his eyebrows. Now they could see headlights coming closer. Two snowmobiles. She instinctively moved closer to the shed and to Dad.

They came up the slope from the lake, pulled up next to each other, and stopped with blinding lights. She raised her hand to shield her eyes. The men revved the engines but didn't move.

"Get the hell out of here!" Dad shouted.

They stood still.

Mom came out on the steps but immediately went back inside. Elsa took out her phone and started taking video, stretching her arm out pointedly. That made one of the men hit the gas and come straight for her. The other followed. Dad grabbed Elsa and pulled her behind the trailer. The snowmobiles skidded by and drove back out onto the road, then cut into the ditch and out through the thickets and back to the lake.

Their engines echoed across the village for a long time before they vanished into the forest on the other side.

Dad slapped the trailer. She waited for him to say that this was all her fault.

CHAPTER FORTY-FOUR

Njealljeloginjeallje

I t was starting to get dark in Jokkmokk, but the crowd around the market stalls was only getting bigger. In early February, the sun set soon after three o'clock. Darkness still had the advantage for the better part of the day. It had been a clear one, and not as cold as yesterday, when the thermometer bottomed out at twenty-five below. Dressing for the market—staying warm and looking good—was an art form. Their gákti, nuvtthahat, and extra-warm woolen shawls turned tourists' heads as Elsa and Anna-Stina walked by. The rajd, a reindeer caravan through town, had taken place a few hours previously, and there had been a reindeer race down on Lake Dálvaddis. Steam rose from the trailers that sold suovas-kebab or hamburgers. The most renowned craftspeople, the duojárat, had taken up their usual places indoors, at the Sámi Educational Centre. It was Friday, and the activity was feverish. The silver jewelry glittered behind display glass or hung from fantastical wooden stands. Liinnit, shawls with fringe and without. Art. Duodji, Sámi handicrafts complete with seals of authenticity.

Elsa and Anna-Stina zigzagged their way through the crowd, down the stairs to the ground floor. They met some cousins and hugged, promising they would see them at the Sámi dance that evening. They were just taking the last step when a middle-aged woman threw out her arms and beamed at them.

"What beautiful clothing! May I take a picture?"

She didn't wait for a response, was already fumbling with her phone, winking and smiling. She asked her husband to hold her bags.

"Closer together, there. Fantastic Sámi costumes!"

Anna-Stina grinned and put her hand on her hip. Elsa sighed and tried to force a smile. This was the third time they'd been stopped for a photo.

"We should charge a fee," she whispered to Anna-Stina when they were finally moving again.

A bustling clamor filled the rooms, whose acoustics couldn't handle the sheer number of voices. The noise exhausted her. She had been looking forward to the market for months, yet here she stood, feeling like she would rather be somewhere else. She took everyone in, could label each one of them. The confident ones glided around in their gákti, every detail of which they'd sewn themselves; silver dangled from their ears and riskun jingled on their chests. The less confident ones—without language, their eyes searching—moved tentatively among the shawls that hung from hangers, eager to buy them but also hesitant. And then there were the others, the ones who wanted to take pictures, clueless about the hierarchies; those who had taken the night bus to Boden and changed buses there; those who had come on the tourist buses or driven in cars. The ones who only admired and likely never reflected. The ones who took pictures for Instagram.

Maybe they had time to pet the reindeer that walked down the streets of Jokkmokk. And what was it again, wasn't there some fight about a mine here? That was here, right? They seemed to recall some conflict that threatened to kill the reindeer industry in the area. But they didn't manage to finish thinking the thought and instead happily paid 1,550 kronor for a silver necklace that had leaves like the brooches for gákti. Authentic Sámi handicraft, they said. The "authentic" part was important. And "Lapp," you don't use that word, they knew that. But sometimes they slipped up, especially if they were of an older generation and heard "Lappish" being spoken.

"Come on, I want some new earrings," Anna-Stina said, tugging on her arm.

Elsa knew that she was one of the confident ones, one of the women who could sew everything, from gákti to belt, who could weave shoe bands and fringe her own shawl. The only thing she had to buy were the brooches and the round silver buttons sewn close together all around her belt. And the earrings Anna-Stina was looking through now.

"Your clothes! So beautiful!" said an English-speaking voice.

The woman who had pushed her way to them was dressed for a polar expedition; she sounded British.

"Thank you."

"Absolutely amazing," she went on, unable to keep from gently touching the fringes.

Elsa took a step back, but it was crowded and she didn't get far. She nodded and turned away, clinging tight to Anna-Stina.

"I can't take much more of this. They're starting to *touch* me."

"But we look good," Anna-Stina said with a grin.

Right, now was the time to show themselves off. Today Jokkmokk was a proud Sámi community, and no one would acknowledge any hatred for the fucking Lapps who had protested the planned mine in Gállok.

"They're so ignorant."

"Come on, chill out, help me find some earrings."

Elsa wished she had slapped the British woman's hand away and told her about the villagers who had no qualms about threatening her, who drove their snowmobiles into her yard to demonstrate that they could do whatever they liked. That would wipe the smile off that woman's face. Elsa fantasized about shaking her, telling her how reindeer were tortured to death.

She knew that she should relax and feel secure. If ever they were in the majority, on their own terms for once, it was here. She understood why none of her friends wanted to talk about or be reminded of unpleasant topics during the best weekend of the year, and yet it was annoying that no one had even mentioned the article about the reindeer cadavers. Almost a month had passed now, and the police hadn't been in touch about those bags, and surely the gloves with their DNA had disappeared. Elsa couldn't bring herself to call Henriksson, couldn't handle listening to his feeble excuses.

It was stifling inside; everyone unbuttoned their jackets and cardigans when they came in, gasping about the temperature difference. Her gákti was warm and there was nothing to loosen; her woolen stockings were just as warm, and her shoe bands wound tight up her calves. Elsa fanned herself with a brochure from the Sámi craftsperson who made the most expensive knives.

Anna-Stina waffled between two pairs of earrings, holding them up to her ears with an expectant expression. Elsa pointed at the right pair, silver with a small blue bead in the center. Anna-Stina didn't look convinced and turned back to the mirror.

People behind them crowded in to see the jewelry. Elsa ignored all their admiring glances, turning her face away when they held up their phones.

"Are you almost done? I want to get out of here."

Anna-Stina turned to look at her, perplexed. "What now?"

"Well, just look at them. It's all so exotic to them. They're colonizing our culture with their gaze. It's revolting."

Anna-Stina laughed out loud. "Have you been drinking already?"

"No, I haven't." She fanned herself harder with the brochure and closed her eyes.

"You're kind of weird sometimes. Do you really think I should get the ones with the blue beads?" Anna-Stina held up the earrings again.

"Yeah, do it. Look, I need to get some air. See you later."

She turned around and headed for the stairs, took them two at a time, and threw open the door. The cold hit her right away and she took a deep breath. She loosened her belt; it felt like she couldn't get enough oxygen. Everything was supposed to fit so snugly, so perfectly, so right.

She was getting looks, not from the tourists now, but from her own people. She stood there with her belt in her hand, an incomplete gákti and a face flushed red. A snowed-in kicksled was parked by the wall of the building and she sat down on it. Presumably they figured she'd already had her first beer. Someone grinned and gave her a thumbs-up from a distance. Snowflakes danced around her face, straightening out the curls she'd so carefully put in her hair this morning. The snow caught on her eyelashes and melted on her cheeks. She looked up at the sky. Her mascara was running onto her temples. Like war paint.

Now no one wanted to talk about her gákti, no one wondered if they could take a picture for Insta. Instead, she got quick glances from passing tourists in the subpar winter boots someone had sold them in some expensive adventure store. She wanted to ask them if they knew this building had once been a folk school that was started as reparations for all the abuse the

Sámi had been forced to withstand. A Christian attempt at a meaningless apology.

"But do you even know what they were apologizing for?"

Elsa sighed and pulled the belt around her waist again, fastened the snaps and tied the band so the tassels hung on her left side. Her hands trembled in the cold. She couldn't go back inside, even though her jacket was still in there; instead she texted Anna-Stina and asked her to bring it out to her. She stood up, crossed her arms over her chest, and hurried for the residential area near the hotel. Eyes on the ground, she pretended not to hear when someone called her name. She just went faster and faster until she was running.

CHAPTER FORTY-FIVE

Njeilljelogivihtta

The reindeer's sightless eyes were wide open and partially covered in the blood that had flowed down from its head and onto its muzzle. The notch in its head was deep, and if you weren't squeamish you could look closely and see how its skull was split in two. The front part of its body, its head and legs, dangled over the sign, hiding JOK and also JÅH. The rest of Swedish "Jokkmokk" and Lule Sámi "Jåhkåmåhkke" was hardly visible underneath the smeared blood. It was as if someone had taken the reindeer's blood and used a paintbrush to insult the Sámi place name of a market that had brought the Sámi people together for over four hundred years.

The rest of the reindeer's body hung down the back side. It was as though it had simply been tossed over the road sign like an article of clothing cast hastily aside on the back of a chair.

It was just past six in the morning when Elsa arrived at the sign. She had been woken by Anna-Stina, who'd been up to use the bathroom, looked at her phone, and saw the picture that had been shared faster than a parade of lemmings in the mountains. Anna-Stina had collapsed back into bed in the guest room they were sharing with two others, who were asleep on mattresses on the floor. The day-after smell was noticeable, and Elsa had battled both nausea and dizziness as she pulled on her jeans and down jacket and headed out.

She wasn't the first one on the scene; a number of older early risers from the village had gathered; a police car was parked closest to the sign, and an agitated older woman with a dog was talking to the officers, a woman and a man in their thirties.

"And well, that made me so scared, thinking that the fool who did this might still be around somewhere with an axe. And so I called you right away," the woman said, her voice shrill.

Elsa looked for tracks in the snow and tentatively approached the group of villagers, heard them discussing when it might have happened. They talked about what time the snow had fallen and how late at night lots of folks had been heading home from the dance, but only now had the reindeer been discovered.

Elsa had stuck around the People's House until closing time, and she had seen the event organizers herding out the last boisterous guest, who expressed thanks for the night by way of a spontaneous joik in the parking lot outside.

"So what do you think of all this, Elsa?"

She turned around, and there stood Minna. The dark circles under her eyes were as prominent as Elsa's. Her cheeks were just as pale. That sweaty weakness that came after a very long and drunken night. They'd had an insanely good time. She hadn't seen Minna since their Sámi confirmation camp days, and when they ran into each other in the crowd they had thrown their arms around each other and hung out all evening. Laughing at old memories and dancing themselves sweaty. They'd had so much to drink that Elsa had trouble focusing her eyes, at which point Minna poured a glass of water down her throat. And then they started dancing again.

Minna embraced her now, and Elsa didn't want to let go.

"You know what I think," Minna said, extricating herself from Elsa's desperate grip with a chuckle. "Once the village settled in for the night and the last of the after-parties petered out, someone loaded a dead reindeer on a trailer, went out to the sign, and tossed it up there. It must have taken at least two people."

"I wonder how many people went by without even bothering to call the police."

"Are you surprised?"

"Not in the least."

Minna grabbed Elsa's arm and pulled her over to the police officers.

The woman with the dog had joined the cluster of villagers and was now recounting the terrible sight she had happened upon in the dark.

The police were discussing the best way to get the reindeer down.

"You've taken pictures, right?"

They turned around to look at Minna.

"You know, because it's a crime scene," she clarified.

"We're aware of that, yes."

"Will you be classifying this as a hate crime? There's no question that it's meant to target the Sámi, the reindeer herders."

The policeman nodded, his face serious.

"We aren't ruling anything out at the present time. It remains to be seen. It could be as you say."

"What do you mean? What else could it be? A prank? A drunken whim? No, this takes planning, by grown men with a motive behind their killing."

"We'll try to get hold of witnesses. Someone must have seen something." He had a strong accent that indicated he was from Luleå, on the northern coast.

"I think the reindeer should stay there all day," Elsa said. "Let everyone see what goes on here."

"But we can't risk people messing up evidence at the scene or taking the reindeer," the officer muttered.

"So you're actually going to gather evidence this time? Evidence that might lead somewhere?"

The policeman fixed his gaze on her, and his voice was no longer passive. "Hey, I don't appreciate your tone. We will do our job, just like we always do."

Minna pressed close to Elsa. They both reeked of old hangover.

"We're not particularly used to that, so you'll have to excuse our skepticism," Minna said.

She wasn't from a reindeer-herding family. Her father was a well-known duojár, and her mother, rumor had it, was from the south and had applied to the Sámi Educational Centre in Jokkmokk to get in touch with her inner Sámi. She turned out to have Sámi roots and met a Sámi man, but still didn't become the whole person she'd hoped to be and went back south. And

Minna, fourteen at the time, ended up with just her dad. Soon afterwards she and Elsa had become friends at confirmation camp, and Minna had revealed that she wasn't looking forward to her mother coming to church and her confirmation.

The officers moved away from them, speaking in low tones.

"We have to call the newspapers and TV before they take the reindeer down," Elsa said.

"I already did."

"So you got up for this too?"

"Yeah, I thought I was going to wake up with someone this morning, but he was gone."

"Johannes."

Elsa gave a crooked smile and pulled her hood up over her hat. Last night, toward the end of the dance, she had lost track of Minna. When she found her again, she was on the dance floor in Johannes's arms. He'd been wasted, the belt of his gákti almost under his butt instead of around his hips. He had stroked Minna's waist-length black hair and kissed her so intensely that Elsa couldn't look away. Johannes was well known in the next village, a little cocky, just like his younger brother. Elsa didn't much care for either of them. The boys in that family always had to act like such hotshots.

"So you live here in Jokkmokk these days?" she asked.

"You don't remember what I told you?" Minna grinned. "Like I said yesterday, I move around a little. Off to Umeå soon. For school. Gonna do something about all this." She gestured at the reindeer.

"Seriously?"

"Yeah, of course. I'm going to be a lawyer. I'll make them change the way these crimes are classified. Because you and I both know this can't be charged as anything more serious than theft. If that. Even that won't be easy, given that the ears have been cut off. Probably won't be any charges at all."

"We've lost so many reindeer."

"Yeah, I saw you in the paper, by the way. Damn good job! Straight up dumping the reindeer at the station. What happened after that?"

"We haven't heard anything, so I'm sure nothing will come of it. As usual."

A man in his twenties came slipping and sliding their way. His topcoat wasn't warm enough, and the very fact that it was a topcoat set him apart. He ran his hand through his hair, stroking the top of his head, as he tried with sleepy eyes to figure out who was standing around the sign. Elsa heard him introduce himself to the police officers as a journalist from *Expressen*.

"*Expressen*," Minna said, raising her eyebrows. "He's only here because the minister of culture competed in the reindeer race yesterday. That's the only time journalists make it all the way up here."

"Wonder what she'll have to say about this?"

"Oh, I know that one. She'll look grim and say it's a very serious matter. And then she'll go home and forget the whole thing. Or she'll tell her friends all about it at some fancy dinner party and say how terrible it is, all the hatred up there."

"Up there. All vague and stuff, because no one knows where Jokkmokk is anyway."

The journalist from the evening paper was shivering as he held out his phone and interviewed the officers. He didn't ask the right questions and received only curt answers. Elsa took out her phone and posted a photo of the reindeer to Insta. She wasn't sure how to caption it at first, but decided to be straightforward and wrote that it was a hate crime. That would probably provoke an avalanche of threatening comments. Mom had begged her time and again to make her account private, but why should she just preach to the choir?

The journalist approached them, shuffling over on his slippery soles. She could practically see what he was thinking. He was smart enough to realize that two young women in front of a killed reindeer was just the shot he needed. Angry young Sámi women, to boot. But there was no way for him to know whether they belonged to the Indigenous population without asking, and Elsa studied him with a certain amount of schadenfreude as he tried to formulate the question.

"This was a hate crime," Minna interrupted him.

His gaze took on a new sharpness and he thrust his phone near her face. "What do you mean?"

"What do you think?"

"You mean it's targeting reindeer herders, which means it's targeting the Sámi as an ethnic group?"

His hair fell over his face and he smiled, knowing to make use of his looks, which were not half bad.

Elsa felt a sudden wave of exhaustion. She had already tried this route; this conversation would only come back to bite her. The journalist, though, he would almost certainly be lauded in his newsroom. A dead, bloody reindeer and an interview with outraged Sámi women with their high cheekbones.

"What do you plan to write?" Minna asked.

"What you tell me. I really want to portray how terrible it is."

"Did the police say it was a hate crime?"

"No, but that doesn't matter much. The important thing is for the voices of victimized Sámi folks to be heard."

"I'm not a reindeer herder," Minna said. "Is your angle victimized reindeer herders, or Sámi?"

He looked uncertain, but gave her an ingratiating smile. "You all are tough up here. No bullshit, just straight to the point. What do you say about a photo?"

"What do you say about telling it like it is?" Minna's voice was cutting.

"Absolutely, but you'll have to say more than just 'it's a hate crime.' What is your reasoning for saying so?"

Elsa crossed her arms. "Will you bother to find out more? Will you ask the police how often this kind of thing happens? Do you understand what it means to see your reindeer killed, tortured to death? That reindeer was struck in the head, and its legs were bent at an angle, so it probably met a long and painful end. Do you understand what it does to a person, to see their animal like this?"

He nodded encouragingly, glancing at his phone to make sure it was recording.

"Yes, yes, of course. I do."

"But how could you?"

"No, sure, I can't totally—"

"No, you can't. But you have the power to write about it, so maybe others will understand. But you might also end up stoking the hatred toward us. Do you see that?"

"Yes, I mean, no."

"Have you written about the Sámi before?"

"No."

"Then be prepared, because you'll get more comments than ever before. Read them carefully and think about where that hate comes from."

He nodded, so cold that his teeth were chattering. "But you two already know all that. Can't you tell me?"

Elsa felt the nausea well up in waves; she was close to puking. A cold sweat broke out between her shoulder blades. She staggered a few steps to the side.

"So how about that photo? It'd be great to have the two of you together."

"No photos," she said. "Take a picture of the reindeer, though."

He looked disappointed and attempted another smile. "But this is your chance."

Elsa bent over and threw up on the snowbank. Her stomach seized and her throat burned. It came out of her nose too, and the sensation of being smothered made her whimper. Minna patted her back.

HALF AN HOUR LATER, the article was online and Minna read it out loud to Elsa, who was lying on the sofa, pale.

"Listen to this: 'I meet two young Sámi women who don't dare be photographed; the hate they will face is too great a threat.'"

Elsa brought her glass of water to dry lips and hoped what went down would stay down.

Minna read in silence and laughed out loud.

"Well, he sure can paint a picture. And no surprise, he uses words like 'lawless land' and 'wilderness.' Good thing we have both ICA and Coop to buy groceries out here in the wilderness. How else would we survive?"

"It's not funny, Minna."

"No, I know. But what else can we do but laugh at that dork? Did you see him hanging around at the Sámi dance yesterday?"

"No, was he there?"

"Um, yes! Did you really miss him? I didn't think someone could walk in without a gákti unnoticed. He was like a lone lighthouse in a stormy sea."

"You can paint a picture with your words too, I hear."

Minna threw her head back and burst into peals of laughter.

"You have to laugh, or you'll die on the inside. Every part of you will store it up, you know. Your body stores pain."

Elsa considered her. She wasn't much taller than Áhkku, her hair fell over her shoulders and wiry bare arms like a black cape. Elsa wanted to say that she couldn't take much more. She wanted to hear Minna promise that everything would be fine. She wanted to laugh out loud with her again.

Yesterday she had laughed as they goofed around drunkenly, stumbling through the Sydis dance. For just a moment she felt free and happy as a guy from Mittådalen whirled her across the dance floor. But even so, toward the end of the night, she found herself sitting on a chair as despair washed over her. How much longer would they manage to sew their gákti, joik along with the songs, and party the night away? Only to wake up to a perfectly ordinary day and nothing had changed.

"Can you fix this, Minna?"

"What?" Minna looked up from her phone.

"All of it."

"Definitely!"

She so badly wanted to believe her.

CHAPTER FORTY-SIX

Njealljelogiguhtta

The trunk of the car was open, and Mom loaded the suitcase and a moving box inside. Elsa was sitting in the backseat with Áhkku. None of them could look her in the eye. Áhkku was clutching an old brown leather bag with well-worn gold buckles. She had packed it herself, so who knew what was inside. Áhkku probably knew where she was going, but she didn't say a word. She remained silent as the car left the village, and Elsa followed her gaze over the snow-covered bogs, the snowmobile trails that crisscrossed each other in the ditch, and the trees that were no longer weighed down by snow from the most recent storm.

As Mom slowed down for a pair of reindeer, Áhkku looked down at her lap and wrung her hands. Her dry skin sounded raspy; the cracks around her fingernails were hard.

It was just getting dark as they drove into town, and the yellow glow of the streetlights settled gently over the roads and snowbanks. The nursing home, a two-story wooden building painted red, had opened quite recently and was in a residential area a few miles from the center of town.

They'd been told that there would be Sámi-speaking staff, but they were welcomed by someone named Britt-Inger who said that particular aide was out with the flu. She herself was a Tornedalian and spoke Miänkieli, a language related to Finnish. She said she was a Mäki from Pajala, a family Elsa's mother certainly knew of. After that, the conversation flowed more easily; you could always find connections, little threads to grab onto.

"People call me Brittis, by the way."

Áhkku stood still, letting her eyes run down corridors and over closed doors. Her ears seemed to perk up at the sound of a television coming from farther down the hall. The air smelled faintly of the day's lunch, which must have been fish. Elsa so badly wanted to embrace her, but on this particular day she wouldn't survive not getting a hug back. She gently took Áhkku by the shoulders and steered her in the right direction to follow Mom and Brittis. This was one of Áhkku's good days, you could see it in her eyes. In one way, that was a positive thing, because maybe she would remember arriving here.

Brittis unlocked the door to a room that held a twin bed with a pale yellow bedspread, a large white bureau, a small kitchen table next to the window, and two white chairs with floral cushions. Brittis followed Elsa's gaze.

"We left the cushions because they were practically new, and the family of the woman who lived here before didn't bother to take them. So if you want them, they can stay."

One out, one in.

Áhkku sat down on the bed and grasped the round handle of her bag, pulling it close. She dangled her legs, but not in a carefree way. No, it was as if she were seeking firm ground beneath her feet.

Brittis and Mom discussed switching out the curtain rod and what the bedtime routine was like. Mom said softly that they should keep the door locked, and for a moment Áhkku's legs stopped swinging. Her eyes narrowed and she began to rhythmically stroke the smooth leather of the bag until Elsa placed a hand over hers. Then she stopped and quickly drew her hand away.

"We won't lock your door, and those of us on staff will always be close at hand," Brittis said reassuringly in Áhkku's direction.

She took Mom out to see the kitchen and other common areas. There was a pattering on the windowsill. Rain. In the middle of February. The roads might be glare ice by the time they drove home.

"It's not right," Áhkku said in a tiny voice.

Elsa sat down beside her, and the soft bed swayed beneath them.

"You'll like it here. They speak Sámi and they make the foods you like, reindeer and moose and fish. It will be like home."

Elsa squeezed her eyes shut. Like home. Why would she say that?

"It's not supposed to rain in February."

"No, I know. It's crazy."

"It's all in the Bible, it's all predetermined. And now it has begun. We will be swallowed alive."

Áhkku's hand fumbled across the bed, as though she were searching for something.

"What will happen to you? No husband yet, and the reindeer, who will die anyway. This can't go on, weather like this. I've been saying so for years and none of you listened and now it's raining in February. At calf-marking time the sun will burn the grazing lands dry instead, I promise you that."

Elsa seized on the part of this that hurt the least. "Áhkku, I don't need a man."

"And you'll end up childless that way. But I suppose that's just as well, because it will all be over soon anyway."

"I think you're being a little too pessimistic," Elsa said. She had to say "pessimistic" in Swedish, because she didn't know the Sámi word for it. And Áhkku raised her sparse eyebrows.

"Pissimistic," she said with a smile. "Now there's a fitting word."

They laughed together as they had done when she was little. That's how Elsa wanted to remember it, that Áhkku had been as funny as the other old ladies in the collective. The ones who laughed until their bellies bobbed and they had to wipe tears from their eyes.

The raindrops struck metal and window. Elsa went to the little sink and filled a glass with cold water, which she handed to Áhkku. She took a few sips and handed the glass back.

"I don't want to have to get up to pee in the middle of the night, because then I have to walk past her."

The filter across the old woman's gaze had returned.

"It's no big deal," said Elsa.

"You're not supposed to pee at night, or else she gets so angry." Her legs were swinging again, faster and faster. "But if I wet the bed she'll notice and get even angrier. And then she hits me. Hard. Here." Áhkku brought her hand to the back of her head. "But maybe she'll tear out my hair too. She mustn't. It's already so thin." Tears sprang to her eyes and she patted her bag again, hard.

"No one will hit you here," Elsa said gently.

"How can you leave me here, Enná?"

"You have your own bathroom here, Áhkku. Look!"

Elsa opened the door to the bathroom but recoiled as the smell of sewage hit her.

"I don't want to stay here. I want to be with you and Dad and my brothers. I don't need to go to school, I can be with the reindeer."

Elsa sank onto the chair and grabbed the edges of the table, which felt greasy.

"This isn't the nomad school," she said, her voice clear and low.

Áhkku was crying. Tears landed on her green skirt. Yet she wasn't trying to escape. She cried quietly and didn't move. Aware that she had no choice. Even back then, she knew.

Elsa stared into the darkness. There was no point in trying to be physical with Áhkku, to comfort her that way; all she could do was let her find her way back from the other world.

"I can't speak Swedish, I can't," Áhkku whimpered, rocking back and forth.

Elsa recognized that movement.

"You need to pee."

"But she'll get angry."

"She'll be even angrier if you wet the bed, and you know she won't change the sheets. You know you'll have to sleep in the cold spot."

Elsa felt sick when she heard herself. But it worked. Áhkku abruptly stopped crying and slid down off the bed. Elsa gently guided her toward the bathroom.

"You can go to the bathroom whenever you want."

Áhkku dropped her skirt to the floor and pushed down her woolen stockings before sitting down carefully and peeing so forcefully that it echoed in the fully tiled bathroom. Elsa made sure she wiped and washed her hands.

Áhkku was smiling when she came out. Her relief was palpable. She walked around the room, looked out the window.

"Where does little sister sleep? Where does everyone else sleep?"

Elsa didn't answer. She took the bag from the bed, but Áhkku hurried over and lifted it back up. She sat next to it, stroking the leather again.

"Maybe you should lie down and have a rest?"

Áhkku nodded and leaned back stiffly. She closed her eyes, but her eyelids fluttered as though she didn't dare to close them all the way. Her face had grown thinner and more wrinkled. The bags under her eyes were fine, and her cheekbones were sharp under taut skin.

Brittis and Mom were on their way back; their laughter drifted in from the hallway and Áhkku opened her eyes to look anxiously at Elsa, who tried to give her a reassuring smile. Áhkku sat up and looked attentively at Brittis, who was the first in the room.

"We got new beds last fall. Isn't it comfy?"

Áhkku looked down at her hands. Elsa whispered a translation into her ear. Then she looked up and nodded.

"Do you understand Meänkieli?" Brittis asked, and Áhkku nodded again.

Indeed, most folks of her generation were bilingual from a young age. And even though Áhkku could speak Meänkieli, she preferred to use Sámi. Now she pursed her lips, and her vigilant gaze followed Brittis as she moved through the room.

"There's a girl on staff who speaks Sámi. It's so important for our residents to be able to speak their own language, especially in cases like this."

Like this. She emphasized those words. When the brain sloshed around untethered, Elsa thought. When it had lost its direction.

"They typically revert to the language of their childhood, back to safety and familiarity, to mother's milk," Brittis went on.

"Where are the others?" Áhkku whispered to Elsa.

"This is your room, you'll sleep here by yourself."

"Alone," she said, her lower lip trembling. "In the dark."

Elsa reached over to turn on the white lamp that was mounted above the bed. "You can keep the light on all night."

"That's not allowed."

"It is here."

Elsa wanted to shake her, make her understand. Mom didn't seem to be listening. She was fully immersed in going through the dresser drawers and planning how to arrange Áhkku's clothes.

"I'll go get her things," she said, quickly vanishing from the room, as if she couldn't stand to be there. Áhkku wasn't her mother, but she was the one who was forced to do this, to take a home away from her mother-in-law.

Brittis stood in the doorway, bending backwards, listening for some sound or another in the hallway.

"I should probably go on a round. But come find me before you go."

Mom was groaning under the weight when she brought in the box and the suitcase. Áhkku looked on as shards of her life ended up on unfamiliar shelves and in drawers that smelled of mothballs. She looked amazed when the curtain that had once hung in her kitchen suddenly hung here. She was so small, sitting with her back against the wall and her legs straight out on the bed. Her gray braid, which had grown skinnier over the years, trailed over her scrawny breast and landed on her stomach. She twisted it absentmindedly, letting its end stroke her palm. Suddenly, out came the Sámi psalm; everyone knew that Áhkku had a beautiful voice, and now she sang so strongly that red spots appeared on her cheeks. Mom stopped mid-motion, her shoulders going stiff, but she soon returned to her task. Elsa was moved and had to turn away. They would never agree on religion. She would never accept it, while Áhkku had done so blindly. They could no longer talk about it, how Áhkku didn't see all the cruel things that the church had done to them. How she could turn to the church at all. At fourteen, Elsa had stood her ground, asked questions, and made Áhkku raise her voice. It wasn't the church she turned to, it was God, and that was something entirely different. Those who had, in God's name, taken what had once belonged to the Sámi, that was a different matter, didn't Elsa understand? She had scoffed at that. That church had nothing to do with her beliefs.

And now she turned to what had brought her the greatest comfort, and her voice was as bright and clear as Elsa had ever heard it. Áhkku took a deep breath and started over.

"Mon almmi guvlui dal geahčadan . . ."

Brittis cracked the door open, cleared her throat discreetly, and mentioned that some people at the nursing home took a nap around this time.

"But it'll sure be delightful to have such a songbird around during our singing hour on Thursday," she said with a smile.

Áhkku fell silent, and Brittis reassured her in Miänkieli that she was welcome to sing, just not so loudly at this particular moment.

"Are you finished?" she asked Mom, who nodded and wiped her palms on her jeans before turning to Áhkku.

"Goodbye, we'll see you next week. Take care, now."

It sounded stiff, and Mom's entire self seemed awkward and brusque. Brittis walked with her, chattering about dinner, which would be homemade meatballs. Elsa was left behind. Áhkku's hands grasped her bag. None of them had looked inside.

"May I see what you brought?"

Áhkku shook her head frantically.

"The others steal."

"Not me though."

Áhkku looked at her for a long time, apparently trying very hard to recognize the young woman who was so like her little sister.

"Are you leaving me now?"

"Yes, we have to go. But you'll like it here."

Mom honked from the car outside. They had to go before it dropped below freezing and the ice wreaked havoc on traffic. It had stopped raining.

Elsa stood up, fighting tears.

"See you soon, Áhkku."

The old woman looked up at her, bewildered.

They didn't say goodbye, and Elsa walked to the door and closed it softly behind her. Brittis waved from a distance as Elsa unlocked the main door and stepped out. A south wind that didn't belong in February stroked her cheek. But she was shivering deep down to the marrow.

In the third window over from the entrance was a familiar figure. Áhkku had pressed her face to the pane, as if to better see in the dark. She pressed both palms to the glass. Panic was on her face. Her mouth was open. Elsa couldn't move. Was she calling out? Her palms struck the window, but it was hardly audible. Elsa turned to go back inside. She couldn't do this; they couldn't leave her like this. Then Brittis popped up behind Áhkku, put an arm around her, and gently held her skinny wrists. And then they were out of sight.

CHAPTER FORTY-SEVEN

Njealljelogičieža

The eagle had been soaring silently above their grounds for days now. Tomorrow it would be March, njukčamánnu, and there weren't yet any calves it could strike and take off with. An eight-pound calf was no match for an eagle. Elsa had never seen it happen with her own eyes, but she'd heard others talk about it.

She forced herself to look once more at the dead cow in the snow. Her belly was open and the unborn calf gone. It could have been a wolverine or some other predator. The cow seemed to have strayed far from the herd, which was roaming free but being fed in the corral. They seldom wandered this close to the next village.

She sank to her knee and ran her hand along the wound in the cow's belly. No predator could slit flesh open in such a neat line. It was straight, like a cut from a blade. She turned the cow over and looked methodically through the fur until she found the hole. The cow had been shot and sliced open with a knife. And the calf—had they taken it?

Red trails of blood in the white snow, a large pool and a long line of drips along a snowmobile trail. Had they shot more than one reindeer? She inspected the snow and found fox tracks. The poachers must have cut open the belly and let the fox take the calf. They had callously counted on a predator feasting on the cow and hiding the evidence of the knife. They hadn't had to worry about the bullet, because it had gone straight through the belly. But the trails of blood suggested that they'd taken something with them.

She took pictures of the cow, bent down to get close-ups of the slit belly, even stuck a finger in the bullet hole and took a shot of that.

She texted Dad to tell him about the reindeer and her location. She couldn't bring herself to call and hear his voice; she wasn't even sure her own would work.

But she couldn't just sit there waiting. She started the snowmobile and drove alongside the trail; the drops of blood grew ever farther apart. A half mile on, she reached the rise with a view down to Robert Isaksson's house and the ramshackle storehouse that had once served as a barn. The snowmobile tracks were fresh and it was clear that the drops of blood led all the way there. The audacity. So close to his own home. She took off her protective earmuffs and listened for sounds from the property.

She called the police and briefly reported what she'd found, that she had followed the drops of blood to Robert Isaksson's house. She emphasized that they had to hurry.

There was no car and no snowmobile in the yard. He wasn't home. She climbed off her snowmobile and looked at the drops of blood, which had sunk slightly into the snow. Where had he been going in such a rush?

Dad texted to say she should turn back. But she stayed put. The police had promised to come. For the first time, a police officer had actually listened to her and promised to send a patrol car as soon as possible. She ignored the part where he'd said she was in luck because the patrol had just been on traffic duty between two other villages and was therefore nearby.

The storehouse was calling out to her. Certainly it was practical to have a big old barn at your disposal, if you needed to do some quick butchering and wanted to avoid doing it in the forest.

She stared at the house without blinking, waiting to spot movement behind the kitchen curtains. Dad called, but she didn't answer. In a few hours, it would be dark.

There was no time to think. She started wading through the snow alongside the snowmobile trail, down the hill. He would just have to shoot her too. She wanted to see it with her own eyes, the blood leading to his place.

Silence settled around the dilapidated house with its crumbling stairs and flaking paint on both the walls and porch. The windowsills could also have used a fresh coat of paint, and the door was so crooked that the cold wind must blow right into the front hall. She had never been so close to his house.

The curtains in the kitchen window were dingy and far too summery; they looked like they had been there for decades. On the table stood a moss-green thermos and a bulky mug with an advertising logo on it. On the counter she could see a pile of dishes.

She saw footprints between the garage and the storehouse and walked alongside them, well aware that he would discover her tracks. If he got home before the police came. The patrol was only thirty miles away, so it wouldn't take long, maybe forty minutes.

As she stood before the storehouse, she argued with herself. She had gloves and wouldn't leave any traces behind. Black fingerprints stained the frames of the white doors with their brass handles. The drops of blood on the ground were tiny. Whatever he'd hauled home was on the other side of these double doors, which opened in either direction. A large padlock held a four-inch-wide steel plate in place. She pulled on the handle and the doors followed, but didn't move enough to create a gap.

She took photos of the drops of blood, but it was hard to make them show up in the pictures. She backed up and took shots of the barn and the house. There would be no doubt about where she'd been.

The barn had once been painted red, but now it was bare and gray, battered by wind and weather. The only window was way up high, near the roof, in what had once been the haymow. She wasn't about to go up there.

Then she heard a snowmobile, still probably a few hundred yards away; she couldn't tell where it was coming from. She ran straight across the yard, making sure to avoid disturbing the trail of blood and trying to step in her earlier footprints. On the hill she fell down, pulled herself up with her hands, pushed off with her feet. She had just made it to the top when the snowmobile pulled into the yard. It wasn't him. This man was too short. He kept his helmet on as he got off the snowmobile and stepped up to the porch. He knocked and tried the door handle, but it was locked.

Elsa lay flat on the rise, next to her snowmobile, which would be fully visible if he chose to glance around the yard and up the hill. Her heart pounded against the snow, and her breath came in fits and starts.

The man appeared to hesitate. He got back on his snowmobile and hit the gas hard to make the vehicle do a 180. Elsa cursed under her breath as snow sprayed over the spots of blood.

She lay where she was until the sound of the snowmobile faded somewhere past the creek. She fumbled for the knife at her belt, the feeling of it in her hand reassuring.

Another snowmobile. This time it was coming from behind her, and she quickly mounted her own snowmobile. She started it, ready to flee, her eyes already on the best path out. But first she would look him in the eye. She turned her upper body but held the handlebars steady, squinting, recognizing that style, a knee on the seat and half standing. Mattias. He was following her trail and stopped behind her, turned off the engine, and took off his protective earmuffs. He stared as intensely as she had at the house.

"Is he in there?"

"No."

He glanced at her. "Are you okay?"

She nodded. "I went down there and followed the blood to the barn. They'll get him this time."

"Don't get your hopes up."

He rubbed his chin.

"Is Dad still with the cow?"

"Yup." He snorted. "He's furious with you."

"So you had to come and save me."

Mattias ignored her. "His place looks awful."

"Are you surprised?"

"Nope."

They heard the car at the same time and both stiffened. The police car came around the crest, drove slowly into the yard, and parked outside the house. Elsa began to trudge down in her own footsteps as Mattias started his snowmobile and drove down the slope. The officers got out of the car, nodded, waited for Mattias to turn off the engine. The man was young, maybe around thirty, and the woman, who looked somewhat older, had an accent that placed her far south of the county line.

"I'm the one who called," said Elsa.

She extended one cold hand and was met by their warm ones.

"I followed a trail all the way from the cow to this barn. The cow was shot and her calf is missing."

"Shot, you say. How do you know?" the woman asked.

Elsa took out her phone and quickly swiped to the picture of the bullet hole. The officers studied it and nodded. Yes, indeed, that could well be a bullet hole.

"I can drive one of you to the cow," Mattias said.

"This is my brother."

He didn't take off his glove to shake hands. His face was tight.

"Do you want to see the trail of blood?"

Elsa led them to the barn, glancing over her shoulder to make sure they weren't walking on the tracks.

"A snowmobile just drove into the yard and some of the blood ended up under the snow." She pointed and moved on. "But here, you can see where it starts again."

The female officer bent down and shone her flashlight as her colleague studied the tracks that led toward the rise.

"Here are more pictures of the cow."

Elsa held her phone out to the male officer.

"Could it have been a predator?" he asked.

Elsa shook her head and saw from the corner of her eye how Mattias's jaw began to work.

"This is a bullet hole, and the cut on her belly is sharp, like from a knife," Elsa said in a tone as calm as she could manage. "They didn't bother to take the cow because the shot must have gone through the stomach, and that ruins the meat. They removed the calf, but I can't tell if they took it with them or left it for a fox, which has also been by."

"So the trail of blood might not have anything to do with the calf?"

"Not sure. My guess is that they shot another reindeer and took that one with them."

Mattias spit in the snow and stared up at the sky. She saw his nostrils flaring, could tell he was breathing hard.

"You should head out into the forest with Mattias and have a look," she said.

The woman went with Mattias, and Elsa stayed behind with the other police officer. He had a sparse, reddish beard that barely hid his pale skin. His eyes were light, and his eyelashes looked white.

"What's your name?"

"Ljungblad."

"You have to go into the barn."

"We'll see. I would need—"

"A warrant. Call a prosecutor."

He raised his eyebrows appreciatively. "Look at that."

"You've checked up on Robert Isaksson, right?"

"Yes, that's being done now."

He took in her clothes and looked at the knife on her belt. "Was it your reindeer?"

She nodded.

"How did you happen to come across it?"

"I was out tracking down some reindeer that got separated from the herd. This one was unusually far away. This one, and a few others. That's why I think they shot more than one." She looked him straight in the eye. "I'm sure you're aware that we've been having issues with poaching in this area for years?"

"So it's happened before?"

"Are you new?"

"Yes, I am. Or, I've been a police officer for a few years now, but I'm new here in the municipality." He smiled kindly. "But Eriksson, my colleague, has been around a little longer."

"Then she should know that this has happened before. That you're sitting on close to a hundred reports from our reindeer collective."

"I see, no, we didn't have time to get a handle on that before we came out. We only got a brief summary of your report. I'm sure there will be an investigation."

"We only ever hear that there's not enough evidence, but this time there *is* evidence. And you came. You should know that this is the first time the police have actually shown up right away when we called."

They heard the snowmobile at the same time, and both cocked their ears toward the village. It wasn't Mattias. Without thinking, Elsa grabbed Ljungblad's arm, but she let go just as fast when she saw how he looked at her.

"If this is him coming now, please don't let him get away."

Suddenly Ljungblad rushed over to the patrol car with his phone to his ear. Elsa froze; she felt like she should run but couldn't.

Ljungblad was talking about guns, and he looked, if possible, even paler. So now he believed her. And now he realized that the perpetrator might be armed.

The snowmobile pulled into the yard in a wide arc, as though Robert wanted to take in the scene before he stopped. He let his eyes wander over the patrol car, the police officer, and Elsa, and then up the hill to where there was a glimpse of her snowmobile. He pulled up right in front of the patrol car but didn't turn off his roaring engine.

Ljungblad approached him but didn't offer a handshake. Elsa managed to move; she instinctively took a few steps toward the hill. Robert had no rifle over his shoulder. Ljungblad pointed at the snowmobile and the engine cut out.

She could hear that he spoke in a much more authoritative tone now, explaining what they were doing there. The two men stood taller, sizing each other up. The dog, perched behind Robert, held its head low and growled.

Now they could hear Mattias's snowmobile, and soon it came slowly down the hill. They received a scornful look from Robert. Ljungblad was noticeably relieved when Eriksson returned and took over the conversation.

Robert didn't look at the officers; instead he glared at Elsa and Mattias.

"You're not getting in without a warrant," he said gruffly, turning his gaze on the officers.

"There's a trail of blood leading to your barn," said Eriksson.

"Oh, really. Says who? These Lapps?"

"You might as well just let us in if you've got nothing to hide, right?"

"No." He turned on his heel and headed for the house. "False accusations are a serious matter. I should report you for slander."

He aimed a mean look at Mattias, then slapped his thigh and gave a low whistle. Immediately the dog leapt from the snowmobile and came up beside him.

"Where did the blood come from?" Ljungblad asked.

"What blood?"

"The blood outside the barn."

"Oh, that. I shot a hare. That's still allowed in this country, isn't it?"

He removed a key from a boot on the front stoop and unlocked the door. He let the dog in and followed after it.

"We're not finished here," Ljungblad said, louder now.

"Come back when you've got a warrant," they heard from the hall.

He was soon back on the front steps, now with a lit cigarette in the corner of his mouth. Elsa noticed that his hand shook as he lowered it from his lips.

"I'd be happy to talk with you more, but I want the Lapps off my property."

"Could you be so kind as to refrain from using that word?" Ljungblad's tone was sharp.

"That isn't allowed in this country nowadays either?"

"Watch yourself," said Eriksson.

Robert grinned and sucked on the cigarette.

"Like I said, we can talk, but we don't need any witnesses."

Ljungblad turned to Elsa, and with his authoritative voice he asked them to leave and promised to be in touch soon.

"What should we do with the cow?" Elsa asked, cursing the tremor in her voice.

The officers exchanged uncertain glances.

"I'll be in touch," Ljungblad barked like a soldier, but his tone softened when he saw the disappointment on her face. "Thank you for all your information."

Mattias accelerated quickly up the hill with Elsa behind him. She squeezed her arms around his waist as she hadn't done since she was little.

CHAPTER FORTY-EIGHT

Njealljelogigávcci

M attias saw the patrol car speed past, lights flashing. The police were already heading back to town. It hadn't been more than half an hour since they left them at Robert's. He knew this couldn't be a good sign. And he had to tell her, if she hadn't already noticed. He trudged heavily across the yard, head hanging.

She was sitting at the kitchen table, laughing at something on her phone. Her hair was wet, just washed, and she smelled good, a smell that permeated the whole kitchen.

He really had to try to sound neutral, keep from raising his voice.

"The police took off."

"Huh?"

She was smiling. She hadn't heard what he said.

"You'll have to call the police. They took off."

He realized it sounded like a command, and her smile faded.

"Are you sure?"

"I mean, hell, they just went by."

She fastened her wet hair up with a clip. She looked so sad. And his irritation grew.

"I told you! You always get your hopes up."

The long look she gave him made him turn away. He slammed the cabinet doors looking for a mug, only to realize that the thermos was empty, then slammed it down hard too.

She dialed and put her phone on speaker; after several rings an officer finally answered.

"I'd like to speak with Ljungblad," Elsa said. "I just saw him, and I want to know what happened with a suspect I reported."

"The patrol had to respond to an urgent call."

"But what does that mean? Wasn't there a warrant?"

Mattias looked at her as she talked to the officer on the line. She stood up, gesturing with one hand, slicing her palm through the air as her tone grew sharper.

"Don't you see that the poacher will just clear the whole yard now? He'll destroy all the evidence!" This was pointless; she sighed. "Can you ask Ljungblad to call me?"

She set her phone on the kitchen table, sat heavily down on the chair, and propped her forehead on her wrists.

"Now he'll drive over all the snowmobile trails and polish that whole fucking barn clean. There won't be a single trace left. If he's got a freezer in there, he'll empty it."

Mattias couldn't respond. He had to get out of there, had to punch something until his knuckles bled.

"But," she said, looking up, "we do have the pictures. They can't ignore pictures of a trail of blood."

Mattias balled up his fists, could have flipped the kitchen table.

She drooped again. "He'll say it was the hare." For a moment, she didn't say anything. "But then he would need to show them a dead hare, wouldn't he? I'll point that out to that Ljungblad."

"Give it up! They're not going back. You know that."

She turned away, stood up, and went to the living room.

"I'll never give up!" she said before closing the door.

CHAPTER FORTY-NINE

Njealljelogiovcci

It had been over a day since they'd last heard from Mattias. All the blinds were down. Elsa knocked and tried the locked door. She was cold without a jacket, but she walked around the house and knocked on the bedroom window, tentatively at first, then loudly. She called his name, then moved on to the bathroom window and rapped just as hard, then to the living-room window, then she was back on the steps, tugging at the door.

She called his phone but got his voicemail.

There was a set of spare keys; she went home and rummaged through the key cabinet Mattias had built in his sixth-grade woodworking class. She dug frantically through the bureau drawers, through hats and mittens. When she finally found the key on a hook under the hat rack, she took off at a gallop across the yard.

Her fingers were shaking violently as she unlocked the door and threw it open so hard it bounced off the inside wall.

"Mattias!"

She hurried into the kitchen, to the living room, and then to the bedroom, where the door was closed. She couldn't bring herself to open it. But she had to be the one to find him, not Mom or Dad. They wouldn't survive it. She pulled down the creaky handle and slowly pushed open the drab brown door and stared into the darkness. Empty. Her body sagged and she hung on to the door handle, then moved on to the bathroom with a fresh set of images in her mind. Her head was spinning, and she pulled down this handle as slowly as the first one. There was a stale odor, likely coming from the mold they suspected was growing in the ceiling.

In the kitchen, she spotted a gap in the trapdoor. The root cellar. She knelt down and lifted the hatch. When the light hit Mattias, he turned up his face and she recoiled. He looked distorted, a fright. She could see the drunkenness in his eyes. He had rested his head against a shelf and was half-lying on the stool that Áhkku had always used to reach the top shelves. It was freezing cold, and he was wearing nothing but a T-shirt and gray long johns.

"Remember how I won hide-and-seek every time, when I hid down here?" he slurred.

"I remember Mom losing her mind because the stairs are dangerous and you might run out of oxygen."

She tried to sound normal, as if it were perfectly natural to be reminiscing.

"I believed her, about the oxygen. But I haven't fucking suffocated yet."

"Come up."

"Did the police call?"

"Yes. Ljungblad admitted that he and his colleague could have decided on their own to search the place, but they chose to wait for instructions from some commander, or maybe it was the prosecutor. Then they got the call to respond in town and they had to go."

A glass bottle flew to the concrete floor, causing shards to fly and clear vodka to splash over canned goods and bottles.

"I fucking give up, unna oabba!"

She looked at him in terror. Unna oabba. She felt a flutter in her chest, in parts of herself she hadn't been able to access for a long time.

"Watch out for the glass. Sit still! What is wrong with you?"

"Why should we go on like this? What the predators don't take, those bastards do. Yesterday the neighboring collective found four reindeer that the wild animals got. And it was raining! In fucking February!" He shouted this last bit at the top of his lungs.

He stood up, legs shaky.

"Sit down!" Elsa shouted. "You aren't even wearing socks. You'll cut your feet to ribbons. I'll come down and pick up the glass."

"But I can't do this anymore. I won't. And Dad, he just ignores the fact that we can't make ends meet. We aren't earning any fucking money, unna oabba."

Unna oabba.

"There will be lots of calves, you know that. This year will be better."

"He cut the calf out of the cow's belly. What kind of sick bastard does something like that?"

He'd kept it together for all these years. He'd been gruff. Kept quiet. Sure, he'd had the occasional outburst, but this, this was something else. Elsa could tell. He was vibrating, he was letting himself go. Maybe it was the alcohol that had caused the dam to burst, but still, he had reached a breaking point. She spoke in a soft voice, asked him to sit down as she went to get gloves and a plastic bag.

She turned on the light, a single dangling bulb that made Mattias blink in irritation. Her legs shook as she climbed backwards down the steep, narrow folding stairs. She first picked up the large shards, dropping them in the plastic bag, her eyes searching the floor and the rag rug Áhkku had kept there for decades. The smell of alcohol was pungent.

"And the new mine. They're saying the deposits are beyond all expectations. They'll plow up new roads right through our grazing lands. You know that, right?"

His face was close to hers as she gingerly picked up yet another gleaming piece of glass. He nearly tipped over, but steadied himself against a shelf.

"I know," she said wearily. "I know."

Finding every last piece of glass was suddenly a matter of life and death.

"I'm going to burn down his house!"

She didn't look up. It was just the liquor talking.

"You thought I was dead, didn't you? When you were running around looking." He laughed. "But it was just hide-and-seek, like when we were little, unna oabba."

The shards of glass clinked against each other in the plastic bag. She carefully rolled up the rag rug and pointed.

"Now you can walk right here, where there's no glass. I'll help you."

He got up and threw an arm around her shoulder. He was so cold that she shivered.

"But you want to do it, so you and Dad can keep it going."

"Stop it. We need you."

"The men in the collective don't like you. Fuck them!" Mattias lashed out with his other arm, his fist clenched. "Lasse always said you were stronger than all the rest of us. Ha! You were nine years old. No way you were stronger than me."

Elsa froze. Her nose stung as she fought tears. "He said that?"

"What? Who said something?" He tried and failed to focus on her. "Right, hell, he talked about you all the time."

And yet, Elsa thought, he chose to leave me.

She supported Mattias, shoving his butt for that last little push up the stairs. When she followed him out, he was laid flat out on the floor and snoring. She took care to close the trapdoor all the way, tied a knot in the bag of glass, and set it next to the bag of trash under the sink. From the living room she fetched a blanket. She found two mismatched boot socks by the kitchen bench and wriggled them onto his bare feet. Maybe he was asleep. Maybe not. Above ground, they couldn't look each other in the eye.

CHAPTER FIFTY

Vihttalogi

T he first text from an unknown number came in just after two in the morning. Elsa reached for the phone on the floor, in the hopes that it would be a sobered-up Mattias texting to put her mind at ease. She blinked, tired, until the letters fell into place.

"You fucking Lapp whore."

She sat up in bed and stared at the sentence. It had to be Robert. She threw the phone down as if it had burned her, struggling to take calm, even breaths, deep into her belly. It wasn't long before the tone sounded again. She squeezed her eyes shut and decided not to look, but in the end she couldn't resist.

"Stay the fuck away."

It was like he was sitting on her bed, hissing threats. Another beep. This time she didn't read it, just put her phone on silent and let it fall to the rug. There was no falling back asleep. She tossed and turned in bed, tempted to look at her phone but also determined to ignore it. She saw the blue glow illuminating from the floor time and again. Until it stopped.

Elsa parked the car outside her old school in the next village. Her eyes burned from too little sleep; her body felt sluggish, and a headache had settled in the back of her skull.

She had been pitching in as a substitute teacher in the village school for the last few weeks. She'd also gotten a few days at the Sámi school, and hoped there would be more. Now, before spring, she had the opportunity to bring in a little extra money.

Hanna parked next to her and they climbed out of their cars at the same time. Elsa noticed that this seemed to be one of her better days. Jon-Isak hopped out of the car and dashed for the school building before Elsa could say hi. She should talk to Hanna about the fights in the schoolyard. But when she saw her smile, she couldn't bear to do it.

"Hi, Elsa! You're looking a little tired. Are the kids being too hard on you?"

"Just a rough night." She smiled wanly. "But it's so good to see you. It's been a while, not since the market, right?"

A shadow fell over Hanna's face. The anniversary had passed just over a month ago, and everyone knew she went downhill in February and March. There would be no rugs outside for airing, and she was hardly ever spotted outside the house. Elsa had heard the kids at school say she stood by the lake at night, howling. That was sheer nonsense, of course, but Elsa should bring up all the other stuff that was said in the schoolyard.

"I'm heading into town for a massage today," Hanna said.

Elsa wriggled her torso and instinctively brought her hand to the painful spot on the back of her head.

"I should do that too."

"Have you seen Anna-Stina? We hardly ever see her anymore. She spends most of her time up at Per-Jonas's. Did you hear she got an offer to work at a café in town? Guess we'll see if she accepts. She can't just hang around waiting . . ."

"To get married," Elsa said, insinuation in her voice, and Hanna laughed out loud.

"Exactly!"

"Yeah, I heard about the café, but I imagine she'll stick around here. I haven't seen much of her either."

Neither said anything for a moment.

"Good thing we've got our reaŋga," Hanna said.

Something chafed in her voice, but Elsa couldn't make out the nuances well enough.

"They turned out to be too far apart in age. It's like they don't have any use for each other."

"It'll be better when he's older."

"Yeah, like me and Lasse."

Elsa wanted to ask how she was doing, really, and say that she missed him. And hated him sometimes too.

"Anyway. Better go if I'm going to make it to my massage."

Hanna opened the car door, and Elsa wished she could smooth things over with some lighthearted comment, but it wouldn't come and their goodbye was awkward.

She walked slowly toward the schoolyard and heard fighting around the corner. Another shriek. Two angry little-boy voices.

"You Lapp bastard!"

"Shut up or I'll kill you!"

"When the mine opens, all the reindeer will die. I hope!"

Then it got quiet, and she suspected they had turned to their fists. She should have hurried to intervene, but instead she looked around for a teacher. Eventually she had to turn the corner, and sure enough, they were in a pile, a hat ripped off and swinging fists.

"Stop that!" she shouted, breaking into a run.

They were little, and she could easily lift one boy off the other.

"He started it," whined the one on the ground, hatless, his cheeks bright red.

"The Lapps always start it. Because you're all stupid bastards!" screamed the boy who was struggling in her arms.

"Don't use that word!" Elsa roared straight into his ear, and he looked frightened. She let go, and both boys stared at her.

"I know you're all related, so obviously you're taking his side," snapped the boy next to her.

"You two have to stop fighting," she said sternly. "I'm serious. This has to stop."

They walked in opposite directions to their respective schools, their faces storm clouds. The schoolyard between them was a war zone. They were only picking up where their fathers had left off once upon a time.

Elsa waited out the adrenaline before going inside. The first person she saw was Jon-Isak, who was standing by the window that faced the school-yard and must have seen the fight. And probably heard it too. His eyes were black.

"It's all your fault!"

She took off her hat and looked at him, bewildered.

"Ever since you were in the paper it got worse."

"What?"

"And it gets worse when you're here. It only reminds them all."

She wanted to reach out her hand and pull him close. He was so terribly like his uncle sometimes, that sulky lower lip she'd seen in pictures of Lasse when he was little. But his eyes, those were his father's. So dark brown you couldn't even make out the pupil.

"We have to speak up—" she began, but he cut her off.

"But that makes it worst on me!"

She had seen him fight too, that she had.

"Dad hates you too! You think you're so special, but you're not!"

What the hell do I care about your dad? she wanted to say, but bit her tongue.

"It's always been like this. We've always heard this stupid stuff at school. Me included. And your sister. We have to put a stop to it. Just like we have to put a stop to the reindeer poaching."

He looked at her, now even angrier. Too many words, she realized. He couldn't see the connection, or didn't want to. He was only nine, she had to remember that.

"I don't want you to be a teacher here!"

That was the last thing he got out before whirling around and dashing down the hall. Elsa sank onto the bench outside the classroom that had once been hers. The snowdrifts came up to the windowsill, then as now. She remembered how she too had wanted to run away and never set foot in the school again.

It never ends, she thought. It was a cycle; everything repeated itself. She rested her head against the wall and felt her phone vibrate in her pocket. The seventh text.

CHAPTER FIFTY-ONE

Vihttalogiokta

A t the very back of the garage, next to big plastic bins, were the skis Elsa had received when she was nine. They looked brand-new, hardly used. The skis were a curse—so she'd thought as a child. They brought misfortune; she and the skis brought death with them. She'd been on them when she found Nástegallu and when Lasse towed her behind his snowmobile for the last time. So it was only right that the skis should stay in a corner until she grew too tall to use them. Mom had wanted to sell them, but how could they allow the accursed skis to be handed over to another child? She couldn't say so to Mom, but she averted her eyes awfully fast and shook her head every time anyone mentioned selling them. So the skis had stayed.

Now she wished they'd been burned up long ago. They were like a branding scar, a reminder of everything she could have, and should have, kept from happening. Still, she let her hand run over one ski before she took out her new ones.

It was years after Lasse's death before she skied again; they hadn't even been able to get her on skis at school. Instead, Mom had to lie and say she was sick anytime outdoor days rolled around.

But then, a few years ago, there had been a sale at the outdoor gear store, which had nearly gone bankrupt, and Elsa found herself standing at the register with skis, poles, and boots. Her first time out had almost broken her, the sound of snow hissing beneath her skis, the creak of the poles, her breath finding its rhythm. Sure, she'd been close to tears that first mile, but now everything fell still and her body was able to take control of that long-standing grief. Nowadays she wouldn't manage without taking time to ski.

Today it was different. Not even the skis could calm her anxiety. The texts had stopped coming, but that didn't mean anything. She'd called the police but hung up. She'd called Minna, who snapped furiously that she had to report the bastard. But it could be anyone. It wasn't necessarily Robert. He was probably smarter than that; he was probably having someone else do his dirty work.

She walked past the car, carrying her skis. She'd discovered the scratch on the passenger-side door of the Škoda at the end of the school day. Eight inches long. There were no cars nearby. It wasn't a plain old parking accident, no matter how much she wished it was. It was probably from a key, maybe a tool. Not even this could she say for sure was his work, but there was no doubt something had been set in motion.

She took out her phone to take a picture of the scratch and sent it to Minna. It was so nice to have her, someone to react, someone who understood. Ever since they met at the Jokkmokk market they'd been in touch several times a week, mostly by text, and she often found herself thinking about what Minna would say and do. Like now—would she be brave enough to go out after all these threatening texts? Vulnerable and alone in the woods on a pair of skis—Elsa was aware that it wasn't the smartest plan, but she couldn't help it. She needed nature, needed to exhaust herself, let her body work.

She seldom chose the trails that led to the old corral. Anyway, her family kept the herd in new places now, spots that were safer, larger, where they could keep a better eye out. Today she planned to follow the snowmobile trails along the lakeshore until she could turn into the forest and follow a loop that went to the clear-cuts, which had recovered over the years.

Mattias was on his porch, sweeping away the snow.

"Don't you want to come along and get some practice in?"

Her voice sounded fake, too cheery. She should ask how he was feeling. She should get up close and see if he smelled like alcohol.

"I could win the ski race between villages without a day of practice."

He was trying to be funny, she could tell. She had to force herself to laugh. They would never, ever talk about the root cellar. She didn't want him to feel ashamed. What she really wanted was to let him know that she was there for him, but instead she laughed.

"You're so lazy," she managed, waving her poles before she skied out of the yard.

HER BREATHING WAS EVEN, and she felt stronger than she had in a long time. The forest was quiet, the wind had died down, but there was no contrast between the snow and the milky white sky. She squinted, wishing she hadn't forgotten her sunglasses, and rested her eyes on the trees, longing for the green foliage of summer, a walk to the river with fishing rod in hand. The fact that she could still look forward to things made her happy. Maybe she would bring Áhkku home this summer and let her pick cloudberries. But preferably in a harness. She had to chuckle. At least she hadn't lost her sense of humor.

Still, it was strange. To think that she could manage, while Lasse couldn't. Then he was there with her. This was nothing unusual or strange. His laughter in her ear, the sensation of him. There were never any words, but she smiled, affirming his presence. He didn't weigh on her, and when he vanished he did so without leaving her feeling abandoned. Just certain that this wasn't the last time she'd feel him there with her. No one knew about these moments, and she didn't want to tell anyone. Not that they would think it was strange, but sometimes talk could ruin a thing.

The sound of snowmobiles in the distance made her freeze. Lasse had warned her, made her stop. At least two of them. They seemed to be making zigzags, their noise swelling and retreating. Elsa looked back along the obvious tracks of her skis in the snowmobile trail. She was easy to find. She must be a little more than two miles from home, too far for anyone to make it in time to help her. The snowmobiles roared closer and she closed her eyes. Her ears blared, like tinnitus, like the wheels of trains screeching against their tracks. But the snowmobiles never appeared; suddenly the sound moved away from her.

She opened her eyes.

This had to stop.

CHAPTER FIFTY-TWO

Vihttalogiguokte

The spring sun was pale and hardly gave any warmth. Still no dripping from roof ridges; the top layer of snow hadn't yet begun to melt. But the light was returning, calling out to them. Maybe that was why this seemed so macabre. In the quiet forest, in the first shimmering light of spring, at the mouth where the creek fed into the little lake, lying side by side almost as if in a ritual sacrifice, were the severed heads of reindeer and pieces of reindeer bodies. They had been placed in a half circle, each piece about three feet away from the next.

Awfully gruesome, yeah, we were honestly shocked, said the villagers who called their discovery in to the police. They'd been on their way out for the first jig-fishing trip of the season. The next call went to the chairman of the reindeer collective, and soon everyone knew.

Elsa had gone out with Dad and Mattias. They turned off their snow-mobiles and sat there for a long time. It was almost surreal. But she had to see it up close. She walked around cautiously; no point in worrying about tracks anymore, not with everyone who had been there before her. That the police would show up last was only to be expected. That they would show up before it got dark was unlikely.

She examined two of the reindeer heads with special care; she recognized them, and she also spotted the bullet hole just beneath the eye of one. These were the reindeer from the bags she had handed over to the police. Evidence from an investigation they hadn't heard a word about since.

"I'm pretty sure these are the reindeer I found," she said, pointing. "Except now the ears are missing."

Neither Dad nor Mattias responded.

She sighed and called Lovisa Wikberg at the newspaper.

"Remember the reindeer I turned over to the police?" she said when Lovisa picked up. "That evidence is now lying out in the forest. Someone has arranged them in an incredibly disturbing way. Will you come?"

She heard rustling on the other end, a zipper closing, a door slamming, quick footsteps on stairs.

"Of course. I'm on my way!"

As Elsa prepared to make her next call, she wandered off the snowmobile trail. Minna didn't say anything at first, but soon found her footing.

"I'm sorry, but I don't have time to talk to you. I have to go blow up a police station."

Minna didn't laugh when she said it, and Elsa tried but it might just as easily have come out as a sob, so she swallowed it down.

"Do you think there's any way of finding out how it happened?"

"Maybe. I'll try."

"A journalist is on her way here, and I have to tell her what I know."

"Well, obviously, no question there!"

Elsa walked along the trail a few steps, sinking into the snow and lifting her heavy boots in annoyance.

"Hello, are you still there?" she heard on the other end.

"On the other hand, I don't know if more publicity is a good thing. I talked to Anna-Stina's little brother, and he's having a rough time at school. Because of me, he says. And what I said. You know, these damn kids are still fighting and calling each other all sorts of names. And he's getting beat up."

"Shit."

"So maybe I shouldn't talk?"

"But this is serious, Elsa. If the police are involved with killing the reindeer, it's really bad. You can't give up now. This is a scandal. For real, a scandal. It's not just going to be the local paper writing about this now. You know that, right?"

Elsa stomped through the snow again; she wanted to scream.

"I can call the TV news, the evening papers, and *Dagens Nyheter,*" Minna said.

"Jon-Isak will get beat up either way, no matter which one of us talks to the media."

"Then I guess I'll have to stop by the school and murder some kids. Or preferably their horrid parents."

"I feel sorry for those kids. They're stuck, there's no way out. Everyone knows what everyone else is up to; everyone knows who's related to who, which means you're expected to be a certain way. It's so freaking stifling."

"You have to keep going. What you've set in motion could change everything."

She snuck a look Dad's way and saw his stooped back, as if all the air had gone out of him.

"I honestly can't see how we can ever make all this stop."

"If the police and the prosecutors start doing their jobs, it will stop. And that's exactly what you should say when the reporter gets there. In this case, it's very clear that someone didn't do their job. Evidence out in the forest. Evidence! Send me a photo, I have to spread it everywhere."

"I wish you were a lawyer already."

Minna laughed and Elsa could picture her throwing her head back. "Soon I'll come and take care of them."

"My battery is dying in this cold. Talk to you later."

"Tell them everything. Including the scratch on your car! Don't forget about that. And report the threats."

"They're not exactly threats."

"They are so. Both against you personally, and as hate speech against an ethnic group, no question."

"They're from an unknown number."

"Elsa." Minna sounded stern. "If you give up now, Jon-Isak will never be able to stop looking over his shoulder. You know that, right? Never."

IN THE END, FIFTEEN reindeer herders from the collective gathered at the site. The cadavers were in a semicircle, and the herders had parked their snowmobiles to create the other half of the circle. Darkness had fallen and they shone their headlights on the reindeer parts.

Lovisa Wikberg stepped cautiously, respectfully around the area and photographed them and the dead reindeer. Elsa looked around, saw the vulnerability the journalist was trying to capture. The old folks with deep furrows in their cheeks and the youngest, hardly a teenager, who sat behind his father, blinking continuously. Elsa was the only woman present, and she allowed herself to be photographed.

Lovisa, as the first journalist on the scene, was the only one who managed to get photos in both daylight and darkness. And she walked around getting quotes from almost everyone. Some of them shook their heads grimly when she posed questions, but others spoke with sadness or outrage.

"How much of this do we have to take?" said Dad's old uncle.

But it wasn't until the arrival of the reporter from Sameradion, the Sámi-language division of Radio Sweden, a young woman with piercings, that they could speak their own language and have a much more nuanced conversation.

"I don't think anyone on the outside can understand how painful this is for us. Our reindeer are our life. They're hitting us where it hurts the most, and they're doing it on purpose. But where are the police? We've been sitting here for hours, and have they shown up? No."

After the interview, Lovisa walked up to Elsa. "My camera battery died. I have to run to my car. Will you come with?"

Elsa glanced at the chairman of the collective, who looked grumpy, and that made up her mind for her.

They walked single file along the trail, their snow pants swishing.

"I've been getting threats. Over text."

"Really?"

"Yes, and someone keyed my car."

"Can I write about it?"

"If you don't use my name this time. That only makes it worse."

"I get it. It's fine without your name. But I need to see the texts."

They had arrived at her car, and Elsa handed Lovisa her phone.

"Can you send me screenshots? I can't believe how nasty these are. Do you know who sent them?"

"I have my suspicions."

"And in the woods—who did that?"

"I don't know. Like I said, at least two of the reindeer are evidence I handed over. For some reason, the police released it. It should be possible to figure out to whom."

"I'll definitely check up on that."

"But can you promise to do some serious digging this time? We need to know how the reindeer ended up here."

Lovisa inserted a fresh battery and looked up.

"I promise to do my best. It's not easy to get the police to talk. I don't exactly have the same contacts as these guys do."

She nodded at a van from SVT, the national TV broadcaster, which was just pulling up. Elsa recognized the middle-aged man, who waved. He was often on screen, but seldom showed any interest in the reindeer industry. Quite the opposite, in fact.

"Then beat them at their own game this time. You can take that guy."

Elsa glared at him and Lovisa let out a surprised laugh.

"They'll send up a drone and get shots I can't."

Elsa shuddered, imagining what the scene would look like from above.

"Can't you call the police now, so I can hear what they tell you?"

For a moment, Lovisa looked hesitant.

"They never listen to us, but I want to hear what they sound like when a journalist calls."

Lovisa nodded and took out her phone. On speaker, they heard the male officer at the regional dispatch center sigh loudly after Lovisa stated her name.

"Here's the deal," he said. "First the patrol responded to an assault, and immediately after that a woman on a kicksled was hit by a car outside the People's House, and they haven't finished up on that call. I hear you, and I understand that you want a comment, but there's no way to give one without my colleagues having been on scene."

"It's a gruesome sight, and we have reindeer herders here who recognize a couple of the reindeer as evidence that was handed over to the police some time ago. I will be forced to write my story without comment from your end, and I can guarantee that you will want to weigh in on what I'm looking at."

Elsa looked at Lovisa in astonishment, mimed a silent *Wow!*

The officer sounded angry. "The patrol's next assignment will be the reindeer. If no other higher priority call comes in. You'll have to settle for that. I understand that you have a deadline, but crime really doesn't take that into consideration. And, as a journalist up there, you know what vast areas our patrols have to cover."

"You mean to say that this isn't important?"

"No, I'm telling you the reality of the situation. All crimes are important, but we have to prioritize. A patrol might be more than a hundred miles from town in one direction when they're suddenly needed a hundred miles in the other direction. It's an impossible equation, and they're well aware of it, the drunk drivers and the thieves, you know, the small-timers."

"Okay, I'll hold off as long as I can, but then I'll file my story."

When Lovisa hung up, Elsa growled. "The small-timers! This is as far from small-time as you could imagine. He can talk all he wants about priorities, but their attitude is awfully telling."

Lovisa nodded. "I know what you mean. I'll give them a little while longer, but then I have to go. I'm going to call the newsroom now. We'll talk later."

When Elsa got back on her snowmobile, the seat was cold. Everyone was still in the semicircle; some had pulled woolen shawls or balaclavas over stiff, frozen faces. Her hands were frigid, even in gloves.

CHAPTER FIFTY-THREE

Vihttalogigolbma

D ead reindeer had been found before, and most of the time there was no more than a news brief. But this time the news spread widely; the articles and stories on TV and radio were shared again and again. Elsa knew it was thanks to the photographs. The image from the drone was a piece of art, an illuminated semicircle in the midst of a dark forest. The photo in the local paper was almost as dramatic. Lovisa Wikberg had stood up on a rise to capture the formation. She had pressed the officers once they arrived, saying that this was evidence, but their responses were noncommittal.

"Come on! It's starting!"

Mom was calling from the sofa, where she, Dad, and Mattias were already sitting. Elsa stopped in the doorway and heard the news anchor say that there were suspicions that the bodies of the reindeer had been police evidence.

The camera swept across the next village, and she saw familiar faces outside the store and the gas station. The villagers' noses were red in the cold and they looked a bit stiff in front of the camera, trying not to hit their consonants too hard on national TV.

"I think the reindeer herders could have done it themselves," said Astrid. The now retired lunch lady's gaze was steady.

"What do you mean?"

"Well, when the reindeer don't bring in enough money, they'll make sure to get paid some other way. And I've also heard that the collectives steal each other's reindeer."

Elsa threw up her hands. "How can they just let her say something like that? Why don't the journalists push back at her? How would laying out dead reindeer make us any money? She's crazy!"

Dad and Mattias shushed her. On the TV was the next villager, the old man who rode his kicksled all around the village early each morning.

"Do you think the police could be involved in the reindeer thefts around here?"

"Nix! We never see the police around here."

Elsa stormed into the kitchen and clenched her fists. "This is such a joke. Do you have any idea how tragically hilarious that answer was?"

From the living room she could hear collective chairman Olle chime in, questioning the actions of the police in a sharp tone. Elsa made her way back to the doorway as a police commissioner responded to the criticism; she was a middle-aged woman with a serious face and a faint wrinkle just above her nose.

"How come all investigations into reindeer theft end up closed?"

"I don't know about all of them. But it's hard to get people in the village to talk."

"The police never even come here. They don't even try!" Elsa exclaimed.

"Can you just be quiet?" Mattias snapped.

"We've got one of the largest jurisdictions in Sweden, and oftentimes there's only one patrol on duty, which makes it difficult," said the commissioner.

"We've heard allegations that the reindeer parts found in the forest are evidence, that these particular reindeer were poached and later handed over by a reindeer collective. How do you respond to that?"

"All preliminary investigations have been closed, so it's not evidence from an ongoing investigation."

"But do you understand why the collective is upset? And who was allowed to take the reindeer?"

For the first time, the commissioner looked flustered. "A private citizen asked if he could have them to use as bait for hunting."

"Who was that?"

"I'm not going to give you a name."

Elsa's phone rang, and Minna was sputtering on the other end.

"Did you see how she weaseled her way out of that? What an embarrassment! Her response is proof of just how bad they are at their jobs."

Elsa headed for her room and closed the door behind her.

"I saw the newspaper wrote about the threats and the scratch on your car too. It's happening, Elsa. They'll nail them now."

"I hope you're right."

She lay down on her bed and could feel a throbbing in the pit of her belly, below her ribs, pulsing as though something were about to burst.

"They won't dare to take more reindeer now."

"But didn't you hear the villagers, the ones who think we torture our own animals for money?"

"But who are those dumbasses? Narrow-minded old farts with no sense at all. I don't even get why the journalists bothered to talk to them. Who cares what they think?"

"Astrid was a lunch lady at my school, and she and her husband tried to press charges against Dad when they hit one of our reindeer."

Minna laughed bitterly. "Well, there you have it, they're idiots."

"She hated me something fierce. I hardly dared to eat at school."

"I hope she falls and breaks a hip," Minna said sharply.

"The pictures and the footage from the forest were good."

"Almost too good. I don't think folks will forget them. So powerful that you all stayed there."

Yes. She closed her eyes. Yes, they'd still been there, shining their headlights on the reindeer when the patrol showed up. The policemen weren't sure how to react at first, hadn't known how to respond to that silence. They had approached the bodies of the reindeer with awkward steps and mumbling voices, clearly bothered about being observed.

The breath of the reindeer herders turned to frosty vapor. In the end, they didn't have the strength to be angry. There was only room for the deepest sorrow. Once the reindeer had been taken away, they turned off their headlights and sat in silence in the dark.

CHAPTER FIFTY-FOUR

Vihttaloginjeallje

P etri should have known better. Especially now. The stories on the news and in all the papers about the poor, poor Lapps. There were eyes everywhere.

He hadn't called Robert. He hadn't said he'd come all the way out from town because he'd received an order. Robert would only say that they should lie low.

The chest freezer back home was filled to the brim with what Robert had rushed over when his home was about to be searched by the police. Petri could have sold some of that meat, but you never knew with Robert. All of a sudden he might want it back, and a hell of a fight would ensue.

Petri hadn't had to search the forest for long. He'd hunted the reindeer a short distance on his snowmobile, zigzagging and tiring it out until it was standing in deep snow and he could simply drive his knife into its neck, followed by a well-aimed stab into its heart. Shooting it would have been easier, but he wasn't that stupid.

Now the reindeer was on his sled and he would soon be back on the road, where his Chevy Suburban was parked with the trailer attached to it. Everything had been carefully planned. He would hide the reindeer under the tarp along with the snowmobile and sled. The villagers knew he came to his cabin most weekends and on his weeks off, so it wouldn't seem suspicious.

He didn't even have to butcher it, just drop it off with the purchaser. He couldn't say no to such an easy job. Robert wouldn't have either. He was sure of it.

Petri turned the key in the ignition but the snowmobile didn't respond. It was totally dead. Not again! He tried once more. That fucking sparkplug. His neighbor had said it was probably a fault in the CDI box, which is meant to send an electrical impulse to the sparkplug to start the engine. Petri knew nothing about engines. He planted himself alongside the snowmobile and tried the pull cord. He yanked it hard again, but the snowmobile was dead.

With every passing minute, the risk of getting caught went up. He took out his phone, then hesitated. No, he couldn't. Robert would be furious. Besides, it was too risky for him to be out on a snowmobile right now.

Petri removed the reindeer from the sled and realized there was only one way out. He had to drag it by hand. He took hold of its antlers and tugged. It was a hefty creature, but as luck would have it the past week's rain and cold had left a layer of smooth ice on the snowmobile trail. He struggled backwards, pulling the reindeer along in fits and starts. At frequent intervals he had to stop and rest, open the zipper of his coat, and let air in as sweat gathered around his neckband. All the while, he kept an ear out. People were on guard; he was well aware of that. And a snowmobile with a sled abandoned in the middle of the trail would be suspicious. Not to mention the blood, which he'd only kicked a little snow over. Shit, maybe he would have to call Robert after all. He couldn't leave the snowmobile and sled there.

He had two hundred yards left to go, and his arms were full of lactic acid. His legs trembled and he felt light-headed, like when he blew up balloons for his sister's kids. He dug in his heels and yanked again. The reindeer was limp and heavy, and slipped this way and that on the trail. The tracks they were leaving behind would likely reveal what had happened. He sank through the snow up to his knees and suddenly there was a tight feeling across his chest. A strained muscle. He gritted his teeth. This wasn't the first time it had happened; all he could do was grin and bear it. He could see the road now, which gave him renewed strength, and he tried a new tactic: getting some speed and jogging with the reindeer dragging behind. There was a welcome dip as he reached the ditch, and the reindeer tumbled down after him. Just as long as a car didn't come by. Panting, he pulled off his hat, wiped the sweat from his forehead and nape. His chest didn't feel good at all; he must have torn some muscles.

The forest was quiet, just a faint breeze rustling the treetops. He opened the car doors with his key fob. The blinking lights were just what he needed to muster his strength and get out of the ditch and across the road to the pull-off. There was only the faintest rustle from the icy road as the reindeer slid right across in his grasp. He muttered the order to himself: first get the reindeer on the trailer and then grab the tarp from the trunk to cover it. He couldn't hear any cars, and he shook out his tired, heavy arms. Bending down, he wrapped his arms around the reindeer's abdomen, trying to keep its eyes aimed away from him. He shoved off with the last of his leg strength and groaned aloud as he wrestled the reindeer onto the trailer. Almost done. He just needed to stop for a little air. But no air made it into his lungs, and suddenly the muscles in his chest flared in pain again. Worse than the first time. That's weird, he had time to think, and then he lost his footing on the icy pull-off and tipped over backwards.

CHAPTER FIFTY-FIVE

Vihttalogivihtta

Eventually, the autopsy would show whether it was his heart or the blow to his head that took Petri's life. Either way, he was dead. Elsa had read the police report so many times she knew it by heart. Petri's name wasn't given, but the village gossip had quickly settled that matter. The dead man in the pull-off was Petri Stålnacke from the green cabin in the next village.

The report contained the phrase "accused individuals not identified" and clarified that he was dead. The investigator stated, in the dry prose of law enforcement, that the crime in question was a suspected theft; the man had stolen a reindeer that did not belong to him. Just as matter-of-fact was the description of the reindeer halfway up on the trailer and the man lying dead on the ground. According to the village gossip, a miner from town had discovered Petri. He had just driven by at first, but immediately turned back and called the police, who arrived on the scene in record time. They contacted the chairman of the reindeer collective, and he in turn called Anna-Stina's father and asked him to identify the reindeer. And now the preliminary investigation into the theft had been closed because the suspect was deceased.

Elsa was in town to visit Áhkku, but she couldn't drive past the police station without going inside. Henriksson agreed to see her but said he could only give her five minutes between meetings.

"Aren't you going to search Petri Stålnacke's place?"

Sergeant Henriksson hadn't aged well. His belly pressed against the edge of his desk and his chin hung slack. He was pale and his nose was streaked red.

"No, we aren't, and I've already told you that we don't have the resources to devote time to a case where the suspect is dead."

"But he wasn't acting alone, killing and stealing reindeer. There might be evidence in his apartment, on his phone. We know there are more of them, we know who they are. You know! We've stated their names so many times."

"I'm honestly sorry, but it's not possible. I can't pull staff out of thin air. We've got a big case right now that's demanding all our resources."

Oh yes, everyone knew that case. A crime of passion—a man had shot and killed his neighbor for having an affair with his ex-wife. His intention had been to shoot himself too, but ultimately he couldn't pull the trigger. And now he was somewhere in the police station, blubbering about being abandoned.

Henriksson turned up his palms and weighed them up and down. "I have to prioritize. But this doesn't mean we're ignoring the reindeer thefts, just that there are crimes that come before theft."

"I've got almost a hundred reports at home, made by those of us in the collective over the last twenty years. There are way more, but that's how many I've gotten hold of. Do you know how many of them have led to charges and convictions?"

Henriksson closed his eyes for a little too long and shook his head slowly.

"None. Not a single one. I can lay them out for you right here, if you like. 'No grounds to proceed,' most of them say, and that can mean that a preliminary investigation was never even opened."

"Yes, I'm familiar with the terminology."

"But do you understand what it means for us, that no one cares that our animals are killed?"

Henriksson's expression didn't change.

"Occasionally there was evidence, and named suspects, but in the end it's always 'no crime can be verified.' How is that possible?"

"I can't account for one hundred reports," Henriksson said wearily.

Elsa clenched the back of the chair she stood behind.

"No, I know that. But can you explain why you didn't search the premises when we had a trail of blood leading to a barn? And who was given the evidence, the reindeer I handed over? Who was it?"

Suddenly, Henriksson's face turned red.

"It was you!" she exclaimed.

He squinted, annoyed. "It wasn't me!"

"But you're the one who okayed the release of the remains."

Henriksson slapped his desk lightly with both palms and looked at the screen in front of him.

"That's all the time I have for you. You came here to discuss the most recent police report, and I've given you my answer. Next time, you can call."

"Can't you just admit it was wrong?"

Henriksson stood up and tugged at the waistband of his pants, but his belly was too big.

"It wasn't wrong. It wasn't illegal," he said grimly. "But perhaps it was inappropriate."

He took a few steps toward the door and opened it.

"Inappropriate," Elsa said, nodding.

She didn't extend her hand and he didn't look her in the eye.

SHE DROVE TO THE home to see Áhkku, who was having one of her better days, so much so that Elsa could get close to her. They sat on the bed, waving their toes, which hardly reached past the edge. She'd inherited her short legs from Áhkku.

"Little dachshunds, that's us," Elsa said, which made Áhkku laugh, and Elsa took the opportunity to nestle a little closer. Áhkku's hair was in a beautiful braid and wound into a bun.

"Who braided your hair?"

"My little sister," she said with a smile.

Elsa sagged, tried to take her hand, but it wandered across the blanket that rested across their laps. The wall was cold through her shirt, and she tilted her head back. Áhkku looked at her quizzically.

"It was Brittis. But she did it like little sister."

"Tell me about your little sister."

"She was my best friend."

"Tell me about when the two of you were little."

"She followed me everywhere, copied me. Learned everything by watching me. But then I left her." Áhkku cast her eyes down. "And I didn't say sorry."

"You started school."

"No one told me I wouldn't be coming back."

"You did come back."

"Not for the rest of that year. She was so lonely."

Elsa hardly dared to breathe; Áhkku might slip away at any moment.

"But you were loneliest of all, weren't you?"

"Eh! I had my brother with me at the school. But they beat him all the time. The teachers and the other children too. I hardly wanted to say that we were related. But of course everyone knew."

"And then little sister came there too."

"I said to Enná, 'Don't let her come. She'll never survive.'" Áhkku's voice squeaked, and her body grew uneasy, rocking back and forth. "It's just like back then. I'm not allowed to speak Sámi here."

"But isn't there someone on staff who knows it?"

Áhkku nodded.

"What's her name?"

"I don't remember. But she's nice."

"That's great. Talk to her."

Her eyes were cloudy, but still Áhkku could drill her gaze into Elsa.

"I want to come home with you."

"When summer comes, we'll go pick cloudberries, you and me."

"I'll be dead by then."

"Don't say that."

Áhkku was working her jaw.

"Maybe you can come this spring too, see the calves," Elsa said. "We're going to let the cows calve in the corral before we head up to the mountains."

The old woman began to cry. She whimpered, and fat tears rolled down her wrinkled cheeks.

Elsa didn't dare to put an arm around her; instead she grabbed her hand even though Áhkku protested at first, splaying her fingers.

"Don't be sad. It'll get better, it will." Her own words made her feel ill. "You know what? One of the men who takes our reindeer was found dead. He was lying beside his car and he had a reindeer with him."

"Serves him right!" Áhkku said softly.

"Not that we're supposed to say so, but absolutely." Elsa took out her phone. "I'll read you the article."

"I can still read, you know."

"I do know, but maybe you haven't read this particular article."

Lovisa Wikberg had taken a tentative approach and Elsa sighed. Maybe it was because Petri had died that the newspaper was toning down the incident. Or maybe it was because the police had closed the case. Fucking Henriksson.

"A man suspected of stealing a reindeer was found dead in a parking pull-off yesterday afternoon. The reindeer that had been killed was hanging halfway off a trailer. The police have no comment on whether there are possible connections to previous reindeer thefts," Elsa read.

Áhkku pulled her braid from its bun and stroked it. "Who was he?"

"Petri. The guy from the green cabin by the river."

Áhkku stopped short, appeared to be taking this in, trying to grasp what she wanted to say. But nothing came out, and Elsa kept reading about crime-scene investigations and the autopsy.

Suddenly she heard gentle snoring, and Áhkku's head fell to her shoulder. She was like a child, falling asleep when things got to be too much, Elsa thought. She took the opportunity to stroke her grandmother's warm, slack cheek.

CHAPTER FIFTY-SIX

Vihttalogiguhtta

Rumors were flying. The villages were always full of rumors when anything happened, and this incident was spectacular, giving way to any number of theories. How *had* Petri died? Was the miner really first on the scene, or had Ante been there first and killed Petri? Ante laughed at that rumor, but confessed to Hanna that he could have given that bastard a real run for his money if he'd caught him red-handed.

"Let them talk," he said before heading out.

And then she was alone again, with too many thoughts. Sometimes she wished it was her job, women's work, to be away with the reindeer for long periods. The men didn't have to be at home thinking; they let physical work take over.

What would Lasse have said, if he were alive? Always that same thought: What would Lasse do? He definitely would have laughed at the rumors, and she would have misunderstood him again, believed that he truly thought it was amusing. All those times he'd laughed, all those times she felt warm inside, thinking that he was their bright light, the one who always urged them on, moved them forward, said it wasn't so bad. But toward the end, Lasse had started talking differently. Sometimes she approached that memory, how he must have tried but she needed his laughter and he acquiesced to her wishes. That thought made it hard to breathe and sometimes made her moan aloud in her quiet, empty kitchen. As time passed, she had become ever more convinced it was all her fault.

"What's on your mind?"

Elsa was sitting in front of her with a cup of cooling coffee; the buns had started to dry out in the woven basket. She got a piece of cling wrap and laid it over the perfectly coiled cinnamon buns.

"Nothing special," she said.

"I've been thinking about Jon-Isak a lot," Elsa said.

They'd been talking around it for a long time now. There was plenty to say about Petri, and she had made an honest effort to seem engaged. She had told Elsa about the rumors surrounding Ante, which made Elsa shake her head indignantly. But they'd avoided the topic for long enough now, and she braced herself for the response to the next question.

"How were things at school after the articles were published? I haven't worked for a few days, and I've been so worried. You know—" Elsa said, but she cut herself off and brought her mug to her lips, grimacing at the cold coffee.

She should get up and put on a new pot, but then Elsa would never leave.

"You know they get in fights, right? He's told you, hasn't he? I don't know if the school has been in touch?" Elsa looked at her expectantly.

Hanna looked up from beneath her bangs—she should have gotten a haircut ages ago. Her hair was down past her shoulders and the threads of gray made her look older.

"He told me," she lied.

Elsa leaned back and exhaled. "Good."

She nodded; that was all she could manage. Jon-Isak hadn't said a word. Just like Lasse.

"And I hardly ever see Anna-Stina. She's only ever with Per-Jonas," Elsa went on.

Hanna eagerly latched onto this topic, grateful not to talk about her son. "No, we don't see her very often either. So how are your parents?"

Elsa lit up. "Mom is like a whole different person. Siessá has been coming by more often, and last time she tricked Mom into going to an aerobics class in the next village, and now she goes there every Tuesday."

"She's so wonderful, your siessá."

"Everything's more fun when she's with us. You know how she laughs."

Elsa quickly glanced down, as if she'd said too much. But it was no secret that Marika was a tough one. How many times had Hanna opened the door to Elsa when she was little and given her what she was missing at home?

"We all need a siessá sometimes."

The muscles at the back of her neck contracted, warning of a migraine.

"Yes! She gets how we have to enjoy everything we have. And besides, we have the best life in the world," Elsa said with a smile. "When the village isn't full of rumors and the kids aren't having fistfights at school."

She knew Elsa was trying to be sarcastic. Her hand went to the back of her neck and she began kneading the muscles there.

They fell into silence; the only sound was the hum of the dishwasher. She saw Elsa's gaze drift to the tarp by the shed, where Lasse's old snowmobile had been for all these years. She braced herself for the question: Why didn't they get rid of it? But Jon-Isak liked to drive the Lynx, even though it was old. He was angry that he'd never gotten to meet his uncle, who everyone said was so nutty and cheerful. She had to get up. The two of them, together. How many times had she pictured them together?

"You know he's with us," Elsa said softly. "I feel him there often."

Hanna was enraged. She had to turn around and steady herself on the counter. She knew that people talked about Elsa. That she was a gunsttar who had special abilities, had the power to heal and stanch blood from a wound. It wasn't as if Lasse had come to Hanna. She had searched for him, in her dreams, in the quiet kitchen, but also in the mountains each summer; he'd been at his happiest there. But, nowhere.

She couldn't turn around. She clattered dishes in the sink and drew up her shoulders.

"Do you remember when Anna-Stina and I were little, and I would come here in the mornings for a treat?" Elsa paused for a moment. "You were important to me."

So here was her thanks. When she couldn't even turn around because the envy was tearing at her body.

"That's nice," she managed.

"And Lasse, if I was lucky, he was over here with you."

She held tight to the dish brush, and water splashed onto the tile and the window as she scrubbed the morning's oatmeal from the pot.

"I just want you to know he's with us. But I'm sure you knew that already."

She forced herself to glance back with a smile. Then she turned the water on full force.

"I'm a little worried about Mattias . . . ," Elsa mumbled. "He's not doing so well."

They heard snowmobiles in the distance. It was almost lunchtime, and Hanna realized she was behind. Elsa didn't continue. Surely Elsa couldn't expect that she would help Mattias if he wasn't doing well? She must realize this was no longer a sanctuary.

"I need to get started on lunch."

Elsa looked at her in disappointment. But what could she do? Mattias had never sought her out as Elsa had. He'd been a wild child who soon grew into a sulky teen. He managed, as boys do. *Boys can manage*, she wanted to scream out loud, to make it true.

The snowmobile drove into the yard and she relaxed. This conversation would soon be over. Finally. The clouds had scattered and the sun broke through; it looked like a nice afternoon. Maybe she would have the energy for a deep clean after all. A thorough one, with rugs outside to air.

CHAPTER FIFTY-SEVEN

Vihttalogičieža

It was a quiet funeral at the church in town. Three wreaths on the grave and a pastor who hadn't had much help to make the service more personal. Not like at Pop's funeral, where the coffee at the reception had almost run out. He supposed there hadn't actually been very many attendees that time either, but to be honest, there were more than Robert had expected. And Ma had sent a telegram, but he'd ripped it up without reading it.

Robert was wearing the same black suit jacket today, but this time it wouldn't button up. There was a stain on the breast pocket of his white shirt, but the jacket hid it.

The smörgåstårta was dry and the salmon badly salted. At least the coffee was strong. Petri's sister and her family, and his elderly mother, sat beside the pastor. His sister's two kids were lively. Once, when drunk, Petri had mentioned that those little ones were like his own kids. They'd never talked about children or family, but that had slipped out. Petri had only been fifty-three, one year older than Robert; it was hard to take in.

The conversation between Robert and his tablemates was forced.

"Could've used a nip about now," he said.

He received *hmms* and small smiles back.

"But then again I've got the car."

Jan-Olov, who owned the house next to Petri's cabin, stooped down and got way too close to Robert's face. His breath was sour.

"What do you think happened to Petri? Was he murdered?"

Robert hesitated; he would love nothing more than to whip up some drama. He glanced toward the family. He'd heard someone say it was a heart attack, but it wasn't his place to spread such information. And really, who could say for sure what did it—the heart attack or the blow to the head? Folks wanted to believe it could have been some Lapp bastard after all, someone who happened by just as Petri was loading the reindeer onto the trailer. Maybe he'd even run him over. Who could say? There could be other injuries to suggest that very thing, broken legs or internal bleeding. So, sure, he could have been killed by a car or at least robbed of his life on account of a violent shove backwards that had caused him to hit his head on the ground.

"Well, you know, who can say? Sure seems shady," he said.

"I've heard there's a new cop with Lapp roots himself who's covering for those Lapps," Jan-Olov said.

Robert looked at him with interest. "Is that so? I'll be damned."

"He's got a Swedish last name, though, Ljungkvist or Ljungblad. I heard he got rid of his Sámi last name."

Robert nodded emphatically. Right, Ljungblad. That whelp who had been out to his place. Changed his name, huh? Well, who the hell wouldn't want to change his name? Of course you'd be ashamed to have Lapp blood in the family. Lots of Sámi had Swedified themselves over the years. He wiped his mouth with the white napkin. He didn't know Jan-Olov well enough to speak freely.

Nevertheless, he said, "I suppose there's a chance all the newspaper reports about those reindeer parts in the forest have caused some madman to take the law into his own hands."

"But everyone knows the collectives steal each other's reindeer. And blame outsiders."

"Sure, that way they can both keep the meat and collect the damages."

Jan-Olov shook his head and poured more coffee.

"But Petri did have a reindeer with him," he said slowly, looking closely at Robert.

"You know, I'm one hundred percent certain that Petri had accidentally run it over and was only trying to do the right thing. I'm sure he planned to take care of it and let the collective know."

Jan-Olov raised his eyebrows and smirked. Robert was furious. He'd misjudged the man. He was nothing but a gossip.

"Well, guess it's about time to head home."

Robert pushed his chair back and stood up. He clenched his jaw and the pain radiated down his back.

BACK AT HOME, HE found himself sitting on the sofa with his suit jacket still on. It wasn't like he was crying, but for some reason his vision was a little blurry.

"Ugh," he said to himself, rubbing his eyes with the back of his wrist.

Four empty cans of Mariestads beer stood on the pine table. He opened a fifth and raised it toward the ceiling.

"Cheers, Petri! You stupid bastard!"

By now the thread on Flashback Forum about Petri's death was fifteen pages long. Robert ran his index finger down the screen. He'd read most of it. A majority of the posts were full of conspiracies, convinced it was murder. Few seemed to know Petri in real life, and Robert wanted to write about him, tell them what a good guy he was. But he didn't know how to create an account and he didn't trust it would remain anonymous. Wasn't worth the risk.

There was a pleasant buzz in his head, and the pain in his shoulder and back wasn't as fierce anymore. Raija struggled her way onto the sofa, then put her head in his lap. He petted her with a firm hand and scratched her ears. *What if she dies?* he thought. But he must not think those things. Had to drain the beer in three big gulps.

He scrolled through the thread again, updating the page, wanting more posts to appear. He wrangled himself out of his jacket and loosened his tie so that it hung around his neck like a slack noose.

If he could have replied to the thread, he would have told them about that Lapp whore who ought to be put in her place. Maybe that would get her to shut up.

He pushed the dog aside and went to the fridge. Behind the row of Mariestads there was a piece of reindeer jerky he'd forgotten about. Petri had smoked it for him. He was good at salting and never took down the meat too soon. Who would smoke his meat for him now?

When Pop died, life became lonely. But in recent years he'd had Petri. They'd met one another back in their twenties while logging. That had been a really nice summer. Hell of a lot of mosquitos, but they'd had a damn good time together. Then came the DUI.

Robert opened the beer and drank some, but the memories wouldn't leave him be.

He'd taken a chance and driven to work even though he'd been drinking all night. It was summer, after all, and he wanted to have a life too, not just work. The sun blinded him as he turned onto a gravel road and the car went into a skid. Gravel sprayed, something hit the car, and an instant later he lurched to a stop in the ditch. The foreman's son had gotten in the way. A snobby asshole who thought he was better than everyone else. It wasn't like he died; he didn't even break anything. But he took a bad fall, split his eyebrow, and broke two teeth.

And then the foreman said it out loud: It had been a serious mistake to hire Robert; he should have known better given that father of his. That family, nothing but alcoholics and jailbirds, the lot of them.

Robert was about to give him a good smack, but Petri grabbed his arms. Instead he bellowed that he didn't need this shit job anyway and got in his car, even though they said he wasn't allowed to drive. They would call the police. But one look at him and they backed off.

That night, the pain started in his neck and back, like red-hot pokers on bare skin. It radiated up, branched out into blood vessels, muscle attachments, and sinews. Had he known then that this was just the beginning, he would have hung himself on the spot. A week later, the pain had faded, but it was only hiding and would return later.

He and Petri lost touch after the forestry job. But then he showed up in the village a year or so after Pop died, and eventually he bought that old cabin by the river. He had a job in town, but he came to the village whenever he had time off. Pop wasn't as capable as he had once been, and Petri was interested in earning some extra cash. And that's how it went. Pop died and Petri took over. It had always been understood that this was Robert's thing, that he helmed the ship. He was in charge.

But now. Now he knew that Petri had taken liberties. Maybe more times than he'd guessed. Robert sank back into the sofa, which swayed considerably.

After Petri died, there was no time to brood or be angry—Robert had to act fast to retrieve the meat he'd dumped at Petri's when the police were threatening to search his property. He'd called Petri's sister to get the key. She hadn't even asked what he was going to do there.

He'd had to sell off most of it, quickly and for way too cheap. He only saved a few steaks for himself, because it would be weird for someone not to have a single cut of meat in the freezer.

Robert sighed and Raija lifted her nose, sniffing the air. Fucking Petri. Why the hell had he gotten it into his head to drag a reindeer halfway through the forest without calling him? Together they could have loaded up the creature in no time, could have left the scene quickly and efficiently. Petri would be alive today. And above all, he wouldn't have lied.

Robert rubbed his meaty fists over his jeans. A sharp odor of sweat rose from his armpits, and he unbuttoned his shirt and tossed his tie to the corner of the sofa. Sitting there bare-chested, he scratched at the back of his neck.

A little while later, as he trudged into the cold in his Crocs, he was still without a shirt, and his nipples, under their sparse but long black hairs, grew hard as birch buds. He went into the garage and opened the gun safe. With the rifle in hand he felt calmer. He went back inside, slipping on the last step and cursing when a burning arrow flared in his shoulder.

He would show those little trolls on Flashback that you could do more than just sit in front of a screen and pretend to be somebody. It wouldn't be long before they were posting in a frenzy about what had happened, what he'd done.

He pulled on a flannel shirt and buttoned it crookedly in his rush. He pulled up the zipper of his jacket and put his fox-fur hat on his head. He couldn't find any gloves. The rifle hung from his shoulder.

CHAPTER FIFTY-EIGHT

Vihttalogigávcci

S iessá was leaning against the kitchen table, watching Mom's scatter-brained dashing from room to room. She winked at Elsa and smiled. "She's not used to leaving."

When she said this, it occurred to Elsa how true that statement was. Mom was always the one who stayed behind. When Dad and Mattias went with the reindeer, when Elsa moved away for school, when Áhkku had to leave them. Mom's cheeks were red and she was searching for her phone. She laughed aloud when she realized she was already holding it in her hand.

"We're going to drink so much wine. And I booked spa time at the hotel, and on Saturday we're going to spend the whole day shopping," Siessá said, waving the car keys.

"You know I can't handle that much alcohol." Mom dragged her suitcase into the hall. "I'm ready. Let's go."

They giggled, crowding in the front hall as they pulled on their shoes, and Elsa wanted to tell Siessá that she was her hero. She hugged them both.

"Will you be okay? Isa and Mattias should be back soon. But the storms have done such a number on the fences."

Elsa shook her head, smiling. "Come on. You're just babbling about stuff that doesn't even matter."

"It just feels so strange to be leaving," she said, but she didn't look sad.

Siessá rolled her eyes and nudged her toward the door. "Dear God, we'll be back on Sunday."

There was talk, in the family, about Siessá's increasingly frequent visits to the village. Elsa had heard whispers of divorce, but she didn't want to ask.

She waved as they honked three times from the yard, and then the car turned south, toward the city on the coast.

Semis thundered by the house at regular intervals, but otherwise there wasn't much traffic. Quiet outside and quiet inside. She lay on the living-room sofa and pulled a soft white blanket over herself. When she was alone, she always found herself drawn to the center of the house. When she was little, this sort of dreariness would prompt her to run over to Áhkku and Áddjá's. Now there was nothing better than having the whole place to herself. She read for a while, dozed off, woke up, and felt unmoored from time.

When she heard a snowmobile, she sat up. Could that be Dad and Mattias? She craned her neck to see if there was light on the snow, but the sound seemed to be coming from the other direction. She padded to the front hall, tried the door handle to make sure it was locked, turned out the lights in the hall and the kitchen. The snowmobile, there was only one, came closer and she waited for it to turn off, but the sound of the engine grew relentlessly near.

And there it was. Elsa stood half-hidden behind the kitchen curtain and saw the headlight. It was going awfully fast. It didn't slow down for the last snow-bank before the main road, kicking up snow and going airborne, then landing hard on the road, followed by a wobble before it stopped in the ditch on the other side. The driver fell off and lay motionless in the snow. Elsa dashed to the living room and grabbed her phone. She had to get back to the kitchen and see where he went, but she felt frozen to the spot. Her hands were icy and her feet unresponsive. It felt like danger was all around her in these dark rooms. Her body betrayed her, and she wanted to roll under the coffee table and close her eyes until it was all over. Someone whimpered. The sound had come from her own throat. Just one step. And another. And another. Don't show yourself in the kitchen window. Her fingernails scratched at the sill, clawing frantically.

He had gotten up and was limping along the road. In his hand, a long, narrow object. A rifle? It couldn't be anyone but Robert Isaksson and he was on his way to their house. The realization hit her like a punch to the gut.

She backed into the kitchen table, fell to her knees, and shoved the rug aside to yank open the hatch and scurry down the steep stairs. The rug tossed into a corner of the kitchen! He would peer in and figure out that she was in the root cellar, trapped like a rat, cowering in a corner.

She dialed 112 and her teeth chattered in the raw, damp cold. The odor of earth forced its way into her nostrils.

"I need help! A man is on his way to my house. I think he has a gun."

The operator had a calm voice, spoke so slowly that Elsa had to interrupt and shout which village they should send the police to. And when she said his name, her voice cracked.

"We live in the first house you see coming from town."

The operator repeated the name of the village, couldn't pronounce it, asked if she had locked the door and whether she was alone.

"Are you sure he was holding a rifle?"

"I don't know, that's what it looked like. Please, please, this time you have to come!"

"Try to remain calm. I've already informed the police and they're on their way as we speak."

"But don't you understand how far out I am?" Her voice was a muffled shriek. "Send a helicopter! A car will never make it! Don't you see?"

There was pounding on the door and then on the kitchen window.

She whispered through clenched teeth. "He's here now. I have to call my dad. You'll never make it in time."

"Don't hang up—"

Her hands shook violently as she touched Dad's name on the phone. It rang, but he didn't pick up. At the same time, she heard the voice coming from outside, muffled and far off, but still terrifyingly close.

"Where are you, you Lapp whore?" He banged on another window, probably in the living room. "You need to learn to keep your mouth shut!"

She called Dad again and this time he answered.

"What is it?"

Her mouth was so dry that her lips stuck to her gums.

"Robert. He's here . . ."

"Helveha . . ."

She heard rustling and crackling on the line; Dad was running. She was crying now, sitting on a narrow step and hugging herself. On the phone she heard a snowmobile start and Dad roaring that he was on his way.

"Don't drive all the way up! He'll shoot you."

"He's got a gun? Elsa, listen to me. I have to hang up and call for help. Stay away from the windows."

"I'm in the root cellar."

A window shattered above her. The phone fell from her hand, bounced off the rug on the concrete floor, and went dark.

"Fucking Lapps, fucking scum! And who killed Petri?"

His voice was so close, just above her. He was slurring. Still no footsteps inside the house. She turned on the flashlight and swept her eyes across the shelves, looking for something she could use as a weapon.

She wondered if she should shout that she'd called the police, maybe it would scare him, but when she opened her mouth no sound came out.

Now there was silence, dangerous silence. She took a firm grip on the cord that hung from the trapdoor. She would hang on it with all her weight if he tried to open it. The old cord cut into her palms. The silence and the waiting were worse than hearing his voice.

Then the sound of a snowmobile. Could that be Dad already? He would be shot. She pulled harder on the cord but dropped it over and over, she was shaking so hard. Her fingers were like jelly.

The snowmobile faded away and she tried to gather her thoughts. It must be Robert taking off, but she couldn't let go of the cord. Not even when the sound of the engine was gone and it had been quiet for a long time. Not even when she heard two snowmobiles in the yard. Not even when she thought she heard the door being unlocked with a key. Only when Dad called her name could she let go.

CHAPTER FIFTY-NINE

Vihttalogiovcci

E lsa pulled her cardigan tighter, alternately sweating and freezing. The teacup was untouched on the kitchen table. Dad paced back and forth, muttering to himself.

The police arrived with lights and sirens; maybe they'd been on all the way from town. Elsa pictured them passing other cars at high speeds, but easing off the gas when they were informed that the immediate threat had passed.

Dad stared out the window. The blue lights had stopped flashing across the cabinets and walls.

"I'll be damned. Henriksson himself. And a colleague."

He met them in the front hall and led them into the kitchen without a word. Heavy footsteps, something rustling—maybe their uniforms—and an unfamiliar smell filled the kitchen.

"Hi, Elsa. We've met before, out here."

She looked up, and sure enough, she recognized those transparent eye-lashes and pale eyes.

"Yes, and on the phone too. About that search warrant that never materialized," she said, her voice wheezy.

Ljungblad deflated a bit. "Yes, unfortunately."

"And now that same person has threatened me."

Henriksson cleared his throat and Ljungberg took a step aside.

"Well, Elsa, this is no good. How are you feeling?"

She shrugged, but her chin trembled.

Ljungblad and Henrikksson pulled out chairs and sat next to each other, across from her. Ljungblad took out a small notepad and Henriksson leaned forward.

"Start at the beginning. What happened?"

"It was Robert Isaksson."

"Are you sure?"

"Yes. He was going to kill me."

"Did he expressly say he was going to kill you?"

"I think so. It all happened so fast. He was shouting horrible things, something about how he was going to teach me to keep my mouth shut."

"Can you remember what he said word for word?"

"He called me a Lapp whore, I remember that much."

Dad cursed.

"If you all don't take care of him now—" He faltered. "Well, I don't actually know what I'll do."

"Try to take it easy. Have a seat," said Ljungblad.

He spoke slowly, but Dad wouldn't be appeased. "He could have killed her!"

"Did you see him?" Henriksson asked. "Start from the beginning, so we understand the sequence of events."

"I was home alone and heard the snowmobile when I was resting on the couch in the living room. I went to the kitchen window and saw him approaching, very fast, and the snowmobile flew out onto the road and he sort of crashed. Then I saw him walking toward the house. He was carrying something, and I'm pretty sure it was a rifle."

Ljungblad looked out the window but saw only his own reflection.

"It's awfully dark out there. Are you sure he was the person you saw?"

"One hundred percent."

"Aren't you listening? She's sure!" Dad blustered.

Ljungblad got to his feet and herded Dad into the living room.

"Why don't you sit in here for a while and let us talk to Elsa? I know you're upset, but we need to have this conversation in peace and quiet."

He blocked the doorway until Dad sat on the sofa.

"I'm sure you can follow the snowmobile tracks to his house," Elsa said.

"Well, the thing is, we don't have a snowmobile with us, so . . ." Henriksson turned up his palms, resigned.

"Then just take ours!" Dad said loudly.

Henriksson nodded at the light switch. "Can we turn out the overhead light and see how dark it is out there and what you might conceivably have seen?"

Elsa saw Ljungblad's jaw set hard as stone.

"Maybe we should start by forming an understanding of what happened. I see that the kitchen window is broken?"

Henriksson looked at him in surprise, clearly not used to a younger colleague taking command.

"Yes, he broke it."

"Was that when he shouted at you?" Henriksson asked.

"Yes. And I just remembered something. He said something about Petri too."

"The stolen reindeer," said Ljungblad. "The guy who was found dead alongside his car with a reindeer on the trailer."

Henriksson glared at him, and his face reddened. But Elsa relaxed a little, let her shoulders drop. She massaged the left one with an icy hand.

"And you were where, exactly? Did you get a close look at him?" Henriksson harped on, but she would only look at Ljungblad from now on.

"I was down in the root cellar, so I heard him."

"Did you recognize his voice?"

"Yes."

"Hmm." Henriksson drummed his hand lightly on the table. "Anyway, we do have to turn out the lights to determine what you saw," he said, standing up.

It felt strange to stand with two police officers in a dark kitchen, but she pointed out where the snowmobile went into the ditch.

"You can go take a look, I'm sure you can see where he ran into the snowbank."

"There are no streetlights here, and that's quite a long distance to make out a face and rifle. Could he have been holding a shovel or something like that?" Henriksson's question hung in the air. "Okay, we can turn the lights back on."

She heard Dad curse in the living room. "It's one thing that you don't believe us when we report poached reindeer, but not believing what Elsa says—you should be ashamed!"

Henriksson sighed. "Nils Johan, that's enough from you. Either you sit there and be quiet or you can go outside and wait. We're not saying we don't believe your daughter. We need to ask questions to clarify what happened."

"I recognized him, and no, I can't be one hundred percent sure of what he was carrying, but it could have been a rifle," Elsa said.

She thought of Mattias. He would have been so disappointed to hear her now. She had the chance to accuse Robert, and she shouldn't back down about the rifle.

Mattias, his eyes black as night, had helped her out of the root cellar. He said he was going to go kill Robert. Dad had dragged him across the yard, shoved him into his house, and slammed the door.

Elsa's knees were shaking and her stomach cramped. She so badly wanted to lie down and just go to sleep, escape all of this. She tried to remember what the object in Robert's hand had looked like, long and narrow. Could it in fact have been a shovel?

"What else would he have brought? It must have been a rifle," she said, looking at Ljungblad. "Can you please just go arrest him now?"

"Do you think anyone else in the village saw him?" he asked.

"We're the farthest out on the curve leading into the village, so it's a ways to the nearest neighbor. If they didn't see the snowmobile, maybe someone else saw him on his way here."

Elsa lay down on the kitchen bench, her heart pounding against the hard wooden lid.

Ljungblad looked concerned. "Are you okay? Do you want some water?"

"I'm just suddenly so tired."

He got a glass from the dish rack, filled it with water, and placed it on the table in front of her.

"Robert has threatened me before, over text. At least I assume it was him. It came from an unknown number."

"Did you save them?"

She sat up, took cautious sips of water, and scrolled through her phone until she found the texts. Ljungbled read them and showed Henriksson.

"Did you file a report?" he asked, handing her phone back.

"Yes, but not right away. At first I thought it would be pointless, because of the unknown number, but then I did anyway."

Out of nowhere, she thought of Mom. Blissfully unaware, at a hotel with Siessá. Dad had snuck back into the kitchen; he took some paper towels and blew his nose.

"We aren't calling Mom," she said in Sámi, and he nodded.

Henriksson looked at them.

"We're going to take a closer look at the footprints outside," he said. "Then we'll swing by Robert's place. And I will be in touch after that."

He emphasized the "I" with a look at Ljungblad.

"Are you going to bring him in, or are we going to have to stay up all night?" Dad asked.

"I'd be willing to bet he's out cold. Not my first time dealing with him," Henriksson said.

"We'd better just hope he doesn't shoot you two."

Henriksson shook his head, looking perfectly confident. "Not when I'm coming."

Ljungblad placed a hand on Elsa's shoulder. "Do you need anything?"

She wanted to cry.

"Just for you to arrest Robert and lock him up."

CHAPTER SIXTY

Guhttalogi

The house reeked of sour dishrag and old fish in the garbage. Beer cans cluttered the counter and some were on the living-room table as well. Out in the yard, Raija barked aggressively.

Robert let them knock for a long time before opening the door in long johns and an old T-shirt with peeling print.

"Aha, so here you are," he said, trying not to slur his words. "And Henriksson himself, I see."

Robert's bangs and the hair around his ears were damp from the cold water he'd splashed on his face as soon as he heard the car pulling up.

"Oh, so you were expecting us," Henriksson said, his eyes taking in the room. "Yet you let me knock multiple times."

"Sure, you're here to ask questions about Petri, aren't you? He didn't die a natural death, I can tell you that much."

Robert felt his stomach roil, and the nausea made him break out in a cold sweat.

He saw Henriksson's young whelp of a partner raise his eyebrows slightly as Henriksson walked around the living room and kitchen. He puffed out his chest. Like in the service. Robert had the urge to bark out an order. He smirked to himself.

"Where have you been over the past two hours?"

"Here, of course. It was the funeral today, and after that I had a few drinks."

Neither Henriksson nor the whelp sat down, nor did he offer them a seat, but in the end Robert himself had to sit on the stool next to the stove. He wiped the sweat from his brow and tried to focus his eyes.

"Is there any chance you were so angry about Petri's death that you've been out threatening folks?"

"As you can see, I'm in no condition to drive."

He coughed, long and wheezy, buying time, then stood up and spit into the sink. He stood there for a long time, his sweaty palms against the cold aluminum.

"Do you have a rifle?" the whelp asked.

That made Robert let out a big, rumbling laugh, until he had to cough again.

"Of course I do. What the hell do you think? Who doesn't, in this village? We're hunters. What kind of colleague did you hire, Henriksson?"

Henriksson came closer and waited until they had made eye contact.

"An individual has told us you rode over on a snowmobile and had a rifle with you. That you threatened her and broke a window."

"You think I can drive in this state?"

Robert threw out his arms and had to take a step to the side to keep from falling over. He grabbed the counter again and smiled, but he knew it was more like a grimace.

"We need to have a look at your snowmobile."

"It's in the shop."

"Then we'll look at your rifle," said Henriksson.

Robert sighed and nodded at the front door.

Raija paced around anxiously when they came out, making her chain clink. They headed for the garage, and Ljungblad inspected the snowmobile tracks in the yard.

"It looks like a snowmobile has been driven here."

"Well, sure. People come through here day in and day out. It's a shortcut to a good fishing lake."

The whelp wouldn't let it go and followed the trail for a bit, heading around the corner of the house and up to the fir trees. The beam of his flashlight played across the snow.

Robert shivered in the cold and tugged at his long johns.

"There are footprints here as well," the whelp said from a distance.

"Well, hell if I know whose they are."

"So it wasn't you, driving the snowmobile into the forest and running back down?"

Robert shook his head and walked to the garage, his legs trembling. Henriksson followed, and Robert showed him that the gun safe was locked up just as it should be, and then he opened it without removing the rifle. Dad's rifle was hidden under a tarp in the corner of the garage. He forced himself not to look in that direction as he swallowed bile.

Henriksson looked around the garage with distaste. "So your old man was the one who kept things in good order, huh?"

Robert felt it was best not to respond.

"And which shop has your snowmobile?"

"Like I can afford a shop? A friend is working on it."

"Okay, what's his name?"

Robert took his time locking the gun safe again.

"A friend in Lainio."

"Name?"

"Joel Pettersson."

"And his phone number?"

"Don't know it offhand. I'll have to check my phone."

Ljungblad came in, let his eyes sweep over the garage; they landed on the big white chest freezer that had been empty for months, ever since it broke down. *Go ahead, you bastard, take a look*, Robert thought.

"Can anyone confirm that you've been home for the past two hours?"

"God."

Ljungblad scoffed and aimed a weary look at him.

"Then let's head in and get your friend's number," Henriksson said. "His snowmobile's in Lainio," he said in a tone Robert didn't care for.

Back inside, Robert dug in the couch cushions for his phone. Dust and grit got caught under his fingernails.

"How's it going?" Henriksson asked, suddenly behind him.

He looked through the contacts list and gave them Joel's number.

Ljungblad sniffed at the air ostentatiously, like a goddamn elkhound.

"I think I smell snowmobile exhaust on you."

"Where all did you say you're from? You're not used to snowmobiles, huh? The smell sticks. It's not me, it's my pants hanging there. It lingers."

He pointed at a pair of black work pants that were hanging askew over one of the kitchen chairs.

"May I take a look at your shoes?"

Robert held out an upturned palm as if to give them free rein in the front hall. He had tossed his Graninge boots under the lower bench in the sauna. But he wouldn't let anyone in there without a search warrant.

Ljungblad turned the shoes every which way, took a picture on his phone.

"So you haven't been threatening anyone in the next village."

Robert's eyes flashed.

"Maybe you should take a look at how many times people have made false accusations against me. It's not like this is your first time here." He aimed a smug look at Ljungblad. "And nothing came of that either. The Lapps claimed there was a trail of blood leading here. Maybe I'm the one who should report them, for slander." He puffed out his chest and raised his chin. "I was kind enough to let you in, but I think we're done here. Besides, I need to take a piss."

"We'll be in touch," Henriksson said, clapping him soundly on the shoulder instead of shaking his hand.

"You do that. Especially once you've arrested Petri's killer."

"Quit it with that kind of talk. No one killed him," Henriksson said, his voice suddenly sharp. "If it's revenge you're after, you can forget it."

Robert ignored him and stared at Ljungblad instead. "You're the one who has Sámi roots, aren't you?"

"No, I don't. What would that have to do with anything anyway?"

"Oh, nothing, just wondering."

Henriksson let Ljungblad go ahead of him, then turned to Robert.

"We'll just have to hope no one in the village saw you on your snowmobile. So it won't turn out you lied to us, I mean. I don't want to have to come back here and bring you in."

CHAPTER SIXTY-ONE

Guhttalogiokta

Hanna saw the patrol car pull into the yard and she ran a brush through her hair. Elsa had called, saying that the police would probably come by.

She opened the door before they could knock, and they all ended up standing in the front hall. She didn't want to invite them in. Elsa already knew she hadn't seen the snowmobile. Now she would have to say so again to the policemen. Sure, she'd heard a snowmobile, but she heard them all the time and the sound didn't send her running to the window for a look. Only if Jon-Isak headed out—then she might twitch the curtains a few times to make sure he didn't go all the way across the lake and vanish from sight. She had that much good sense.

"So you didn't see anyone driving past here on a snowmobile?" the older policeman asked.

He studied her face too intently for it to feel comfortable.

"No. Didn't anyone but Elsa see him?"

"No, no one. We've been knocking on doors where he should have gone by, but no one saw anything. A man in the white house . . ." The younger officer paged through a notepad. "To be sure, he said he'd seen a snowmobile, but then his wife said he gets just about everything mixed up, and that they hadn't seen a thing."

Hanna nodded slowly. "You know the only way you'll get Robert Isaksson is to catch him in the act. You need to spend more time out here."

"Yes, we've heard that a number of times now. But it's also possible to help us by being a witness."

The older officer said this with a certain sharpness.

"I would have reported it immediately, believe me, but unfortunately I didn't look out when I heard the snowmobile. The others are too scared. These small villages, you don't want to end up in a fight with your neighbor."

"What rumors are going around the village that might have prompted all this?"

"Elsa isn't making things up, let me make that clear." Now Hanna was the one speaking sharply. "She's been receiving threats for a long time. Someone keyed her car, and she gets these horrible texts. And now that fool thinks someone killed his friend. They're even saying it was my husband, because he was the one who identified the reindeer on behalf of the collective."

She fell silent and suddenly had to grab the door frame. Robert could just as easily have turned off at her house, looking for Ante. She could have been shot. Or Jon-Isak. They seldom locked their door, only at night.

"He's dangerous, for real," she mumbled.

"Well, unfortunately, there's not much we can do without witnesses."

"What did he have to say for himself, then?"

"We can't get into that. Except to say that at the present time it's her word against his, which is why we need witnesses."

"So he's going to get away with it again."

ONCE THE PATROL CAR left, Hanna sat down on the kitchen stool closest to the window. For a long time she stared out into the darkness. She texted Elsa and asked how she was, received an "okay" in response. The next text went to Jon-Isak, asking if he and Isa had had a good day up at the cabin. Her child sent a pleasant reply, ending, as always, with a hopeful heart at the end. She sent three in return.

CHAPTER SIXTY-TWO

Guhttalogiguokte

Elsa woke up every night in a cold sweat, sometimes with a sob in her throat. They were all light sleepers these days. She heard Dad's footsteps long past midnight, and sometimes Mattias didn't turn off the lights at all. The glow seeped out from behind closed blinds. They locked all the doors, and the shed, and put a padlock on the smoke goahti.

One night, someone went by and honked, a protracted beep as they passed the house, and she dashed to the window but couldn't see the car for all the snow it had kicked up—just two red dots that quickly vanished.

She spent each day angry, clenching her jaw so hard her teeth ached. But at night, the fear cut through and woke her up with a cold forehead and wet bangs.

Ljungblad called to say they had checked up on Robert.

"The snowmobile is in Lainio. And the shoes in his front hall didn't match the footprints outside the house. Besides, Robert's shoes were a size smaller."

"You don't think he could have more than one pair of shoes?"

She sounded sarcastic, and Ljungblad sighed on the other end.

"It's hard when it's your word against his, and we don't have any material evidence."

"So what do you think I should do now?"

"I know this must be an anxious time for you. I wish I was calling with better news. You'll simply have to give us a call if anything else happens."

"I'm not getting more than three hours of sleep a night, and it's been a week now."

"I'm not going to drop this, Elsa. Who knows, maybe some witness will work up the courage to call us."

She doubted it, but she still thanked him before they ended the call. At least he was taking their situation more seriously than any other cop had before.

The wardrobe door was slightly ajar. She thought for a moment, then opened up the wardrobe, pulled out the boxes of old schoolbooks she should have tossed, and took out the board game she'd managed to rescue when Mom was weeding out the storage shed. Clue had been her favorite as a kid. She opened the lid, lifted the board from the box, and picked up the little plastic bag that held the miniature murder weapons: a rope, a knife, a revolver, a lead pipe, a wrench, a candlestick. And also a piece of ear.

CHAPTER SIXTY-THREE

Guhttalogigolbma

The notice in the local circular was brief, but no one in the whole municipality missed it. There would be a temporary ban on snowmobiles in the reindeer pasturage, where the pregnant cows needed peace and quiet. Just in time for Easter break. It was like dropping a bomb on the community. Each spring, the same old story.

Elsa sat in the car at the gas station; on the radio indignant voices were saying that Easter was ruined. She gripped the steering wheel tight, forcing herself to keep listening.

The municipal commissioner was on the critics' side. "Animals are no more important than people, and being able to get out and enjoy nature is a holy thing for our community. Besides, it's more than just a ban on snowmobiles—it's discriminatory that not all Sámi have the right to practice reindeer husbandry and the right to this land. In other words, it's been decided that some Sámi are better than others and those ones get to control everyone else's access to the great outdoors."

Elsa slapped the steering wheel with both palms. "And who was it that took away the Sámi's rights? It wasn't us, it was the state! And it's not about pitting animals against people!"

The men clustered around the kiosk glanced in her direction. Maybe she'd shouted so loudly that they'd heard her. Or else she just looked unhinged. She glared back.

She was disgusted by the commissioner's self-righteous tone. He was well aware that he was riling up folks who very much wanted to be riled up. He was feeding the flames of hatred and dividing the population.

"I've done what I can, and we've appealed the decision. I want the citizens of our community to know that. I'm just as upset as everyone else who's affected by this."

Elsa took out her phone and looked up the post about the snowmobile ban on Facebook, where the comments were still streaming in.

"I'm sure as hell not letting one tiny group of Lapps tell me what to do at Easter. Just run over the fucking reindeer!!!"

"How the everlasting hell can those mountain gypsies be called the only Indigenous people of Europe? All this goddamn whining about the need for traditional reindeer herding, and they go zipping around on their snowmobiles and four-wheelers to keep their herd in line!"

She had to read this last comment again and again.

"We all live up here for one reason and one reason only: we want to be out in the forests and fields as soon as we've got a day off from the mines or whatever. The Sámi want to work alongside us PLUS decide we can't go where we want. If you get to have extra rights like that you should damn sure have to live off the forest and the reindeer there and not work in LKAB's mines and shove all the subsidies a person can get in our fucking faces. The only answer is to shoot on sight. No reindeer=No rights."

She took a screenshot and sent it to Minna. Her sense of Lasse was so strong she had to squeeze her eyes shut. His final days at the mine—what had he had to endure there?

She climbed out of the car, opened the gas cap, and inserted the nozzle. The men at the kiosk were talking loudly, eager for her to overhear.

"But their fucking reindeer are tame. They're used to snowmobiles."

She leaned her back against the car with her arms crossed and her gaze steady on them. The meter ticked up, filling the tank. Water was dripping off the gas station canopy, creating puddles on the ground. *Do you think we like attracting all this hate every year?* she wanted to call out to them. *We just want to protect our reindeer.* The handle clicked out and she let the last few drops fall. She screwed the cap back on, head held high.

She got in the car and let the engine roar. The villagers stared at her; it would be so easy to run them down. She let out the clutch, snow and gravel spraying behind the car. In the rearview mirror she saw one of them wave a fist at her. They moved, closing ranks, grinning like wolves.

"IT SHOULD BE ALLOWED to shoot reindeer just like moose."

Daniel's shoulders were broad, almost like a full-grown man's. He said this nonchalantly and loudly as he passed Elsa in the school hallway. She saw the younger children press up against the walls and cast their eyes down. Jon-Isak was one of them. Daniel shoved into him as he walked past, and Jon-Isak had to grab the wall to steady himself. Elsa opened her mouth to protest, but the look Jon-Isak shot her was so dark that she fell silent.

Daniel turned around and shouted: "I'm going to run down every god-damn reindeer over Easter. We have as much right to the land as you do."

His sparse entourage of pimply kids laughed. Elsa met the gaze of one of them, was aware of his roots, knew he was Sámi. His smile froze, and he quickly averted his eyes. Maybe she felt sorriest for the ones like him. The deniers.

Jon-Isak ran past her, but she had time to see the sheen in his eyes.

This is unsustainable, she thought. *This has to end.* She knew Daniel well, knew which family he came from. That was just it—everyone knew who you were. There was no way out.

The notice from the circular was posted on the bulletin board in the hall-way closest to the cafeteria, and someone had written on it with sprawling letters: "A good Lapp is a dead Lapp."

She ripped down the paper and crumpled it up. But then she smoothed it out again, had to show the principal. The sentence was out of order; the usual formulation was "A dead Lapp is a good Lapp." But the message was still loud and clear.

THE ATMOSPHERE IN THE teachers' lounge was tense. The village school and the Sámi school shared a staff room. Everyone said they were working toward the same goals, that they fought to unite the children and do away with conflict. The principal whizzed by on clacking heels. Olivia was from the south, didn't have the cultural compass, always missed the nuances of what was said. She never understood when someone was insulting another. She often walked fast to avoid being stopped. But Elsa grabbed her upper arm and held on when Olivia looked at her in surprise.

"This was on the bulletin board."

The principal put on her reading glasses, expensive brand-name ones that hung around her neck from a cord. She frowned and nodded.

"I'll handle it."

"How?"

"I'll handle it, Elsa."

That meant a halfhearted email would go out to all the parents. An email that certain types would respond to—those who didn't appreciate that their well-behaved children should have to be caught up in a collective punishment even though they were always obedient. And those who felt a jab of pain in their chests and wondered if they shouldn't just give up, move to town, and start over. They wrote in on occasion, demanding action, but what could be done when the hatred didn't actually come from the children?

Elsa would have the first-graders today. Among those children, there was hope. They were still too little to pass on what they heard at home. In fact, they were sometimes so full of passion for fairness and consideration that she wanted to lock them in and preserve them as they were forever.

She heard shouting and looked out into the hallway. The seasoned teachers waited for the shouting to reach a higher decibel.

Jon-Isak was bright red, screaming. "Your drunk fat dad! He snowmobiles drunk!"

He dashed off, leaving behind an equally bright red boy, Liam, tears welling up in his eyes.

"He's always so mean," Liam managed to sputter between clenched teeth.

Elsa put an arm around his shoulders. She was well aware that the shouting came from both sides. The principal's clacking heels vanished down the hall; it almost sounded like she was running.

It wasn't always like this; it came in waves, according to the teachers who were here every day. But it was always around this time of year when the conflicts became more apparent, when the circular made dads pound their fists on the table.

And they forgot about the children. The ones on the precipice of a new life. Yes, that was how Elsa thought of it, a precipice they must choose to fly over or fall. She well knew that big, boorish Daniel had a tough time at school and wouldn't continue his education past the obligatory nine grades. And then what could you do, sixteen years old and facing an uncertain future?

Or the teenagers who were hesitant to choose the reindeer because they didn't want to be the last generation in the reindeer forest, when everything went to hell once and for all. Being forced to choose something other than your family's inheritance, out of fear.

Elsa sighed and handed the crying Liam over to a teacher. She continued down the hall, opened bathroom doors, and peered into the rec room where the Ping-Pong table was. As she passed the row of windows that faced the parking lot, she was startled to see someone moving among the cars. It was Jon-Isak. He came running, bounding up the stairs two at a time, and was in the building. She let him go. She gazed out at the cars; she didn't want to go look, but did anyway.

Indeed, a fresh scratch, longer and deeper this time, all the way across the passenger door. She ran her finger along the white groove.

CHAPTER SIXTY-FOUR

Guhttaloginjeallje

They had to move the male reindeer and the yearling calves away from the pregnant cows. It was still over a month before calving time, in Miessemánnu—May—but it was time to separate them now. Males and yearlings could kick newborn calves to death.

Elsa closed her eyes, and the sound of the reindeer's clicking tendons filled her with memories from a time when she was still unaware. Back when she didn't notice her parents' anxiety and when Áddjá still had the strength to come to the forest.

She found her way back to the feeling of surrender, of being part of something greater than herself. How their lives were governed by the animals' lives, but in a good way. When everything was a scent or a sense of belonging that filled her stomach with butterflies.

Everything changed once she found Nástegallu dead, when the grown-ups could no longer shield her from brutal reality, when she learned to see that their smiles weren't genuine. The silence between Enná and Isa started gradually, creeping in like an autumn fog and settling over them both like a blanket, and only they knew what lay beneath it. And Mom's crying, which Elsa never dared to ask about, but only adapted to. The more Mom cried, the quieter Dad got. She couldn't remember ever having seen them touch each other, embrace each other. Never did Dad go after her when she was sad. Mom didn't cry nearly as often when he was away with the reindeer for long periods, and Elsa wanted to tell him when he came home, just in case he had been worried about her. But she was afraid it would come out wrong.

Elsa sighed, annoyed with herself for always letting her mind wander toward dark thoughts. She looked up at the sky, where tufts of clouds sailed by and the sun was warm. Virggo the dog lived up to her lively name and was darting around her, begging for attention, rubbing her warm, black fur against Elsa's legs. This was their best boazobeana ever. She was still eager to work after moving the herd, still had plenty of bounce left in her body. She asked for a task and wouldn't be pacified by repeated pats down her head and neck.

The forest road was muddy; the deep puddles had sent gray splatters up the sides of the vehicles. Elsa hopped over the worst of the puddles as she went to fetch the lasso. She was the only woman there today, and hard work awaited. The male reindeer weighed up to 220 pounds by now. Her sights were set on the calves, and that was probably what folks expected of her as well.

Several of the cousins had brought along their kids, who were hanging on the fence and pointing in excitement at yearlings they recognized as their own. They wanted in, and were allowed in too. Fed reindeer weren't as skittish and would let the little ones come close. The smaller kids toddled after their older siblings or cousins, who had done this many times before. The littlest ones weren't afraid, sharp antlers notwithstanding; they petted whatever they could reach. Two reindeer reared up and clashed their hooves. Mattias called out, and they calmed down. The children didn't let themselves be frightened by the showdown. They backed up a ways, but as soon as it was over they approached again, feeling bold.

"Is it time?" Elsa called.

Mattias nodded.

The kids watched as they began the separation. No one could be in the way in a corral, as the familiar saying went. Even so, some managed. The ones who regretted not taking their origins seriously and wanted to join in now, to strut around the corral and pretend to know what needed doing. They seldom knew, but it made for good shots on Insta. To keep them from traipsing around with the reindeer, the experienced herders let them stand at the openings to the gates where the males and the calves were set free one by one. But Elsa didn't feel derision for these folks; she never had. She imagined there must be some grief there. Maybe it hadn't been their choice to go a different direction; there were so many choices that no one had made out of free will. But she also didn't want them to come here and pretend; no, they should show a little humility when they made a guest appearance during an activity whose importance they didn't understand.

"Look, it survived," she said to Mattias, pointing at a yearling, a čearpmat, they'd been worried about.

"Oh, nice. Looking good this year."

It was almost time to begin. The atmosphere was easy; there was no tension or stress. Elsa wound the lasso in her hand.

"So you came instead of Nils Johan," said Olle.

"He's on his way too."

The feeling of taking up too much space overcame her. He didn't sound unpleasant, he didn't look surly, but his displeasure was still evident in the way he moved. He tilted his head back and wouldn't look her in the eye when he spoke. The fact that she wanted to be there wasn't the point.

She turned her back on him and approached Dad's cousins, joked with them, and sure enough a mustache or two twitched. She could have a dirty mouth when the occasion called for it. But she wasn't about to chase their laughter.

"See that? She's thrown her calf."

Elsa pointed again and Mattias went to get a closer look. The placenta hung out, striking the cow's hind legs, red and slimy.

One of the cousins' kids, Elle-Karin, a freckled little towhead, came up to Elsa and was gazing curiously at the cow. "Didn't it want its calf?"

"Something might have frightened it. The younger cows especially can throw their calves if they get scared."

Elsa stopped herself before she said that the cow might not be made for birthing calves, in which case slaughter awaited her. It struck her that she was acting like her parents and protecting the child. But the fact was, nature had its own way of solving problems.

"She'll have another calf next year," Elle-Karin said confidently.

Elsa set her eye on a nice yearling. She threw the lasso and caught it. Pulling slowly, methodically, doing her best to keep the calf's discomfort to a minimum. It couldn't have weighed more than sixty-five pounds, but it resisted, didn't understand what was happening. And it wasn't ready to leave its mother. Some hung on longer than necessary. But new calves would take their place.

She put her legs into it as she hauled the calf to the opening, where the gate-opener gave her a hand and the calf bounded out to freedom.

"Can't you work the gate instead?" Olle asked in passing. "It's already too crowded."

She pretended not to hear him and walked purposefully back among the reindeer, lasso at the ready. She picked out one of the reindeer that looked to weigh 120 or 130 pounds. She threw the rope and lassoed it, almost pulling her shoulder out of joint. She planted her heels but slipped on a patch of snow the sun hadn't reached yet. This was easier done on bare ground. The reindeer leapt sideways and tossed its head, trying to get loose. She pulled, but the reindeer pulled harder. Then Mattias was there, and they pulled together. He was smiling and shaking his head at her. She didn't want his help, but she supposed falling on her face would have been worse.

"You always have to play badass," he said as they released the reindeer.

"I learned from the best."

"If you mean me, then you're far from done learning."

They exchanged grins. Elsa wanted so much more. She wanted to talk about Jon-Isak. About her fear of Robert. But she didn't dare.

PART III

GIÐÐAGEASSI

SPRING–SUMMER 2019

CHAPTER SIXTY-FIVE

Guhttalogivihtta

Gidda became Giddageassi, spring became spring-summer. In past years, the river would have been creaking with ice floes that had broken free from the banks, but ice-out wasn't the same anymore. The ice gave up listlessly, with no vigor. And now the river was open and the birches had tentatively leafed out. If they were lucky, the mosquitos would hold off until Midsummer.

Elsa cut down the tired blue, green, yellow, and red balloons that were reminders of an end-of-term ceremony that had been far too chilly this year. The kids had been set free, and they no longer had to take sides in conflicts that had begun at a time that no one could quite recall. The ninth-graders had the whole summer to get used to the idea of moving away to attend high school in town. Some wouldn't be able to handle it and would stay home in the village or return after a month or two, maybe try again next year, or not.

Her black, knee-length skirt flapped around her legs, which were covered in goose bumps thanks to the cold wind. There was still no scent of summer in the air.

The end of May had been horrid as usual—it was too late in the year to go snowmobiling, the water in the river was too high for fishing, and just as all of Sweden appeared to be in bloom the snow paid another visit. They'd watched the winter snow melt and the hopeful blades of grass stretching skyward. The mercury unexpectedly climbed above eighteen degrees Celsius for a few days, only to dip back down to a few measly degrees above freezing. Now it was around fifteen degrees, but the icy winds from the north kept them all inside.

But Miessemánnu was also their best month, because it was calving time. It was the start of the reindeer herder's year. Everything started afresh in May, and with the calves came the hope of a good year. Elsa always got goose bumps when she watched the calves being born, saw how they lay on the ground for a moment, bewildered, but still—those tiny creatures scrambled up so quickly on gangly legs and learned to recognize their mama's ruovgat.

Elsa looked out at the parking lot; hers was the only car there. When the principal had called to ask if she would help clean up after the ceremony, she'd hesitated. But now she felt safe in the car, and she could lock herself inside the school. Still, she had to look around before locking the door behind her. Her family knew she didn't go out unless it was necessary, and preferably not on her own. It made her angry that he had that much control over her. Sometimes she drove to town just to feel a sense of freedom. Town was the only place she could be another Elsa. She would call up her high school friends and grab a coffee with them. She never told them about Robert. It struck her that maybe that was what Lasse had been chasing—the space between, where he could be someone else.

She poked holes in the balloons, which slowly deflated. She walked around the teachers' lounge, watering wilted flowers. She took a few forgotten mugs from the dishwasher and tied up the garbage bag. She couldn't shake her memories of Lasse. His trips to Mediterranean beaches. The sandcastles he claimed to have built. She smiled, but her chest was heavy. It didn't help that it had been a different Lasse, the one who built sandcastles. And in the end, none of it was enough.

She wandered the hallways and stopped just outside the lunchroom, where a mural had been painted on the concrete wall. It depicted reindeer, ptarmigans, and mountains, but in the bottom corner there was a kiwi bird. Lasse had painted it late one afternoon after his classmates had gone home. After it was graffitied a number of times, the art teacher had come up with the idea of letting the ninth-grade students paint it for real, and almost all of them had taken turns in groups, arguing about motifs, but agreeing in the end. Elsa knew all of this—one day when she was mute with grief after Lasse's death, the art teacher had brought her to see the mural and pointed out the kiwi.

"Guess who painted that lovely bird?"

Now, once again, Elsa knelt down and patted the cold wall. That little brown bird, incapable of flight.

SHE PUT HER BLINKER on in good time before turning off into the yard. The sun gleamed off the new kitchen window, and a fence had been erected around the house. Hammers had echoed for days, and afterwards it felt all wrong. It was as if they'd drawn a circle around themselves, showing everyone where fear lived.

The shock had stayed with her long after Robert's attack, but somehow life still went on. Officer Ljungblad had been persistent, tracking down witnesses and paying visits to Robert. Never had the villagers seen the patrol car as often as they had this past spring. But Ljungblad never turned off at Elsa's place, because he never had any words of hope. When he finally did call, he told her it was impossible to prove anything when it was her word against his.

"You shouldn't have hung up when you called the emergency line. If we'd been able to record his voice, we might have had enough for unlawful intimidation."

And that was how it became her fault.

She locked the door behind her. The floor creaked under her as she walked through every room. The kitchen was warm from Mom's gáhkku baking, but Elsa would never crack the windows to air it out if she was home alone. Too often she found herself standing at a window to see who was driving by. The sound of a four-wheeler down by the lake would make her stomach seize up.

Minna answered on the second ring. Elsa's body relaxed.

"Are you ready for the calf marking?" She tried to sound cheerful.

"I'm already packed."

The silence that followed lasted too long.

"How are you doing?" Minna sounded worried.

At first, Elsa had lived life as usual, out of habit but also maybe denial.

But then she had seen him. Outside the gas station, his cap pulled low and a wolfish grin on his lips. Her body had been reminded of the terror in the root cellar. Suddenly, there was no air and her heart pounded in her ears. She didn't complete her turn into the gas station; instead she braked hard and shifted into the wrong gear, the engine howling before she sped off, the gravel on the shoulder crunching under the tires. She ended up calling Minna. And Minna was the one she kept calling, each time her body relived the panic.

"I'm always looking over my shoulder for him."

"I think he's scared; he's the one who's hiding out. You're living your life like normal."

"Not quite like normal."

In her nightmares, she saw his smile. The hours of sleep were fewer and farther between. Her world was shrinking.

"He doesn't know that. You have to keep your head up. Assholes like him are looking for weakness. You can never give him the satisfaction."

"I'm glad you'll be here soon."

After they hung up, she checked the front door again, tugged at it three times to make sure it was locked. At first she had naïvely hoped that the police would be successful. Then came the inexplicable shame. Of not being believed. Of not being worth more. And her equally shame-filled father, who couldn't protect his family, was so full of a despair he could never allow anyone to see that he'd built a fence around the house. She had watched him hammer with a furious energy, paint with a spattering brush. The grass would be speckled white for a long time.

And Giđđa became Giđđageassi.

CHAPTER SIXTY-SIX

Guhttalogiguhtta

The bang echoed dully across the mountainside. Every five minutes, the propane cannon sounded to keep predators away from the newborn calves.

Elsa was sitting beside Anna-Stina and Minna at the kitchen table in Per-Jonas's cabin. This year, for the first time, her reindeer collective would be marking the calves in the winter grazing lands before the herd was let back up to the mountains.

The bangs scared off both eagles and foxes. The fox was wily; it knew how to frighten especially the young cows. It would lift its red tail and shriek, then nab the calf.

"Hopefully marking down here will save more calves from the predators," Elsa said, looking at Minna.

She still hadn't gotten used to her shaved head. Minna had laughed at her wide eyes when they met at the bus stop.

"It's just hair," she'd said.

Minna looked through the binoculars. "Isn't it expensive to feed them?"

"Better to feed than to find reindeer with their eyes plucked out by ravens, or with bloody, torn bellies from the wolverines, or the tiny pile a bear leaves behind. The worst is when you find them half-dead and you know they might have been lying there injured and in pain for days."

"Shit."

"When I was eleven, we lost sixty reindeer in three days. There was a storm, and no one could make it out to them. The reindeer lie there in the snow, struggling, easy prey for wolverines. When the storm died down, Dad found bodies everywhere."

When he had come home, he could barely speak. At first. Eventually he was overcome with rage, and in his fury, he had ranted about selling the land and quitting. His anger settled over all of them; they cowered in silence. Elsa had cried because she knew no other life than this one. She didn't want anything different.

"What a horrible sight that must have been," Minna said, putting down the binoculars.

"Yeah, and if it's not predators it's those assholes shooting our reindeer," said Anna-Stina. "By the way, Elsa, did you hear that Robert Isaksson got committed for his drinking?"

Instantly her stomach was in knots. He hadn't been seen for quite some time. It was general knowledge, in the village, that he drank.

"Are you sure?"

Anna-Stina shrugged. "Well, he wouldn't come up here, anyway. We'd see him long before he saw us."

Minna moved to the sofa, squeezing Elsa's shoulder gently when she walked by her.

This was the best time of year for the reindeer collective. She wouldn't let him rob her of that feeling. When her heart wanted to flutter, she reminded herself of the security of family, that her whole sohka was gathered now.

Minna lay stretched out on the sofa, wiggling her toes, apparently deeply absorbed in her phone. She wasn't as boisterous as usual; she seemed more thoughtful and observant.

Anna-Stina had a growing bump under her shirt, and Elsa had seen Minna gazing at her for long stretches. *Why, look at that, Anna-Stina was going to be a mother.* She frequently stroked the little rise.

"Remember when the old guys said riding snowmobiles might hurt our ovaries, that we shouldn't become herders because it was dangerous? We wouldn't have any babies." Anna-Stina made a face and nudged Elsa with her shoulder.

"Just one of the many idiotic things they said," Elsa muttered.

"But look here, I'm proof that you can absolutely ride a snowmobile and still get pregnant."

Anna-Stina's hips had swelled, and her chin had grown soft and round. The cabin was nice and tidy, and she moved around it with a different sort of calm energy than the last time Elsa had been here.

"Is Hanna the one who comes up here to clean?" she asked jokingly.

A shadow passed over Anna-Stina's face and Elsa regretted her words. Hanna had nothing to say about her expected grandchild and she never rested a hand on her daughter's belly. But Elsa had noticed Anna-Stina's longing, how she approached Hanna, looking for her touch.

"I do it all myself," Anna-Stina said curtly.

Elsa had to smooth things over. "But, the house! It's so great—soon you'll get to start building."

Anna-Stina lit up. "Yes, in the spring. We got our hands on a lot near the river, with a fantastic view," she said in Minna's direction.

There was a sour taste in Elsa's mouth. Not just anyone could get hold of such a lot, but Per-Jonas's family could.

"Oh, a house," Minna said slowly.

Anna-Stina didn't perceive her tone the same way Elsa did. Surely Minna thought Anna-Stina was too young, that at twenty-two she was settling down too soon.

"Per-Jonas says I get to make all the decisions—wallpaper, cupboards, flooring, furniture, everything. The plus side of having a man who doesn't care about décor is that I get to do exactly what I want." She gestured around the room, beaming.

Minna nodded and gave a kind smile.

Elsa, too, sometimes thought Anna-Stina was too young, but who was she to judge anyone, living as she still did in her childhood bedroom? She'd gotten nowhere.

"How about you, do you work?" Anna-Stina asked.

"I'm moving to Umeå soon to study law."

"She's going to save us all, make sure Robert goes to prison and that online hate crimes will result in strict punishment," said Elsa.

"Wow! Good luck with that." Anna-Stina looked impressed. "And Elsa will still be in the forest with the men. I don't know how you manage; they're so bullheaded."

"I don't give a single fuck. I'm there for me, not for them."

"As long as you don't turn into a bachelor like that brother of yours." She burst into laughter. "No, not a bachelor. A spinster!"

"Lay off."

Elsa rolled her eyes and Anna-Stina turned to Minna.

"Has Elsa mentioned Niko, who's interested in her? He's been after her for ages." She gave Elsa a sly look. "Just so you know, he's not going to wait forever."

"Oh my God, tell him to move on. Today."

Minna threw her head back and laughed. Elsa missed her long hair, but she also wanted to reach out and feel those short bristles.

The sputtering sound of a dirt bike approached the cabin. Anna-Stina opened the door and stood with her legs planted wide, her hands on her hips. The mosquitos got in. They were tangled in Elsa's hair, and biting her hands when she tried to wave them off. Rather than sit up, Minna appeared to be making herself even more comfortable.

Per-Jonas came in, making a spectacle of himself in the hall, calling and whistling, then closing the door behind him. He took Anna-Stina by the back of the neck and kissed her on the lips, then downed a big glass of water before he headed for the coffeemaker and filled a big mug.

"It's looking good," he said.

Like all of them, except Minna, his cheeks were tanned dark and he had white circles around his eyes from his sunglasses. His stubble was a shadow over his chin. He sat down at the table.

"Niko's here," he said meaningfully.

Elsa sighed. Of course he was. Everyone was here. Minna clucked in irritation and Per-Jonas shot her a look, then leaned back in his chair.

Anna-Stina took out milk, butter, cheese, and homemade bread that Elsa recognized as Hanna's.

Minna got up and took a seat across from Anna-Stina, who held up her palms with a smile, inviting everyone to partake with a "Help yourselves."

"It's way too warm now, so we'll wait until later tonight, maybe until midnight, before we start," Per-Jonas said in Minna's direction, as if she needed to be taught. "Nights are best."

"Especially now, perfectly clear, sun all night long," Anna-Stina added.

Minna smiled at her. "I used to go with my grandfather to the calf marking, and he said I didn't have to go to sleep if I didn't want to. I was allowed to stay up around the clock if I could handle it. And I could."

"Which family are you from again?"

Anna-Stina asked like the old men in the corrals, the ones who wanted to know your family connections before they invited you in, Elsa thought.

"We don't have reindeer, if that's what you mean. We came along to help out anyway."

Anna-Stina blushed and hurriedly shook her head. "I just meant, maybe we're family, that's all."

"I guess you'll have to check in that famous family book."

"I will." She burst out in another short peal of laughter. "Per-Jonas and I were very nervous paging through that book when we first met. It could easily have turned out we were too closely related."

Per-Jonas bent over and pressed his lips to her temple.

"So you are related?" Minna asked in an innocent tone, and Elsa had to bite the inside of her cheek to keep from chuckling.

"Oh, we're so many times removed that it's fine. It has to be at least six, right, Elsa?"

They giggled as they had when they were little, building snow forts.

"Maybe seven, just to be on the safe side."

CHAPTER SIXTY-SEVEN

Guhttalogičieža

The smell of fresh blood on her fingers. The calf trembling under her. Elsa stroked its soft fur and wiped a drop of blood from its ear, where she had just made her mark. She let the little one go and it staggered off, found its voice, and called out for its mother. They would soon find each other again. The ground rumbled as the herd resumed their counterclockwise run. Elsa's eyes followed them as she wiped the knife on the ground.

It was just after midnight and the sun shone above them. Against the light she could see black clouds of mosquitos. The temperature had dropped a few degrees, but not as much as they'd hoped. It was warm and there were swarms of mosquitos and gnats. Elsa rubbed another layer of insect repellant around her wrists and neck, and dabbed a little on her wide red headband.

Minna stood nearby as Elsa caught the calves and marked them. She got down on her knees, sat quietly, and studied Elsa's deft hands. Listened as she whispered to them, just before she set them free.

"I don't own you, you belong to yourself. You are only mine on loan."

The reindeer were biekka oapmi, belonging to the wind. Áddjá had explained this to her carefully when she was little. You must never brag about your reindeer herd, and you must be aware that your good fortune with them could vanish at any moment. You must take nothing for granted; a reindeer herd was never a constant.

Elsa couldn't resist any longer. She let her hand brush Minna's hair, and it reminded her of the time Mattias shaved his head when he was a teenager.

"You should wear a hat, you're getting eaten up," she said, brushing away the mosquitos.

Minna was bleeding behind one ear from gnat bites. The blood trickled down her neck but didn't get far before it stopped and dried.

"Look at Jon-Isak," Elsa said, pointing.

He was focused; he grabbed a calf and didn't need any adults to show him how to do anything, even though Ante hovered nearby. He gently laid the calf down, took out his knife, and made the cuts. When he stood up, he puffed out his chest, planted his feet wide, and spit over one shoulder.

"I've been talking to Johannes," said Minna. "The Jokkmokk Market, remember? Somehow he came home with me then disappeared in the middle of the night."

"Yeah, I remember." Elsa smiled. "So, what, is there something going on between you?"

"Maybe. Or maybe not."

"Well, what does he say?"

"Yeah, what do macho guys say? Not much." She snorted and laughed at the same time. "He mostly wondered why I shaved my head."

"Oh, he's such an idiot."

"Is he?"

"He's basically Per-Jonas."

"Ouch."

Elsa laughed. "Nah, I guess he's better than that."

"I really think he is. He says he might want to move, do something else."

"Yeah, people talk about him. He doesn't join in. His mom would never admit it, but there are rumors he doesn't want to work with reindeer anymore."

Minna looked at her closely. "Well, obviously he should be able to choose what he wants to do."

Elsa swatted at the mosquitos and weighed her words carefully. "It's not that simple. Especially not since his little brother seems to want something else too. You know, it would be a disaster for their family."

"Then I feel sorry for him, if he's forced to stay."

Her voice was firm, and Elsa wanted to end the discussion.

"Come on, we have to go this way. One of my calves." She pointed and strode off.

"It's kind of like an honor culture, not being able to choose for yourself," Minna persisted.

Elsa stopped short and scratched her temple, under the headband, in irritation.

"Okay, you probably shouldn't say that stuff here. Or anywhere. You can't compare us to . . ." She stared at her. "You know, all the backwards stuff about an honor culture."

"Okay, okay, sorry." Minna raised her palms.

Elsa looked out at the herd but kept losing focus. She had *just* seen her calf. Mattias called from the other side, and pointed, and she gave him a thumbs-up. The herd calmed down, and she was able to easily catch the calf with her stávrá, its loop closing around a hind leg. The calf fought it, buckling and pulling back, but she soon had it down on the ground. This time her hand trembled a little as she made the cuts. Minna had stopped a few yards away with her arms crossed and her gaze in a totally different direction. She leapt aside as Mattias tugged at a calf. She laughed out loud and apologized.

As Elsa released her calf and headed for the fire to get some coffee, Minna came up beside her.

"Look, I can be kind of argumentative, I'm sorry. I really don't mean anything by it."

Elsa had a tendency to hold grudges, and found it hard to let go even when someone apologized. Minna linked arms with her.

"It's just frustrating," Elsa said. "This is all I want, but I'll probably never get voting rights in the reindeer collective."

Minna took a breath, but Elsa quickly put a hand over her mouth.

"No, don't say anything. Let's just drop it."

By the fire, she took her mug from her belt and filled it with steaming hot coffee.

"It's torture, not being able to say what I think," Minna said, but there was a smile playing at her lips.

Elsa burned the tip of her tongue and swore. The smoke from the fire forced her to hold her breath. The mug warmed her fingers. Mattias was in the center of the herd, relaxed, strong, standing straight as a pine, alternately laughing and cursing. This was how she wanted to see him, and herself. She would never doubt, like Johannes, never abandon this life. But Mattias? When she looked at him now, he was far from the big brother breaking down in the root cellar. Minna's talk had awakened an old worry, and she didn't like it.

CHAPTER SIXTY-EIGHT

Guhttalogigávcci

Áhkku came to the calf marking. She looked tiny in the front seat next to Dad, and she wasn't wearing a seatbelt. When the car door opened, her spindly little legs were the first thing they saw. And there she stood. The wind took hold of long strands of hair that had come loose from her braid; they whirled up and brushed her face. The skin was drawn tight over her cheekbones and her eyes had sunk deeper into her face. She had lost another few pounds.

Elsa took her by the arm and together they walked toward the sound of reindeer. Áhkku pricked up her ears, opened her eyes wide, and tugged at Elsa to move faster.

"This isn't where we usually are," she said.

"No, we're taking them to the mountains later."

Áhkku looked at the reindeer and stopped. Her nostrils flared as she took deep breaths.

"It's too warm."

"I know, way too warm."

She was wearing the gákti she hadn't worn since Áddjá's funeral. Never again, she'd said after. It was marked by her sorrow.

"I have to make sure they get their coffee." She hurried toward the fire. Reminded of the jobs that had once been hers. "But I don't think I have the strength to pull reindeer today."

"No, you probably shouldn't." Elsa rubbed Áhkku's back and felt her arch it, sticking out her chest.

Áhkku gazed with concern at Hanna, who was standing by the fire with the thermos in her hand.

"Give me that," Áhkku said.

Hanna handed over the thermos, looking pleased.

"It's so nice to see you here."

Áhkku eyed the thermos, weighing its heft as if to gauge how much coffee was left inside. She looked around for a place to sit that wasn't in the smoke. She let go of Elsa and sat down. Dissatisfied, she got up, gazed out across the corral, and shook her head.

"It's too warm. We should be in the mountains."

Elsa held out her mug, and Áhkku, with a stern expression, filled it exactly halfway.

"Did Isa get coffee? Otherwise we need to make more. This isn't enough."

"He's right over there," Elsa said, pointing.

Áhkku hugged the thermos to her chest.

"Not him. My Isa."

Hanna glanced at Elsa and gave a quick shake of her head, then took a few steps away to light a cigarette.

"Look at what we baked—gáhkku."

Elsa held out the plastic tub, which was full of flat white rounds of bread.

"Did I bake those?"

"No. Or, yeah. Yes, you did."

The old woman nodded and took a piece. She set the thermos down and brought the bread to her nose. The scent made her smile, and her wrinkled face came to life.

Elsa had shaved a sizable pat of butter onto the knife and gave it to Áhkku. They sat beside each other, and Áhkku got butter in her long, loose strands of hair as she took a big bite of the gáhkku.

"Can I stay this time?"

Elsa didn't have a chance to answer before Áhkku caught sight of Minna, who was walking toward the fire.

"Whose boy is he? Or what sort of ugly girl is that?"

"That's my friend Minna. I'm sure you know who her dad is; he's a duojár."

When Elsa said his name, Áhkku screwed up her eyes.

"Right, right, the one who talked too much."

"What do you mean?"

"You don't always have to say what you know." She grabbed Elsa's upper arm. "That goes for you too. You don't want to lose the power."

Hanna's mouth became a line; she tossed her head, ground the cigarette out with her boot, and walked off.

"Did you hear me?"

Áhkku pinched her again; it hurt. Elsa nodded. The power. It was difficult to mention it without being afraid of saying too much. She still hadn't worked up the nerve to consider what people claimed Áddjá had passed on to her—the power to heal and stanch blood. That she was a gunsttar. In the villages you knew who to call, who could heal. Talk went around about Elsa, among the relations, but she resisted. Not yet, she always thought, not yet.

She dropped the thought, as she had done so many times before, when Minna walked up to them, legs planted wide, and introduced herself to Áhkku with a warm smile.

"Girls aren't supposed to look like that," Áhkku said.

Minna raised her eyebrows, but the smile didn't fade from her eyes. "Sure, girls these days can, you know."

"Well, I suppose it could be practical. No need to wash your hair."

Áhkku let out a hoarse laugh, which made them laugh right along with her.

"Well, where's your mug? I have the coffee."

Minna held out a green plastic mug and Áhkku filled it less than halfway this time.

"The rest is for Elsa's isa, my boy."

Elsa clasped her hands together to keep from giving in to the urge to put her arm around Áhkku and feel her back bend away from her.

Mom waved from a distance and was making her way toward them.

"It's her, that rivgu," said Áhkku. She looked displeased. "She thinks she can handle this life, but she's wrong. Nils Johan ought to pick someone better."

"But Áhkku, they fell in love, and there's no stopping love."

The old woman's eyes flitted this way and that, as if they were seeking a stable resting point from her drifting mind.

"Are they married already?"

"Who's getting married?" Mom asked, holding out her mug.

Elsa shook her head at her, raised her hands, wanted her to back off and not ask any more questions. Minna was staring down at the fire, moving the logs with a stick.

"A rivgu can't understand," Áhkku said, not relinquishing the thermos.

Mom's hand lowered slowly.

"Don't listen to her," Elsa mumbled.

The fire crackled between them, the smoke shifting directions, and they took turns holding their breath and turning their faces away. The heat made their cheeks glow and kept the mosquitos away.

"But this rivgu managed pretty well. Just look at your grandchildren, how clever they are. Elsa is the strongest girl of all."

Her voice was calm and collected. Mom sat down and put out her mug again, but Áhkku hid the thermos behind her back.

"Elsa, grab me a Coke instead."

Elsa rummaged through a bin, tossing cinnamon rolls and can openers aside until she found the plastic bottle.

Suddenly Áhkku began to sing in a loud, clear voice. A Sámi psalm. Hanna was standing quite far away, but she turned around to listen and deflated, looked as if she might fall over.

"We sang that at Lasse's funeral," Mom whispered.

Áhkku's gaze was far away and her voice faded. She took a huge bite of gáhkku and handed the thermos to Elsa.

"I need to rest now, so you take over. Give some to your enná. She can't drink only soda."

She beamed at Marika as if no hurtful words had been said. And Mom smiled, as she'd done a thousand times before.

CHAPTER SIXTY-NINE

Guhttalogiovcci

In late August, when the forest glowed red and gold, she could breathe again. Elsa loved autumn-summer—čakčageassi—most of all. The summer had been way too hot and the forest fires that had ravaged their area had burned away all the reindeer lichen. Still, they hadn't been hit as hard as the south Sámi lands, where thousands of acres of forest had burned. It would take twenty or thirty years before the lichen grew back. If it ever did.

The lawn needed mowing and the blades of grass brushed Elsa's nose each time she did a push-up. She groaned but forced herself to keep going. The muscles between her shoulder blades were burning and her arms were starting to shake. She landed on her belly and panted loudly.

Mom's green skirt fluttered by. "You should come to aerobics with me. We're starting back up on Tuesday."

"I don't think you old ladies can quite match my tempo."

Mom laughed at her. The shed door opened. The gravel crunched as she walked back.

"Are you sure about that? You're wrecked."

Elsa rolled onto her back, lifted her legs, and began to do sit-ups. The sky above her was gray.

On the whole, the family had had a good summer. Almost all the calves had survived, and the herd had been moved to a safer spot in the mountains. But in a few months, they would come back down to their winter grazing area.

With čakča, autumn, would come the clear air, but also the memories that had been repressed. Elsa doubled her efforts, didn't want to think, couldn't slip back into the fear of last spring. But as the midnight sun left them and the evenings grew darker, worry crept in.

They filled up the freezers. Whitefish, char, lingonberries, blueberries, but hardly any cloudberries. This year too the cloudberry blossoms had been hit by some unusually cold and frosty nights. Mom was making space for the moose steaks. She lugged around some overfilled bags of bread that would be stored in the house instead.

"So what's the plan? Are you going on the moose hunt?"

"Only on the weekends. I'm going to sub at school as often as I can."

Sweat trickled down her temples as Elsa drank from her water bottle.

"There's a rumor that Robert Isaksson has been banned from the hunting party this year," Mom yelled just before she disappeared inside.

Elsa waited for her to come back out.

"He's back? I thought he was committed."

"Oh, I don't know, there's always so much talk. But I heard someone called the police when they saw him swerving on the road a week or so ago."

Elsa rolled her eyes. Because they were so far away, people could drive drunk around the villages. The police never made it in time. And as long as the villagers had each other's back and raised the alarm if they saw a patrol car, no one would get caught. So they drove drunk, without licenses, in unregistered vehicles.

She stretched her upper arm and felt a pleasant pull. She ought to let herself feel relieved to know that he wouldn't be out hunting moose. But a frustrated man was an unpredictable man.

Her phone lay next to her in the grass. She couldn't show Mom. She'd hardly come back from the mountains before she received a text consisting of just two words: *Lapp cunt.* She would have to start looking over her shoulder again.

"Jon-Isak is refusing to go to school. Did you hear?"

Mom was carrying sheets to hang on the clothesline. Elsa got up, brushed away the grass, and followed her.

"What happened?" she asked, picking up a sheet.

"Weren't you working yesterday? Someone beat him up so badly that he had to go to town and get two stitches in his forehead."

Elsa's grip on the white sheet tightened, and she tossed it over the clothesline and secured it with two wooden clothespins.

"Who beat him up?"

"Someone from the village school, I suppose."

"Shit!"

"It's been reported to the police, Hanna said. I ran into her at the store."

"How is he?"

"Not so good. He's going to quit school and be with his dad full-time, he says. Poor kid."

"I have to talk to them."

Mom tossed the last sheet onto the line and spun the clothesline, inspecting their work.

"It's starting again. I don't know how I'm going to make it through another winter." There, she'd said it. Elsa didn't dare look up.

Mom picked up the empty basket and made her way toward the house. Her old, worn brown clogs clattered against the stone pavers that would soon be overgrown with grass.

"We'll do what we've always done: we'll manage," she said, her voice tense. "All we can do is file police reports and hope they'll get caught eventually."

Elsa sank onto the grass and let the sheets brush her face. She pressed the cold, wet fabric over her eyes, squeezing them shut as hard as she could, picturing Jon-Isak, the laughter in his eyes at calf-marking.

She stood up and crossed the yard, walking to the road and up the rise. The house looked dark and silent. It was in need of a fresh coat of paint, and the yard was a jumble of rakes, buckets of water, a broken shovel, and a snowmobile that had never made it into the shed. There was sure to be speculation, around the village, of what it looked like inside if the yard was in such poor shape. Elsa was one of the few who knew that the floor was still scrubbed with bleach.

Before Elsa had reached the house, Hanna met her on the steps, her eyes tired and her chin full of tiny red pimples. Her hair was loose, its part messy, and she ran her hands over the strands to smooth it over.

"I just wanted to see how Jon-Isak was doing."

"You know what, Elsa, it's best if you don't come over right now."

Elsa stopped on the gravel path just below the stairs, unsure whether she should back up. She searched for words, but it felt like a knife was stabbing her just beneath her ribs.

"I understand," she lied.

Hanna twisted a dishrag, her knuckles red and chapped. Elsa blushed. Waited.

"Jon-Isak is really upset. So it's for the best."

"With me?"

Hanna walked down a few steps. To get closer, to protect what she was about to say. She spoke in a low voice.

"He's too little to understand. He thinks we adults are making things harder for him, that we make a fuss about the reindeer being killed and then he has a rough time at school."

"He means me."

Hanna's lower lip trembled, but then she set her jaw and clenched her teeth.

"You've reported it to the police, right? You have to," said Elsa.

Hanna nodded but kept twisting the dishrag, harder and harder.

"Can you tell him," Elsa cleared her throat, "that I'm sorry. That I won't make a fuss anymore. I just wanted to make things better."

Hanna turned around, one hand on the door handle.

"Is he very upset?"

"We'll talk more later."

Hanna slipped inside and closed the door silently behind her.

Elsa lingered, peering in the windows. Looking for his little face.

CHAPTER SEVENTY

Čiežalogi

She had to get out. She had to get away, go to the forest.

She changed quickly, rummaging around the storage area under the seat of the kitchen bench until she found the gray knitted socks that kept her feet from sliding around inside her boots. Mom was going from room to room, pinching dead leaves from the houseplants, wiping down the handles of the fridge and freezer, and sneaking looks her way. She wasn't going to ask, even though she had noticed the angry red under her eyes. But when Elsa took the key to the gun safe, Mom gasped.

"Where are you going with the rifle?" She followed Elsa, watching as she unlocked the safe and took out the gun. "Are you going hunting right now?"

Elsa snorted and went to the front hall. She shoved her feet into her boots, took her cap and pressed it so low on her head that her eyes were almost hidden.

"Elsa . . ."

"I don't feel safe out in the forest. It's just for security."

"Take Mattias instead."

"No. He's not even home."

She slammed the door behind her, but Mom opened it immediately. Her arms were crossed and her shoulders raised as Elsa got into the car.

"Don't be late. We're having an early dinner today."

THE FOREST ROAD WAS bumpy and it scraped the undercarriage of the car. The open, grassy area where the fishermen usually parked their cars was deserted, and she sighed in relief.

It took only seconds for the mosquitos and gnats to find her. One big horsefly was buzzing in tight circles around her. She slapped at it, ducked under branches as she trod down the path. The sound of the river could be heard from a long way off; dry twigs crunched beneath her boots. The anthill was teeming with life. And out on the bog she knew just where to step without sinking. She leapt and balanced with equal amounts of agility. It had been a long time since anyone needed to carry unna oabba. The thought made her throat constrict with tears. Most of the time, it used to be Dad who held her high above dangerous sinkholes, but once Mattias was big enough he let her ride on his back. That is how unna oabba got to know the invisible paths until she was ready to walk them herself. Not once did she make a misstep, and the entire forest was hers.

The rifle thudded against her back. There were bears; one could surely see her now. Sniffed the air, scared but curious. When she was little, Áhkku told her to sing in the forest. You must never sneak up and surprise a bear. Her steps were sure, but when there was a sudden crack in the forest, her song faltered. Just sing louder, said Áhkku.

She was moving fast and breathing even harder; sweat broke out on her back. If it weren't for the rifle, she would have run and shouted until there was no more air left to breathe.

Her body protested, couldn't take any more; panting, she slowed down and bent over with her hands on her knees.

The sound of the rapids drew her in. She should have brought her fishing rod, to find the soothing calm in the repetitive movements: cast and reel in, cast and reel in. The river was always loud enough to quiet her anxious thoughts.

Her breathing was back to normal. And she heard something in the silence. A dog's whine? She stood still, following the tree trunks with her eyes, looking for movement. There it was again, but this time it sounded more like a human whimpering. She took a few cautious steps on the softest spots, then held her breath and looked side to side, trying to locate the sounds. Each place was familiar, trees and paths, boulders and stumps. She noticed the odor of exhaust, stopped, listened. And there it was, twenty or so yards on: an overturned four-wheeler. A leg sticking out from underneath it.

A dog was dashing around and whining; it seemed to have a limp. The wind carried her scent and the dog froze; a growling bark erupted from deep inside its chest.

She lifted the strap over her head and held the gun in one hand as she approached the four-wheeler. The dog kept growling, but she ignored it. She recognized it, though; she knew whose it was.

As she rounded the vehicle, she saw the back of a head and two out-stretched arms; the torso and legs were under the four-wheeler. A cap lay nearby. The man gasped loudly, as if the last of his breath was leaving him.

He had heard her, and he struggled to turn his head, looking at her with bloodshot eyes. It was Robert Isaksson.

She gripped the rifle harder.

"Fucking help me, don't just stand there!" His lips were cracked and dry. "My legs are caught, and you can lift it."

She didn't move, but her thighs and abdominal muscles tensed. Her heart was pounding wildly in her chest.

"At least give me my phone, if you're not going to help."

He nodded to the left and there, half-visible in the moss, was his phone. *Help*, she thought, *he's asking me to help. Him.* Her legs began to tingle, and it spread through her body like bubbles.

She raised her rifle and disengaged the safety. His eyes went wide. She aimed the barrel at his head, from a distance of two yards.

She wanted to ask if he remembered how he had killed Nástegallu. She wanted to remind him how he had threatened her, a child. But her voice wouldn't come.

The elkhound growled louder and pulled back its upper lip, baring its sharp canine teeth. Then she aimed the rifle at the dog.

Robert grabbed at the moss. "Leave her the fuck alone!"

"I wonder if it's theft, if theft is all it is, if I shoot her and take the body," she said quietly. "Do you think a dog is worth more than a reindeer?"

He swore in Meänkieli, spit flying from his lips. "Saatanan perkele. Hel-vetin vittu!"

He shoved off with his hands in an attempt to budge the four-wheeler.

"If I shoot you, it's murder, or at least manslaughter. But I can't take you with me. Her, though . . ."

She closed one eye as she once again aimed the rifle at the dog.

"For fuck's sake. You're fucking nuts. And the minute I get out from here . . ."

He wiggled forward and backward but groaned and dropped his head.

Without thinking, she took a few steps in his direction and pressed the barrel to the back of his head. He started and his breath came in gasps.

"Is this what you do with the reindeer? When you run them over and torture them slowly to death?"

The dog growled and took one limping step her way. She kicked at the air and it shrank back.

She moved the barrel through Robert's hair and pressed it hard against his skull. Suddenly she felt a wave of dizziness and her legs became unsteady. She took a step back and swallowed the sudden nausea, walked around the four-wheeler so he couldn't see her anymore, then leaned one hand against a tree trunk and waited for her head to stop spinning.

She took out her phone, but her hands were shaking so violently that she dropped it. She picked it up and went back to him. Pressed the record button.

"I want you to confess to everything you've done. All the reindeer you've killed. Threatening me. Coming to our house to kill me."

His forehead was glistening with sweat and his skin was pale. He croaked out a laugh.

"You fucking Lapp cunt."

It was a like a slap, a diabolical force that made her take a step backwards to keep from falling. She turned around, her face contracting in tiny twitches around her eyes and mouth. She pictured Nástegallu, walking across bare ground and patches of snow with her long legs. And Lasse. Smiling, no walleye. She headed for the river. Robert called out, but she couldn't hear what he said. By the time she stopped and looked down at the rifle, it was decided. What had been predestined for so long. Her steps back were silent; unna oabba knew exactly where to put her feet.

This was her land.

CHAPTER SEVENTY-ONE

Čiežalogiokta

The waders were draped over the back of the chair. Mattias drank another cup of coffee and the pit of his stomach burned. He ran his hands over his lower back, massaging the muscles there. His tongue prodded his unbrushed teeth. His eyes stung after last night's insomnia.

He found the tackle box in the hall closet. He opened the lid and rooted among the gold-colored salmon lures that he'd had such luck with over the years. Fishing for salmon in the fall wasn't like early summer, when the salmon were moving upstream, jumping along the riverbanks and waving their tail fins in the air. He was still kicking himself over the female that must have weighed fifteen or sixteen pounds, which he'd released in accordance with the laws. You weren't allowed to keep females. His cousins had laughed at him, saying no one was that honest. The fish had given him a run for his money, fighting for its life for almost twenty minutes. Mattias knew when to let out the line and knew when to resist, tire it out. When the salmon finally landed on the sandy bank of the river, he had lifted it up with a simple grip on its tail fins. It was a female.

He would take the fishing rod along today. Do the usual things, seem normal. But he would pack the waders at the bottom of his backpack. He held his hand against their cool, smooth surface. Remembered Áddjá wearing them. In waterways, streams, and by the river. Explaining how to tire out a salmon, pointing out the rocks they rested behind, showing him how to lift them by the tail.

Mattias rolled up the waders and held them tight to his chest, closing his eyes, but he felt silly and opened them again. His movements almost frantic, he shoved them into the backpack and slung it over his shoulder. He stopped in the hall—something that had been gnawing at him all morning. There was no doubt that he'd made up his mind, except about the note.

He'd never written anything about himself; he'd hardly written at all since leaving school. The pen skidded like a slippery fish and his handwriting was horrible, all angular like a child's. Oh well, they were only words. He'd made an attempt, and he had crumpled up the paper, smoothed it out, crumpled it again. First he left the farewell note on the kitchen table, but there was a chance Mom would come into the house. Before it was done. So it was better if they had to search, he thought, putting it under his pillow.

But now that felt wrong. Under his pillow, it wouldn't work. If he'd had a girlfriend who slept by his side every night, she would have looked underneath it. But for his family it would be too intimate and wrong.

He dropped the backpack on the floor, went to the bedroom, and dug one hand underneath the pillow. The coffee can was more his style, but who would look there? He thought of Áddjá, who sipped coffee from a saucer with a sugar cube between his lips. Mattias had started drinking coffee when he was eight. There was a sense of comfort in the smell, and the taste was only a problem the first few times.

An accident, people would say, the waders weren't safe. The family would cling to that explanation. Avoid the shame. And eventually believe it themselves. So he'd thought. He wrote another few lines anyway, but now he had made up his mind—there would be no explanation. He crumpled the paper in his palm, went to the bathroom, and flushed his angular handwriting away.

THE SPUTTERING MOTORBIKE ECHOED noisily across the village. He'd always enjoyed that, especially when he was with Lasse. The sound of their bikes drowning out all other noise, silencing conversations and making heads turn to watch them go.

He was going fast. A truck was the other option, but there weren't any. He didn't see a single car on the highway before taking a right onto the gravel path that ran for a mile or so along the river. Then he took another turn onto the bumpy forest road, and decided to take the motorbike all the way to the river. It was hard to maneuver the fishing rod and the handle-bars, and he nearly tipped over a few times. When he finally parked by the rapids, he sat down for a while. The river's roar could fill your thoughts. The campfire site was waiting for him, the place he had knelt a thousand times to get kindling to take light. Today he didn't have the energy to make a fire, but he had to go over there. His steps were slow; his feet dragging.

Someone had left some birchwood behind. He took off his backpack and sat down on the round stone that had served as a seat by the fire for generations before him. Áhkku usually set out a sit-upon to avoid any is-sues with her "waterworks," as she said. She seldom did any fishing, but she might wander off to look for cloudberries. And now. Now she was unreach-able.

He took out the waders and spread them before him, smoothing them out on the ground.

A crow landed on the small grassy island just beyond the riverbank, its wing-beats heavy, only to take off again almost immediately. That island had drawn him in so many times as a child. It was no bigger than their yard, and it shouldn't have been able to hide any secrets, but still. The grown-ups had always made all sorts of threats if you even mentioned trying to get to the island. There was a dangerous, steep drop near the bank. There were big boulders at the very edge, but just beyond the water was black, and the current was full of fast eddies. Lethal ones. Not even boats would go that way; instead they passed the island on the other side. But the island was only five or six yards away, so close.

Áddjá had said that you could get there if you knew the right rocks, but Áhkku had quickly smacked him on the shoulder and said that it wasn't true.

HE DIDN'T KNOW HOW long he sat there, but when the silence was bro-ken by a barking dog every muscle in his body contracted. He gazed down the river and into the forest. Maybe he'd misheard. There could be fowl hunters nearby. It was no good to be sitting around idly if someone showed up, he thought, searching for some kindling under the pile of wood and finding a few measly bits of birch bark. He stripped thin splinters from the logs and added the bark. He blew on the small flame, added more wood, and watched the fire flare up.

When he heard the shot, he jumped. Usually no one hunted so close to the river. He got up and peered into the forest. There, the sound of something approaching fast. A dog. Its ears flat, limping, terror in its eyes. It was easy to recognize; there was only one elkhound with that distinct shift of color in its fur. It was Robert Isaksson's.

Mattias crouched down and called to her, holding out his hand, fingers curled as if he had something for her. The dog dashed around herself, limping, then plopped down, panting. He went over to her, grabbed her collar, held it more firmly when she growled. There was some blood spatter on her fur. He lifted her enough to drag her to the river. As if it had been planned. But really, he just felt empty as he gave it his all and tossed the dog across the river. She landed with a tumble on the island, whined, and then fell silent.

Mattias fell backwards. What the hell had he done that for? He stared at the dog, regretting his actions. He wasn't the type to hurt animals, especially not dogs.

Robert must have shot a reindeer. Mattias went back to the fire, his shoulder aching like he'd seriously pulled a muscle. The smoke would give him away. He ran down to the riverbank, filled the coffeepot with water, and drenched the fire. It billowed with smoke and he shook his head at himself. He was so stupid sometimes.

The forest was silent. But the dog was standing now, dipping its front paws in the water and letting out a pathetic bark. It wasn't a sound Robert would miss. Mattias's hand went to the knife hanging at his belt.

The dog unleashed a tormented howl that the rush of the river couldn't drown out. Mattias scrambled to collect the coffeepot, black with soot, and the tackle box, and grabbed the fishing rod. He paused—if Robert had in fact shot a reindeer, this might be his chance to catch him red-handed. He dropped everything and took the small rise in three steps, moving quickly in the direction he thought the shot had come from. It was impossible, of course; the forest stretched out for miles in every direction. The howling continued and Robert wouldn't ignore it for much longer. But why had the dog run off? It should have stayed nearby. Something was off. Mattias stopped. Not a sound from anywhere. Robert, with a gun. That was synonymous with risk. He held his breath, the better to listen, but the sound of his own pulse was louder than everything else.

CHAPTER SEVENTY-TWO

Čiežalogiguokte

The shower spray was strong and it stung as it hit her shoulders, but Elsa only increased the pressure until it made her cry. She had to prop herself against the walls of the stall and sob quietly, because Mom might be pressed up against the bathroom door, eavesdropping. She sank to the floor. Steam rose around her. She turned off the water and crouched down again, her arms hugging her knees. The walls of the stall weren't joined perfectly, and there was a cold draft. Goose bumps spread across her skin and soon she was shivering. She managed to reach for the towel that was draped over one wall. She huddled under the soft pink terry cloth and slowly warmed up again.

In the mirror, which she had to wipe off with her hand, her face was glowing red, and the whites of her eyes were just as inflamed. She dropped the towel on the floor and pulled on her underwear.

The phone was in her jeans, on the floor. It was a beat-up old Samsung. She'd brought it with her, shoved it into her pocket and run all the way to the car. She missed all the steps on the bog, and the water splashed up over her boots, leaving spots on her pants.

She left the bathroom in her underwear, holding the jeans far from her body as if they were contaminated.

"Those must need washing."

Mom popped up behind her, reaching out a hand.

"Yeah, but I'm just going to empty the pockets first."

"And where on earth is Mattias? He was going to eat with us today."

Mom was muttering to herself; she didn't really expect an answer. Elsa was already out of earshot and dropped the phone into a dresser drawer.

Had to click it, see if it needed a code. It did, of course. She put it on silent and her fingertips felt sullied, contaminated. The phone smelled distinctly of diesel, and it would permeate the clothes in her dresser. Pretty soon she would have to wash everything.

Her hair sent cold drips down her back, and she took out a white knitted sweater and black jeans from the wardrobe and quickly got dressed.

In the kitchen, she scrubbed her hands for a long time.

"It's going to be below freezing tonight," said Mom, who had already sat down to peel her potatoes. "Now sit, I don't want to eat alone. You look frozen."

Elsa avoided her eyes and helped herself to potatoes, boiled carrots, and a scoop of reindeer hash.

"Below freezing," Mom said again.

"How cold?"

"Might get down to four or five below. It's ridiculous. Might as well snow."

The carrots were so soft she hardly needed to chew them; the potatoes burned her tongue, but the reindeer hash was perfectly salty. She chewed and swallowed, chewed and swallowed.

"I'm glad you came home so quickly." Mom looked at her, trying to make eye contact. "But is something wrong? You're so quiet."

"No, nothing much. I'm just a little tired."

"Did you lock up the rifle?"

"Yup."

She drank her water with audible gulps, managed to eat all her food, and licked her fork to get the last of the gravy. What kind of person was she, eating at a time like this?

"The evenings are getting so dark." Mom twitched the curtain a bit. "Haven't heard from Dad, it's been a few days. But that probably means everything is fine."

Elsa stood up with her plate, rinsed it, and put it in the dishwasher.

"You ate so fast."

"Thanks, it was good."

What kind of person was she, chatting as if nothing had happened?

"I'm going to Anna-Stina's."

"I saw her the other day. Her belly was so nice and round. It could well be twins."

"I'll be late."

"Tell her hi."

Once her outerwear was on, she went back to her room and put on her gloves so she could pick up the clothes and the phone, letting it fall into her coat pocket. Letting it become a weight that struck her hip as she walked.

She started the car, adjusted the rearview mirror, even though it didn't need adjusting, pulled the seat forward one notch, fastened her seatbelt, and put the car in reverse.

What kind of person was she?

She drove to the next village and passed Anna-Stina's apartment. All the windows were dark, and she kept driving.

She turned around at the gas station. On her way back, she let up on the gas when she spotted the gravel road from a distance. A buzz in her coat pocket. A call. For him. No sound, just a vibration against her hip. It stopped. But soon it started again. She turned off at the gravel road and braked hard. She took out the phone and saw two missed calls from an unknown number.

She had to keep going, couldn't stand here with her bright red parking lights on. The road was too narrow to turn around, and she had to drive on a bit. The temperature was just at the freezing point now.

The car drifted to the wrong side of the gravel road as she took out her own phone. She looked up Minna, pressed the green "call" button, but hung up before it started ringing.

The phone began to ring, and she jumped, then found herself staring at the picture of Hanna with a tiny Jon-Isak in her arms. She hadn't seen that picture for a long time; Hanna didn't typically call. Her vision went blurry. Jon-Isak.

She didn't answer and pressed the gas instead.

Internal injuries.

Frozen to death.

Was it a crime to leave him there? Oh, Minna, you would have known, she thought.

She rolled down the window and cold air filled the car. The river was black in the darkness. Maybe she should have thrown his phone in. Let it vanish into the depths.

Saving him meant risking her own life. She hit the brakes again, suddenly. Dialed the number to the police. She might as well leave an anonymous tip.

But what if he was dead? No one needed to know she had been there. He was trapped under a heavy four-wheeler. An accident.

But.

She could have saved his life.

She opened the car door and staggered out. A north wind had picked up and she was cold. Birch leaves rustled across the road.

She pictured his expression again. How life seemed to drain from him when she came back and aimed at his head. And then she turned the rifle away and shot into the sky. And Lasse caught the bullet.

Afterwards she bent down, grabbed his phone, and ran.

Robert didn't raise his face from the ground; he lay with his head turned to the side, his eyes glassy.

Who just left another person like that?

DESPITE THE DARKNESS, SHE could find her way through the forest. She wasn't afraid of bears. Now she was only afraid of herself.

The clouds parted and let the moon peer out. Enough so she could see the four-wheeler from a distance, its metal gleaming in the moonlight. She had taken his phone so he wouldn't be able to call for help, had robbed him of any chance at survival. The dog had taken off like a bat out of hell when she fired. A behavior she'd never seen before. Maybe she'd aimed the gun at the dog after that; it was hard to remember.

She took the last few steps and saw a boot under the four-wheeler. But no legs now. He wasn't there. The four-wheeler looked like it had been moved, she thought, but she wasn't entirely sure. Elsa stared, without blinking. He was gone. It was quiet and she looked all around—had he managed to get himself out? Was he lying hurt nearby? She bent down and thought she could see blood on the ground, by the handlebars. Had he freed himself, or had someone else come by and helped? Was he at the police station, telling them about her?

She ran around, looking behind fallen trees and boulders. Then another buzz came from her pocket and she stopped.

It had to be him, calling his own phone. She dropped it and began to run.

CHAPTER SEVENTY-THREE

Čiežalogigolbma

Mattias stumbled as his foot came down wrong on the slope; he was skidding down to the fire. Above him stood Robert. He had only one boot on, and his pants were wet at the crotch, but also at the knee. The wet patches at his knees looked like blood. He was holding his chest and grimacing. The dog, having caught sight of her master, was whining and limping back and forth, wanting to cross the river.

"*Stop*, Raija! Stay!"

Robert's voice was gravelly and he grabbed his chest again. He shuffled down the slope with one leg held out unnaturally. He kicked off his boot and, without a glance at Mattias, picked up the waders.

"Those aren't safe."

"How the fuck did Raija end up on the island?"

He already had one leg in the waders. The pungent smell of urine hit Mattias.

"As soon as I get back here, you're fucking . . ."

A loud groan as he tried to get the other leg in. He pulled the straps over his shoulders and buckled them.

"You can't use those waders."

Mattias's voice was flat, not urgent, not full of panic, just toneless. He knew he should say more. But Robert shoved him brusquely aside.

"Shut up!"

The dog stood with her front paws in the water and Robert called to her.

As Mattias would remember it, the current caught them both at about the same time. Robert screamed as the eddies took the dog. He went in too deep and in an instant the waders filled with river water. He flipped upside down. That was when Mattias began to run along the bank, and when he reached the spit he rushed straight out to intercept them. The river was more shallow there, and he splashed in. The icy water took his breath away. He couldn't see the dog; it was below the surface, but the waders came sailing toward him at a high speed and he threw himself forward with all his might, his hands outstretched, and grabbed. At nothing. Only his own fists. And the moment was gone.

CHAPTER SEVENTY-FOUR

Čiežaloginjeallje

Hanna held Anna-Stina's hand in her own. Her daughter's fingers were cold, and she shivered as if the chill were coming from within. Hanna had spread two blankets over her and asked to let go of her hand so she could use the phone.

She dialed 112, and blurted that her little girl needed help, that she was bleeding.

"Yes, she's pregnant. I told you that already, aren't you listening?!"

But there was no ambulance at the nearest station. The staff had packed up and headed home at five, so now an ambulance would have to be dispatched from town. It meant a wait of more than an hour.

"What about a helicopter then?" she whimpered. "We can't wait an hour."

"How many weeks along is she? Unfortunately, the risk of miscarriage is . . ."

Hanna let the phone fall. She didn't have a car at home; Ante was out repairing the fence, getting ready for autumn and winter, and a cousin had borrowed Anna-Stina's car. She was all on her own, as usual. Thank goodness Jon-Isak was out with his father and wouldn't have to see the blood and the panic.

"It'll be fine, it'll be fine," she heard herself saying over and over to Anna-Stina.

She had to fix this. She must not fail. But panic was about to set in. Her fingers were going numb and nausea washed over her. She had to move, so she stood up.

Elsa had the power. She could stanch blood. Although she seemed hesitant to accept it, everyone knew she was a gunsttar. Hanna searched through her contacts and pressed her name. The phone rang, but there was no answer. Anna-Stina's face was draining of color right before her eyes.

Shame burned within Hanna like a wild flame. Five minutes ago, her daughter had taken control of the situation in the midst of her own panic. Anna-Stina had come out of the bathroom and collapsed in a heap on the hall floor, screaming that she was losing the baby. Hanna had instinctively covered her ears.

When she didn't immediately come to her daughter's aid, Anna-Stina had roared even louder. "You have to help me!"

Hanna had grabbed the phone from the kitchen table and gone to get blankets from the living room and towels from the bedroom while her daughter's terrified howls followed her from room to room.

She looked down at her beautiful little girl, her hands so frantically clamped over her round belly as blood stained the towel beneath her.

Anna-Stina pulled her near, wanted her close by now. Hanna found herself on her knees, holding Anna-Stina's hands, their fingers intertwined.

"I'll call—" Hanna's voice broke. "I'll call someone else, who can make the bleeding stop. Elsa didn't pick up."

What she really wanted to do was tear herself away, open the door, and run without ever looking back. She couldn't handle this. Anna-Stina squeezed her hands harder and stared into her eyes.

"You have to be my mother right now! You have to!"

CHAPTER SEVENTY-FIVE

Čiežalogivihtta

M attias drove home in his wet clothing, which stiffened in the wind and nearly froze to his body. But he wasn't cold. He didn't feel a thing. He parked by the house that would never feel like his. He went inside, avoided looking at his parents' house, locked the door, and didn't turn on any lights.

In the bathroom he struggled with the single button on his jeans, but his fingers were too stiff. His sweater went over his head, and he shivered as the cold, wet fabric ran up his rib cage. He rinsed his hands in hot water until they were full of pins and needles. His jeans hardly fit over his hips and got stuck halfway down his thighs. He opened the medicine cabinet to look for a pair of scissors—he might as well cut them off—but didn't find any and had to tug and yank so hard at the wet denim around his ankles that it felt like they would break clean off. His thighs were red but bloodless. Naked, he walked through the dark house to the bedroom and pulled out the dresser drawers. Underwear and a T-shirt would do. Once he was dressed, he could breathe again. From his bed he had a view of the lake, its surface a smooth mirror in the moonlight. He had no sense of time; it might just as easily be night.

He had lingered by the river, unable to stop staring at a rock surrounded by foaming white water. He couldn't complete a single thought. The wind tried to dry his wet clothes, but the river water clung to him. His ears turned red and his lips blue.

In Áddjá and Áhkku's house, his body slowly thawed. But his feet were still ice-cold. His heels and toes hurt as he walked around the bed and rolled down the pale gray bedspread. He folded it and hung it over a chair. He forced himself to lift the blanket and lie down. Let his head sink into the pillow.

ELSA LAY FLAT ON her back in bed, fully dressed. Robert would turn up tonight, she was sure of it. Maybe set fire to their house. Shoot her. Shoot them all. This time he wouldn't let any windows or doors stop him.

It was impossible to lie still. She got up and paced back and forth, weighing her options. But her thoughts got all tangled up in one another, forming labyrinths. Should she warn Mattias, who was all alone in his house? She'd heard him come home on his motorbike. Should she warn Mom and Dad, who were sleeping? Or should she just call the police and tell them everything?

Under the bed was the axe she had taken from the garage. She lay down and flopped over the edge, rehearsing how fast she could grab it.

She could have killed him and brought them all peace. Instead, she had unleashed his madness.

She sat up again and slapped her knees, swaying back and forth. She should have shot him and explained that there was no other way out.

Which God had helped him move the four-wheeler? A jolt ran through her belly. She hadn't searched the forest thoroughly. What if he had staggered off, all beat up, and maybe passed out from the pain? She had seen blood, hadn't she?

CHAPTER SEVENTY-SIX

Čiežalogiguhtta

It was a broken blood vessel that had caused the heavy bleeding. The baby's little heart was still beating. Quick little drumrolls filled the room, and Hanna cried. She cried in a way that made the nurses exchange glances.

Anna-Stina's hair was spread like a tangled skein of yarn across the white pillow and down her shoulders. The big hospital gown made her look tiny, and her hands rested over her belly, on top of the blanket. She trusted the doctors and allowed the warm, stroking hands of the nurses to calm her.

They patted Hanna too, but someone said, in a harsher tone, that she should probably dry her tears. After all, everything had turned out fine.

"Enná . . ." Anna-Stina held her limp hand. "What's the matter?"

But how could she respond? She didn't know. She was crying because she was happy the baby was alive. But she was also crying because she would never again feel peace. Anxiety was already growing within her like a volcano.

This child, who wasn't even born yet, would keep her awake at night from now on. And once the baby was in her arms, warm and smelling like vanilla, Hanna would never be able to breathe calmly again.

The nurses had stopped giving her tissues to blow her nose. It was probably time to pull herself together. But they knew nothing about her life. They had no idea that she couldn't manage to keep everyone alive. They had no clue that she couldn't sleep when her husband was off with the reindeer and Jon-Isak was hers to keep alive. They didn't know that she had let her daughter move out too soon.

"Enná, they're going to send you up to the psych ward soon."

Anna-Stina smiled as though she were joking, and Hanna had to squeeze her hand tighter. It was slim and narrow, with those nails she made way too fancy. Her hands were cold, and she wanted to ask the nurses if that was normal. From now on, everything would be a question: Normal or not? Each time her daughter went to the bathroom, she would be waiting for a scream, waiting to see blood again.

The psych ward. Yes, that was probably where she belonged. But no one there would understand her. They didn't know what it meant to be a reindeer herder's wife. She supposed they knew, thanks to their line of work, how difficult it was to have family members who took their own lives, but they wouldn't understand the situation Lasse had been in. There was no understanding her life if they didn't speak her language. They would prescribe antidepressants and offer one therapy session a month.

"Should we call the father instead?" one of the nurses' aides said pointedly to Anna-Stina, who shook her head.

"I already called him. We'll be okay."

They were left alone in the room. The smell of disinfectant made Hanna feel vaguely nauseated.

"The baby is fine. Áhkku."

Anna-Stina had said it for the first time. She pushed down the blanket and took Hanna's hand to place it on her belly.

"You haven't even felt it kicking."

Right away she wanted to yank her hand back, but her daughter pressed it down, holding her in place. Together they slid over her belly until they found a tiny, squirming foot. Hanna jumped, as though the little baby's kicks were rippling through her own body, through all her cells. Anna-Stina smiled and closed her eyes for a moment. Hanna wanted to feel the foot again, so she pressed gently, calling to the little one. And there! A kick, the fluttering of tiny soles.

"It can still do somersaults," Anna-Stina said in a sleepy voice.

"Get some sleep now, you must be exhausted. I'll keep an eye on her."

Anna-Stina opened one eye.

"You think it's a girl?"

Hanna nodded. It couldn't be another boy. It had to be a girl.

"I'm hoping we have a daughter. But don't tell Per-Jonas."

"Never."

She forced herself to look at Anna-Stina for a long time. At her freckles, at the dark shadows under her eyes, her cheeks with their new plumpness, the birthmark just above her right eyebrow, which, if you looked right up close, was shaped like a little heart.

How had she ever gotten the idea that Anna-Stina wasn't strong? She was a force of nature. Hanna had seen that today, that explosive rage. But Hanna knew too that this rage was partially directed at her.

And still. She was the one who would be Áhkku; she was the one who would keep them all alive.

Anna-Stina's breathing grew even, and her legs twitched. Her dreams were near. Hanna stroked her belly and used her other hand to wipe her own tears.

CHAPTER SEVENTY-SEVEN

Ciežalogicieza

T wo days later, Robert was on the front page of the local paper, missing and wanted. The newspaper had borrowed the photo from someone in the hunting league; it had been taken when the guys gathered for a picture after a successful moose hunt a few years previously. Robert was unshaven and wearing a cap and a big smile, showing all his teeth.

Elsa shuddered when she saw his face: that wolfish grin. Mom and Mattias took turns reading in silence.

There had been buzz in the village about how strange it was that Robert hadn't showed up to talk to the hunting league before the moose hunt. The guys had readied themselves for a battle and honed their arguments, but he never turned up. Then someone had peeked into his mailbox and found that the mail hadn't been collected, and that seemed like reason enough to start wondering. Maybe someone should even take it upon themselves to contact the police? Not that Robert was well liked, or even particularly missed. But call they did, and the police sounded rather weary; the name was a familiar one, after all, and they asked the caller to stop by Robert's house and knock on the door. The caller did, and found the door unlocked. On the kitchen table was a half-empty cup of coffee and part of a cinnamon loaf, now dry. The chair wasn't pushed in, as though he had just stood up. They walked around the house, nose wrinkling at the stench of garbage. They tried the locked garage door, and tugged at the padlock on the barn. But neither Robert nor his pup was anywhere to be found.

So in the end, the police had to make a trip out to the village and confirmed that he was missing. The old Jeep was still there, but the four-wheeler was gone.

That's when the rumors began in the village, about the cars with Polish license plates that other villages had heard warnings about, the types that seemed like they were scouting houses to rob. Not to mention the way they seemed to be disappearing one by one, first Petri and now Robert. It was an open secret that Robert shot a reindeer now and again, so it wasn't beyond the realm of imagination that the Sámi had had enough.

And now he was on the front page of the paper. In the article, the police asked the general public to call in any tips or sightings. There was a description of the four-wheeler, as well as the elkhound, which was missing too.

Mom read select paragraphs aloud. She didn't quite know what to think of this news. She laughed at the description of him. "A skilled timberman back in the day," said one. "Unbelievable," said another. "In our little village."

Mom brought her hand to her mouth; she shouldn't be laughing if he was dead.

Elsa filled her mouth with food, chewed until it seemed to expand. She tried to meet Mattias's gaze across the table, but he was looking down at his plate, all his focus on eating. He hadn't come over for a few days. Her guilty conscience nagged at her again. She should have searched in the forest; he was surely lying somewhere, bleeding and dying.

"The police say his phone must have run out of battery, because their calls aren't going through."

Mom looked up and leaned back on the kitchen bench.

"I'm so glad to see you eating again, Mattias. That sure was a stubborn stomach bug you caught. It even looks like you lost a pound or two."

He didn't respond, just drank the last of his water. The thin skin under his eyes was dark purple, Elsa noticed. And he hadn't looked at her once.

"Will you feel up to going out and working with Isa tonight?"

Mom had a toothpick between her lips. Mattias shook his head and Mom quit poking between her front teeth.

"What about you, Elsa?"

"I have to go to Anna-Stina's. The baby."

"Yes, my God. So fortunate that it turned out okay."

She put away the bread and butter, humming some tune.

"I've got aerobics again this evening. Maybe you should come along, Elsa. You're so pale."

"I told you—"

"Yes, yes, Anna-Stina." She rinsed out the pasta pot. "He must be dead."

Mattias quickly vanished into the bathroom and Elsa heard him turn on the tap.

She rubbed her tense shoulders and the pain radiated up to her ears until she felt dizzy. The water was still running full force in the bathroom, and the kitchen faucet splashing in the pasta pot was just as loud. The volume of the radio was way up. Elsa held her ears until Mom turned around and looked at her.

"What are you doing?"

"Nothing. I've got a headache and all this noise isn't helping."

"I just want to hear the news. In case they found him."

Elsa pulled on her white cardigan and wrapped her red shawl twice around her neck. Leaving her plate on the table, she went to the front hall; she heard Mom sigh and pick up after her.

She leaned her head against the bathroom door, wanting so desperately to talk to him.

"They found something!" Mom cried.

The water in the bathroom stopped running. Elsa waited. Mom called out again.

"Did you hear that? They found the four-wheeler, not far from the river. Overturned."

"I have to go," Elsa said, opening the front door.

Mom popped up in the hallway.

"Isn't it strange that they found the four-wheeler, but not him?"

"Yeah, but maybe he wasn't the one riding it. Maybe someone stole it, and flipped it."

Elsa heard herself speaking, heard herself lying so casually.

Mom nodded. "Sure, that's true. It could have been the Poles. The police did say they suspect foul play."

Elsa turned her back and waved one hand. "I'll be back late."

"Everything okay, Mattias? Are you feeling sick again?"

There was a rustle and he mumbled something inaudible. Mom grabbed Elsa's arm.

"I'm worried," she whispered, nodding toward the door. "Could he have become gluten intolerant?"

"Oh my God, why would you think that?"

She closed the front door before Mom could say anything else. Her steps down were jerky, as though her legs were flailing uncontrollably. Her hands trembled inside the mittens Áhkku had knitted once upon a time.

CHAPTER SEVENTY-EIGHT

Čiežalogigávcci

Then the body got tangled in a net set out by fish poachers, way downstream. The report was first broadcast over the radio and then on the evening news. By then there was a map with a black X marking the spot where Robert had been found, and a red X for the four-wheeler. Signs seemed to point to an accidental drowning, but of course there were questions. The police would have to investigate, and the villagers were full of speculation, talking through all the facts and perhaps fabricating a detail or two once the discovery had been endlessly rehashed; everyone wanted to contribute something to the story.

If he had, in fact, flipped the four-wheeler, why would he continue on foot to the river? There had been a trail of blood that led all the way to the river's edge. Maybe he wanted to wash out a wound? Maybe. But presumably he'd been drunk, which made the most unreasonable actions perfectly reasonable. Of course he hadn't been acting rationally. He must have tripped and fallen into the rapids, and was unable to get out.

So it probably wouldn't be long before it was determined that Robert had died in an accidental drowning. "A tragic accident," the papers would say. And the villagers would be relieved not to have to worry about foreigners.

Dad watched the news intently; he didn't miss a word.

"Well, he may not have been the only one who took our reindeer, but he was the worst," he said. "Things will have to calm down now."

It was as though he was trying to convince himself. Elsa agreed with him, yet she couldn't sit still. She wanted to flee the house, but at the same time she didn't want to spend a second alone with her thoughts. The villagers' speculation had followed Dad home from the gas station, and he repeated what he'd heard.

"What do you think, Elsa?"

"I honestly have no idea."

She couldn't let herself even think about the truth, but it was impossible to defend herself against it; it just kept coming back. She had walked away from an injured man who had stumbled into the rapids and died.

Dad channel-surfed, looking for news, wanting to hear it all again, all the different theories. He picked up his phone now and then, refreshing the newspapers' websites. He read each new sentence aloud, even though it was totally pointless. The police were tight-lipped and there were no witnesses.

Elsa had to settle down, or she would soon crack and shout that it was all her fault.

"Do you think I could call Áhkku?"

Dad shrugged and pointed out that it was late.

For some reason, she needed to hear Áhkku's voice. She called the facility, and Brittis answered.

"I'd like to see Áhkku. Could you help her with FaceTime?"

"FaceTime?" Dad scoffed from the sofa. "How is she supposed to understand that?"

Brittis's Tornedal dialect comforted her; as always she was sure everything would work out fine. The picture zoomed this way and that, and Elsa heard her giving Áhkku instructions. Whenever Áhkku got too gloomy and Brittis could see that the old woman needed to anchor herself in her family, she would call and say they needed to hear a familiar voice. Brittis had quickly learned that it was Elsa, not Mom or Dad, who would take the call.

She saw Áhkku on the screen, her cloudy eyes peering at her.

"Hi, Áhkku! Can you see me?"

She smiled and waved.

"Sure can!"

"How are you?"

"Good. We had potato dumplings today, and they were delicious. And Brittis had picked the lingonberries herself."

There was a glimpse of Brittis in the background. She gave a thumbs-up and a smile.

Elsa was dangerously close to tears, and she swung the phone around to show Dad.

"Look who's here."

Dad waved and Áhkku twittered with delight.

"It's almost moose-hunting time. Remember when Áddjá shot the twelve-pointer?" Elsa asked as she pointed the phone back at herself.

Áhkku's face brightened and she chuckled, yes, that hunting story was one worth repeating. How Áddjá was relieving himself against a tree when the moose suddenly came crashing through the woods, and Áddjá picked up his rifle to shoot.

"With his pants down!"

Elsa glanced at Dad, who was grinning as well. For a moment, everything was normal.

"Did you hear the news about Robert? He's dead," Dad called.

"Brittis read the article at breakfast. Way too loudly. My hearing is perfectly fine."

Áhkku let her braid slip through her fingers, trying to remove the elastic.

"Nu lat dea," she said. "You can't be cruel to animals and get away with it. That's the truth."

Brittis's hands appeared. She carefully took the braid from Áhkku's hand and gently arranged it into a bun.

"Can I have a mirror?"

Áhkku looked at her reflection, turning her head this way and that and smiling.

"Look how pretty, unna oabba."

CHAPTER SEVENTY-NINE

Čiežalogiovcci

The doctor at the clinic looked first at Mattias's hands, which were drumming at his knees, and then at his right leg, which was bouncing up and down. But she couldn't make eye contact. When she asked him questions, he gazed past her and out the window.

"Heart and lungs sound good, blood pressure is normal, the CRP test didn't indicate infection. We'll see what the blood tests show. They'll be sent to the lab and you'll get the results in a few days."

"But I have chest pain," he muttered.

"Walks and fresh air are good. Exercise three times per week to get your pulse up."

He looked up and sighed heavily. "I get out and get my pulse up every day. Like I said, I'm a reindeer herder. I'm still feeling pressure over my chest."

Moments ago, she had slid her cold stethoscope over his back and chest.

"Your heart is perfectly strong."

"I'm exhausted."

He had never said it out loud, and it made his leg bounce uncontrollably.

"How are you sleeping?"

"Not getting much sleep."

"Sleep is important. What is your workday like? You might need to bring it down a notch or two. I'm thinking this might be stress-related. Do you feel stressed?"

"I can't bring it down a notch. It's up to the reindeer, what my days are like."

"Yes, but that's the thing about stress, you know? It demands a lot of lifestyle change. You have to learn to say no. Can you do that?"

He grabbed the armrests of the chair, cold metal that quickly dampened under his palms.

"You can't take time off from the reindeer."

He shoved the chair back, and it scraped loudly in the spartan room. The doctor frowned.

"I can put you down for sick leave so you can rest for two weeks. I can also write you a prescription for Atarax, which is a mild sedative that can help you sleep."

She had already turned to the computer and was filling out the prescription. Mattias looked at her hands; her knuckles looked dry and her cuticles were ugly. Her dark hair was short, her ears large.

"I can't take sick time right now."

She stopped typing.

"Then, Mattias, what do *you* want?"

"Just some peace and quiet."

"Maybe you can go away for a while, so you don't have to think about the reindeer."

The room fell silent. Outside he could hear clacking steps and voices. One of the nurses had been in his class back in school. She had waved at him in the hall when he came in, and he very nearly did an about-face. But he slunk into the bathroom and waited there until the doctor was ready to see him.

He couldn't fill a prescription for Atarax at the pharmacy here, because one of his cousins worked there. He'd have to go into town.

"Would you say you feel depressed, listless, sad?"

He heard the words, but he couldn't connect them to what he felt. Hopelessness.

"I don't know."

"Anxiety?"

He nodded. "Yeah."

"What makes you anxious? Can you tell me about specific situations?"

She was young, this doctor, a little older than him, but there were oceans of life and time between them. She was a locum physician, from some big hospital down in southern Sweden, and she was very expensive, he'd heard. He was sure she and her colleagues would laugh when she got back to the big city and told them about him.

"A lot of our reindeer die," he said. "It makes me worry each time I go out."

She nodded and gazed at him solemnly.

"I can refer you to a psychologist, but the wait list is three months. Do you want me to do that? In the meantime we have a counselor who you can get in to see faster."

She said the name and he sank back in his chair.

"I know her."

"Oh, all right, that won't work then. The psychologist it is. There's a new one who's supposed to be very good."

She turned to the computer again and began to type.

Was she smiling? It looked like it. Why was she smiling? He couldn't stop looking at her small white teeth. He stood up suddenly and dropped his hat on the floor. Bent down to pick it up.

"I have to go."

"No, wait. Sit down, we're just getting somewhere."

"I'm done."

"What about the Atarax? Should I write you the prescription?"

He nodded and shoved his hat down over his head.

"You can just forget the psychologist."

"Are you sure? Because I really think you should—"

He was already out of the room and closed the door behind him. His former classmate was talking to a stooped, white-haired man with a rollator. She smiled at Mattias and rolled her eyes. She looked good. Maybe she could have been the kind of girl for him, back in the day. Now he wasn't much of a catch. He nodded at her without smiling. But she only gave him an even bigger smile in return.

CHAPTER EIGHTY

Gávccilogi

S he knew she shouldn't do it, but she couldn't help herself. Elsa dialed his direct number and he answered after three rings. In an authoritative voice. With his full name, Alexander Ljungblad. She wondered if his friends called him Alex. His tone softened when he realized it was her. Once the pleasantries were out of the way, she told him why she was calling.

"Have you found Robert's phone? There must be evidence on it that he was killing reindeer. Maybe you'll find some contacts. People he sold the meat to."

"We've started working on that, but for the time being that's all I can say."

"I expect it's not much of a priority, since he's dead."

"It got prioritized anyway." He was quiet for a moment. "Once we found him."

"What do you mean?"

Her heart beat faster and she had to lean against the wall. Had she dropped something? Had she left evidence near the four-wheeler?

He put a hand over the receiver and she heard mumbling before he returned.

"Sorry, that was a colleague. Elsa, I can't tell you any more right now, but the investigation isn't over."

"But it said in the newspaper—"

"Yes, I know, but the situation has changed."

"How so?"

"We'll talk about it in person."

"In person?"

"Yes, we're coming to the village this afternoon. We need to talk to you all."

" 'You all'?"

"Yes, your family." He paused. She could tell that he was mustering his authority again. "So, great, we'll see you in an hour or so. Really appreciate it if you could all make sure to be at home."

"Were you planning to call and let us know, or were you just planning to show up?"

"Does it matter?"

"You know it does."

She heard him breathing, and he could surely hear her too.

"We're all home," she said.

DAD'S HAIR HAD GONE so gray, not only at his temples but everywhere. And it was long at the ears, needed a trim. Mom had lost weight, and it didn't suit her. There were dumbbells under her bed. Dad was sleeping in Mattias's old room. Mom had turned their room into some strange sanctuary that didn't fit with the rest of the house. She had filled it with books and orchids which bloomed best this time of year, thanks to the drafty windows. She'd switched out the wall art and bought a new pink bedspread. It was as if she had made a little life of her own, alongside her family's. They all left her to it. Just as long as she didn't cry like before, Elsa thought, they could accept anything.

Her parents filled their coffee cups for the second time, and Dad stared out at the sleety snow, which had come on suddenly, more than a month earlier than normal. Not that it would stick. But today the snow mixed with the blazing yellow of the leaves. Two of eight seasons fighting for space, way too early. It wasn't yet time for the shift from čakča to čakčadálvi, autumn to autumn-winter.

They called Mattias, but he didn't pick up. His car was in the yard and the blinds were down.

"I'm sure he'll come when he sees the patrol car," said Dad.

"They probably don't have winter tires," said Mom.

"It's not slippery; the snow isn't sticking at all. Just look at the road."

Elsa held tight to her cup of tea and didn't refill it, even though it had gone cold. She looked at them—Enná and Isa had such high hopes for her and Mattias. Hopes that they would carry on their parents' life work.

They laughed together. They were relieved, believing that they were facing a bright new future now. Maybe they wouldn't have to guard the reindeer this winter. Robert Isaksson was dead. Of course, it was wrong to wish someone dead and wrong to celebrate their death after it happened, but they could laugh again now, together. Feel relief.

But soon that moment would pass. Soon their daughter would be getting into a police car. She took a sip of cold tea, surprised at how clear her thoughts were, sure that she would give only honest answers.

Yes, I was by the four-wheeler.

Yes, I walked away from him.

No, he wasn't dead at that time.

Why did I do it?

Silence would descend around the table. Everyone's eyes would be on her. How would she answer that question? What sort of person would do that?

"Maybe they're going to apologize for all the reindeer thefts they never investigated," Dad said.

"I'm sure they went through his house and found reindeer," Mom added.

Dad's hands, with their rough calluses, made Mom's delicate, floral coffee service look tiny. His thumb and index finger didn't fit through the handles of the cup; instead he enveloped the whole thing in his fist. He drank with all his senses, especially loudly, and with his eyes closed for a brief moment.

Then the patrol car turned into the yard. They stretched their backs and Dad cleared his throat.

"It's Henriksson, so it must be serious."

He called "come in" when the knock came, and there they stood in the front hall, Henriksson and Ljungblad. Mom told them they could leave their shoes on, it seemed like it would be more trouble than it was worth to remove them, and the floor hadn't just been cleaned or anything. She was full of expectation, having already set out a mug for each of them. They greeted one another with firm handshakes, except when Elsa took Ljungblad's hand, which was gentle and warm. They let the officers know that Mattias wasn't home and wasn't answering his phone, but they would try again. Elsa had a feeling he actually was home. She imagined he'd come over soon. But could he forgive her? Would he understand? Soon everyone would look at her with new eyes. She tried not to look in the mirror these days.

She had called Minna, snuck out to stand shivering by the lake, which was black beneath the dark clouds. She'd asked if it was a crime to walk away from an injured person, and Minna's voice grew tense when she asked what had happened. She couldn't say it out loud, not even to Minna. So instead she just said she had to go and had hung up on Minna's anxious voice, then put her phone on silent.

Ljungblad had let his beard grow, but it was trimmed neatly up to his ears. He was sweating in his uniform.

Henriksson instructed him to take notes. Why didn't they just call her into town to interrogate her alone? Did they suspect the whole family was involved?

"How is it going? Did you look through his freezers?"

Dad sounded so confident that it pained her physically, like a stomach cramp. He never got to have the upper hand, but right now he believed he did. He leaned back, at ease, and the coffee cup disappeared in his large hand.

"Our colleagues have started on that, yes," Henriksson said.

"Thought I spotted a patrol car yesterday as well. We were just saying that we have never seen so many cops in the village. It's about time you found your way here."

Henriksson didn't look amused. Ljungblad took a cautious sip of his coffee, but Henriksson put a hand over his cup when Mom tried to pour him some.

"My colleague and I, we're taking a closer look at Robert's death," he said.

"Oh, was it not an accident after all?"

Dad leaned forward, turning his left ear toward them. He didn't want to admit that his hearing had gotten worse.

"Yes, presumably it was, but to be on the safe side we still want to check up on a few loose ends."

Elsa glanced at Ljungblad, whose expression didn't change.

"We examined what Isaksson was wearing, and that raised a few questions. I would like to start by asking if you recognize this phone number."

Henriksson took his notepad from the table, flipped back a few pages, and pushed it over to Dad. A number, with area code—one they all knew by heart but hadn't used in years.

"That's my parents' landline, to the house next door. But we canceled it a long time ago. Cell phones are enough these days, even if you can't always depend on getting reception," said Dad.

"And these initials, are they your father's?"

"Yep, I suppose they are."

"The initials and the phone number were in the waders Isaksson had on. Can you explain why Robert was wearing your father's waders when he died?"

Dad's jaw dropped; he looked at Mom, whose eyes went wide. Elsa and Ljungblad looked at one another, but she wasn't seeing him; her gaze went right through him.

"What? He was? But . . ." Dad shrugged. "Didn't we toss those out ages ago?"

Mom seemed to be frozen to her chair. Her eyes looked down first, then at Elsa. They were screaming inside: *Mattias.*

"Maybe he stole those too, from the recycling," Dad said tentatively.

"Robert did?"

"Yes, that's the only explanation I can think of. Do you have another idea?"

Mom was slow to respond, as though she had to think through every word first.

"That must be what happened."

"Anyway, we threw them out," Dad declared.

"They were old and torn," Mom went on, just as slowly.

"Yes, that's just it. We took a closer look at them, and they were a death trap. Old waders with no belt. If water gets into the legs, it'll flip a man upside down, with minimal chances of recovery."

"Right, that's why we threw them out," Dad said.

He couldn't put the pieces of the puzzle together, and looked quizzically at Elsa, who avoided eye contact and looked out the window instead. She could feel Mattias's presence. Ljungblad followed her gaze.

"Do you by any chance know where Mattias is?"

"No." Mom and Elsa responded in unison.

"So he died in those waders?"

Dad tilted his head again and watched Ljungblad's lips as he replied.

"Yes, he did. And we found a boot down by the water, so our theory is he changed into the waders. Why, we don't know. He didn't have a fishing rod with him."

"Strange," Dad said.

"Yes, we can't quite put it together," said Henriksson.

"Well, how should we know? Like I said, we tossed those waders."

"Are you sure they went to the recycling? Where did you keep them before you got rid of them?"

In Mattias's house. Elsa bit the inside of her cheek until it hurt.

"In the storage shed, right, Marika?"

Mom nodded.

"Would you like any more coffee?" she asked.

She had already stood up and turned her back to them. She filled the kettle with water and measured out the grounds with a steady hand but took her time doing it.

"We must have thrown them in the recycling center," Dad said. "I hauled several bags of stuff."

"You were aware they were dangerous?"

This was Ljungblad. Mom shot a quick glance over her shoulder but didn't meet anyone's eyes.

"We knew they didn't have a belt, so no one used them," said Mom.

"They were awfully old, and outdated," said Dad.

He still sounded confident, but there was a watchfulness to his tone now. Elsa had gotten up too, and was filling a pot with water.

"Maybe you'd like some tea. After all, not everyone drinks coffee," she said to Henriksson.

"There's no need, it's too late for caffeine."

"We've got rooibos as well."

Mom and Elsa stood side by side, shoulders propped together. No one would fall today. The kettle whistled and Mom pulled it aside. She poured the coffee through the strainer and into a cup, then poured the dash of coffee back into the kettle, moved the strainer to the thermos, and filled it all the way up with coffee. The grounds came out with the last drops and formed a little pyramid in the strainer; with a quick rap she dumped them in the trash. She served Ljungblad, Dad, and herself. Elsa got down a striped teacup and filled it halfway with water, then dipped in the teabag of African rooibos.

"It stopped snowing," Mom said as she sat down again.

There was silence around the table as they all waited for Elsa to take her seat. Henriksson didn't touch the tea she set before him.

"Are we suspects?" Dad asked. "Because I'm starting to think it sounds that way."

His voice was a rumble from somewhere deep down. Elsa recognized the sound and squeezed her legs together, folding her arms in toward her body.

"We just think it's worth noting that he had waders that belonged to you all, and since no one saw him fall into the rapids we do have to try to figure out what happened."

Henriksson's tone was neutral, but Elsa could see the tension in his eyes. The scent of the trail that had brought him here. He was waiting for a misstep.

"Worth noting," Dad mimicked. "The only thing worth noting is that you've come here to interrogate us about a plain old accidental drowning, even though you basically never bothered to show up when our animals were killed. And you let him get away with it when he threatened my daughter!"

His fist struck the table. Only Elsa jumped.

"Who was the last to see the waders?" Ljungblad asked.

"Me," Mom hurried to say.

"Where was that?"

"I was clearing out the storage shed and they went into the 'toss' pile, which we took to the next village. There's a recycling station there, and we don't have one here, so we have to go there. Which we do pretty often."

She was babbling, and Elsa wanted to put a hand on her arm, make her stop. Instead she gently pressed her thigh to Mom's beneath the table.

"And you never know, there might be folks who go digging through the recycling," she concluded.

"I'm sure that miserable shit found his way there," Dad muttered without looking at them. His arms were crossed, and he had a firm grip on his own muscles. "If you think Robert Isaksson was the kind of guy you could force into a pair of waders, you're dead wrong. You should know that, Henriksson. He put them on voluntarily. Caused his own death."

"We found waders at his house," Ljungblad said. "So it's strange that he would have put on your old ones."

Dad looked pointedly at the clock on the wall, stood up, and went to the front hall. He returned with his boots in hand, sat down on the chair by the door, and began to lace them up.

"All you've got is speculation. How should we know why he wasn't wearing his own waders?"

"Maybe someone tricked him into it," said Ljungblad. "Are you in a rush to get somewhere?"

Dad didn't look up, just kept calmly lacing his boots.

"I've got a job to take care of."

Henriksson looked at him with displeasure; his eyes narrowed, but he wasn't going to fight about it.

"What about Mattias, can you try him again?"

Ljungblad looked at Elsa, who obediently called Mattias and let it ring on speakerphone so everyone could hear.

Mom sat with her back straight, looking from one officer to the other. She smiled and asked if they wouldn't like to try a bun with their beverages. Ljungblad gave a dismissive wave.

"Can you ask Mattias to give us a call?"

Mom nodded, still smiling. "Of course."

"Well, I guess we'd better get going."

Henriksson was the first to stand up. His tea was untouched and cold. Ljungblad had sugar in his beard.

CHAPTER EIGHTY-ONE

Gávccilogiokta

E lsa walked through the little puddles the officers had left behind on the floor, and her socks got wet at the heels. Mom kept tucking strands of hair behind her ears. She'd just gotten a haircut and wasn't quite used to having a pageboy yet.

"He couldn't have killed him, could he?" she said.

Elsa shook her head. It was worse than that. Now she understood. He had kept the waders to die in them.

"But he must have taken them, right? Because I never found them in the 'toss' pile after." Mom tugged at her bangs, drawing them firmly aside.

Elsa stared at the floor. "I think he wanted them as a memento of Áddjá."

"A memento! We've got boxes full of guksi and knives. Why would he save a pair of waders?"

But Elsa too had memories attached to them. Áddjá lifting Mattias over the stream, when the warm weather took them by surprise up in the mountains, melting sheets of snow and making narrow streams that were hard to cross. Áddjá knew never to go too deep with those waders, but he picked up his grandchildren and stepped into waterways. Sometimes he lifted both of them at once and didn't stagger, despite the current around his legs. And she had never been afraid. Mattias had been too big to be lifted over that last time, but Áddjá must have seen that he too wanted to be in his arms even though his legs were too long. So he picked him up and the siblings laughed out loud as they clung to his neck.

"Must have been a memento."

"But how did Robert get ahold of them?"

"It doesn't matter. It's like Dad says, no one could have forced that man to put them on."

"What if . . ."

"What?"

Mom looked at her in horror.

"I don't want to say it out loud." She was near tears and brought her hand to her forehead. "But what if he killed him first and then put the waders on him and threw him into the river to make it look like an accident?"

"No way."

"How do you know?"

"Because it would be stupid, considering that Áddjá's name and phone number were in the waders. Besides, they would have said so, the cops, if they thought he died some other way. They say Robert drowned, so he must have had water in his lungs and no injuries that would suggest violence."

"But I heard something around the village about how there was internal bleeding."

"Sure, but just think of all the rocks he must have hit as he went down the rapids. It's a miracle his skull wasn't crushed."

Elsa's voice was low and calm. But behind her back she was digging her nails into her palms, and her knees were vibrating beneath her long, black down skirt.

"But how, Elsa? How did this happen?"

"Don't say anything to Dad. I'll talk to Mattias."

"I should do it."

"No, I'll do it."

"But where is he?"

The house still looked empty. Snow was melting on the car and trickling down the windows.

"I'll find him."

She felt her phone vibrating in her skirt pocket. Minna. She rejected the call.

"Go get some rest, Enná. I'll clean up here."

Mom scoffed, her hands already on the cookie plate and carton of milk.

CHAPTER EIGHTY-TWO

Gávccilogiguokte

He lay on the bed, a black bag on the floor next to him. The room was dark, but the angular green digits on Áhkku and Áddjá's old clock radio glowed from the windowsill. It had been half an hour since the patrol car left the yard. They had knocked on his door before they took off.

His phone was on silent, but its blue light flashed often from the night-stand with incoming texts and calls. Before the police came, Elsa had texted to say that they were on their way and he should come over. Mom had called three times. And Elsa had called once the cops had arrived. Once they left, she called again, and then she was standing on the stoop, banging on the door, only to tap her nails on his bedroom window seconds later. He had taken their spare key away, placed it in his own key cabinet by the front door. He couldn't live like this. Next door to his parents, who had a key that never allowed him independence. He thought of what he'd said to the locum doctor, that he wanted some peace and quiet. To close his eyes and not have to think about everything that led straight to anxiety.

He could ride out into the forest, freeze to death. After all, he was too much of a coward to use the rifle. Robert Isaksson had taken his solution, the only way to be at peace forever. It was almost laughable, so fucking typical.

"I will break this window, Mattias!" called Elsa from outside.

She was back, and he had no doubt she would do it. But his body was pressed to the bed, his shoulders ached, his neck was stiff and his fists clenched. It was impossible to get up. But his voice surprised him. It rang out clear as a bell.

"Vuordde veahaš." Hold on a sec.

He wasn't sure she'd heard him. He waited for the shards of glass to come flying over the bed. Elsa was stronger than him. So he could go now, secure in the knowledge that she wanted to stay with the reindeer. He had watched her through the years; unna oabba had been his shadow ever since she could walk. He had seen how she carried the lasso with a determined gaze—or, rather, dragged it behind her those first few years. And he had seen how she always stood her ground when someone said her place was anywhere but the reindeer forest. He was proud of her. He should have said so a long time ago. Why hadn't he? Because you didn't say stuff like that. You weren't supposed to praise and admire freely, for it came with a price, as Áhkku always said.

There was another knock, and he had no choice but to haul himself up. The latch was stubborn, but he finally got the window open and cold air streamed in over his bare arms. Elsa's eyes were full of worry. He told her to climb in. She looked at him like he was an idiot but grabbed the windowsill and jumped up with her belly pressed to it, then swung her legs over. She noticed the bag immediately and kicked at it.

"Going somewhere?"

"I was thinking maybe."

He closed the window and she turned on the ceiling light, then sat on the bed. He had to keep his distance, so he leaned against the dresser.

"The police were here. They want you to give them a call."

He tried to look nonchalant. She dangled her legs and kicked at the bag again, harder this time. Then the dam burst and she was sobbing. In a way he hadn't seen her cry for years. Snot flowing, tears spurting, and she seemed to have trouble breathing; the howls came in waves. Her fists hammered the bed.

She had to repeat herself several times before he could tell what she was saying.

"You were going to kill yourself. You were! Weren't you?"

He let his arms fall. He should feel something, but he was dead inside. She didn't wait for his response.

"You were going to put on the waders and drown."

She wiped her nose with the back of her hand and pulled up the bed-spread to wipe the tears from her face.

"I was there! Don't you get it? I was there!"

He was still numb.

She stood up and struck his upper arm with a well-aimed fist, buffeting him, but he stood steady. Because his feet had grown into the floor. His arm didn't hurt. She staggered back to the bed, threw herself down on her side and rolled into a ball, her knees tucked to her chin. She stared vacantly at nothing.

"I thought he died because of me. I found him and he was hurt and I left him there. And then it turns out it was you."

She heaved herself up onto one elbow and gazed at him anxiously.

"I don't believe you killed Robert! But I was about to shoot him." She stared defiantly at him. "And I did fire the gun."

"I heard the shot," he mumbled.

"Lasse told me not to shoot him, so I pointed the rifle at the sky."

Mattias looked down at his feet, at his white socks that had turned dingy gray.

Lasse.

He swallowed hard. He must not think.

"It was no coincidence that we were both there," she went on. "I could feel Lasse so strongly. He must have—"

Mattias growled. "Stop it!"

It was getting hard to stand still, but he curled his toes against the floor.

"You should have shot him."

"If I had killed him, you wouldn't be here right now, would you?"

Her eyes were shiny, feverish.

"You would have put on the waders and let the rapids take you."

He stared at his feet, which weren't listening to him anymore.

"Because you were planning to kill yourself, weren't you?" Her voice almost didn't hold. "He was really stuck under that four-wheeler. There was no way he could have gotten out. But Lasse—"

"Stop talking about him!"

He couldn't stand still any longer. Elsa called after him as he went to the kitchen sink and let the cold water flow over his wrists; he filled a glass and drank it down fast. All the blinds were down. It was like a prison.

She had followed him to the kitchen, slid onto one of the chairs, and stared at him in the dark. They could hardly see each other, but he thought her eyes glowed like two dots. When she turned on the light by the window, he wanted to tell her not to. But there she sat, unna oabba. Her eyes puffy, red streaks all down her face, and her hair hanging lank over skinny shoulders.

"He killed Nástegallu. I saw him."

Mattias held his breath.

"Everything would be different right now if I had been brave enough to say something. Maybe he would have gone to jail. But he threatened me— I thought he was going to kill us all."

It felt like someone was standing on his chest. Her voice was the same now as it was back then.

"So it's all my fault. And Lasse, he asked me about Robert. Not long before he took himself away. I was so close to telling, and I should have done it. They could have caught Robert and convicted him."

She had her knees pulled up to her chin again. So pale and tiny.

Mattias forced himself to speak. "He never would have gone to jail. It only would have been theft, after all. It wouldn't have made a difference."

"You don't know that."

"Yes, I do. We've filed over one hundred reports, and none of them led anywhere."

"But I saw him, that's the difference. I was a witness."

"Still just theft. Maybe he would have had to pay a fine. And then what? He would have been worse than ever, I bet."

Mattias made an effort to sound confident, but he wished he was better at expressing himself. He should say he loved her, but you didn't say stuff like that. He wanted to say he was sorry, he should have understood, he should have helped her.

"You saved us from that," he finally managed.

She rested her forehead on her knees, hiding her face, and gave a deep sigh. He had the strong urge to break something again. He wanted her to leave so he could yell and hit something. He forced himself to look at her; his guilty conscience was back.

He had failed to take care of her. Elsa had been his unna oabba and then one day she wasn't. Now he wanted to remind her of how he used to tickle her, carry her around, and chase her through rooms only to catch her and squeeze the air out of that little body. But once she got bigger, he couldn't find any new ways to touch her. So he had backed off. Let her go.

Elsa sighed again.

"You can't leave me," she said.

And with that, his legs gave way. He had to sit down on the floor. He hated himself. He already *had* abandoned her. A long time ago.

"I just don't know what to do," he said, rubbing his hands over his thighs, back and forth.

"You have to get help."

"I've already been to the clinic. They thought I should take some time off, spend a weekend catching my breath."

He croaked, but she didn't understand that it was a laugh.

"They have no idea what they're talking about. You have to go to Norway, to SANKS." The Sami Norwegian National Advisory Unit on Mental Health and Substance Abuse.

"I can't go anywhere."

"You have to. I'll take over. I'll be with Dad. You need help. And at SANKS they have psychologists who understand our life."

Elsa was steady now. She spoke rapidly, talking about the Sámi center for mental illness, telling him how they saved lives, how so many Sámi received help there. He watched her lips moving, and her eyes were bloodshot but resolute. The strength had returned to them.

"I'll drive you to Karasjok," she concluded.

"But maybe I'll get that vacation after all. In prison. For negligent manslaughter."

The silence between them felt endless.

"What happened?" she asked.

His throat constricted.

"I left him under the four-wheeler," she said. "How did he get to the river?"

Mattias ran his fingers through his hair, from his forehead and all the way down to his nape. The way Mom used to do when he was little. He would always shiver when her fingertips reached his neck. He stroked his hair again and again.

"How did he end up in the waders?"

"He put them on himself."

"Why?"

"I had thrown his dog across to the island."

"You did what?" She snickered then quickly covered her mouth. "Poor pup."

"I don't know, I just grabbed it by the collar and launched it. I had no idea what was going on. I heard a shot and the dog came bolting by. I saw whose dog it was and I guess . . . I got scared." He cleared his throat. "Yeah, shit, poor pup."

"Then what?"

"He showed up, saw the dog, and took the waders. I tried to tell him he shouldn't. But he wouldn't listen." Mattias slapped the floor. The sting of pain was immediate. He closed his eyes. "I should have said more, taken the waders away from him."

"What happened?"

"He slipped on the rocks and fell in. I ran to the spit, thinking I could rescue him. I threw myself straight in." He stopped. "But I missed."

Elsa stood up. He heard her soft footsteps and saw out of the corner of his eye that she had sunk to her knees beside him. He wanted to pull away; he couldn't handle more right now.

"It wasn't your fault."

"The police won't agree."

"Are you going to tell them?"

"I have to. It's all I can do."

Elsa's skirt rustled beneath her.

"What about me? I'm the one who left him there, injured. Do I have to tell?"

"No! This has nothing to do with you."

This time, he wouldn't fail to protect her. He glanced up, but looked away just as quickly. She was too close.

"Ljungblad is a good policeman, I think. We'll talk to him," she said.

They remained on the floor, silent now. Mattias thought about how they used to play in that kitchen. Áhkku and Áddjá had told stories, filled Elsa and Mattias with fantasies that turned into games. He wanted to ask if she remembered too. But Elsa spoke first.

"First the police, and then SANKS," she said.

He nodded. Sure. It was unna oabba's turn to take charge.

CHAPTER EIGHTY-THREE

Gávccilogigolbma

The knitting needles clicked in her hands. Hanna had finished the tiny, pale green pants and now she was working on the white cardigan.

She sat in the kitchen, spending most of her time looking toward the living room and the sofa, where Anna-Stina was lying, asleep. Just as often, she craned her neck to see into the yard, to check on Jon-Isak.

Rumors were flying again. Rumors that quickly spread from village to village. When the police went by with a trailer, imaginations knew no limits, and what people were saying must be true. It wasn't made up; it was fact, because everyone had heard.

Reindeer carcasses, moose steaks, even a bear's head. Yes, there had been a bear's head in Robert Isaksson's freezers.

She shuddered and pulled on her pink fleece.

Robert was dead and buried, but the tale of him would live on a long time, she was sure of it. His house would fall to ruins; the curtains would first fade in the sun and then disintegrate in the window. Unless one of his few relatives took pity on the wretched place. His mother wouldn't be one of them, that much was certain.

The roof of the former barn that was now a storehouse would collapse, and small animals would take refuge there. Village children would find their way there, frighten each other by claiming he still haunted the house, still came out to kill reindeer. Only the most reckless ones would dare to enter the barn, stand there with their knees trembling to hear rustling in the corners and alarming creaks above their heads.

She couldn't see Jon-Isak anymore and had to get up to look out the other kitchen window. There he was, with a soccer ball, as usual. He could keep it in the air with endless kicks, always trying to set a new record.

She sat down again, letting the yarn slip through her hands.

There was already talk of kids being drawn to Robert's house. Jon-Isak's friends had been there, and she had expected he would be in the lead, throwing rocks and dragging pieces of charcoal across the wall.

But no, Jon-Isak stuck close to home, close to his father. He still didn't want to go to school. For among the rumors were whispers about a murderer who had thrown Robert into the river.

She wasn't about to force him to go to school. He would grow up to be like his father, anyway, so he wouldn't need schooling. These days she reached for her son and squeezed him hard. At first he had been stiff, unsure how long it would last or why Mom was clinging to him. It took a few times before he relaxed and trusted her. And then he squeezed back, cautiously. Now he sought out her presence, came right up to her when she was cooking, wiggling closer on the sofa, leaning his head against her shoulder and falling asleep.

Anna-Stina's belly would soon be as big as she was tall. Her face was round and soft, but her hands and feet were swollen. She sometimes confessed that she was afraid of giving birth. Hanna had promised to be there with her, if Per-Jonas wasn't home. Let him be home.

At the store she'd heard that Mattias had gone to SANKS. The gossip-monger who passed this on, expression full of concern, didn't know the reason, but Hanna had her suspicions. No one had watched over that sixteen-year-old who lost his friend. Who was left behind without Lasse.

She let her knitting rest on the table for a moment. It was painful to think about Mattias; it reminded her of how terrifyingly easy it would be for her to lose her balance. Everything she'd been so sure of was built on no stronger grounds than that. But now she gathered her flock, did what was expected of her, expected of an áhkku. She picked herself up, did it for her kids and her coming grandchild, but it wasn't as if she was whole. She could only hope she wouldn't break down again. Some evening she would talk to Ante. Say she was sorry. She hoped he would say he was sorry too.

If Lasse had told her he'd needed help, she would have driven him to

Karasjok. She grabbed a tissue that was on the table and gingerly wiped her nose and dabbed her eyes.

She looked out the kitchen window, down to the main road where Elsa zipped by with her reflective vest on. She took long runs along the village roads. Someone had said she was training for a marathon in Stockholm. Hanna had to smile. That girl was bullheaded enough to do anything. Elsa had been training her whole life, walking with her head held high and preparing to take over, take the space she deserved.

Hanna stood up and got Lasse's confirmation picture, placing it on the kitchen table in front of her. There. Now she could keep an eye on all of her kids. She counted her stitches and the needles began to click again.

CHAPTER EIGHTY-FOUR

Gávcciloginjeallje

The Sámi flag waved outside the People's House. Sámi folks in gákti hurried past Elsa toward the building; many of them recognized her and said hello. Today was the last day the Sámi Parliament was in session, and Minna was in town, had come from Umeå to listen.

They hugged for a long time.

"You truly do the word 'nomad' justice," Elsa said, letting her hand glide over Minna's shawl and its fringe down her back. "How do you manage?"

"Someone has to," she said with a smile.

Her hair was longer, but it was still a short style. Her eyes were just as sharp as ever.

She had been traveling a lot. There were mine protests, human rights demonstrations, and many long days in Stockholm at the Supreme Court, where agents of the state shamelessly referred to the Sámi as "Lapps." Elsa still felt rage boil up inside her when she thought about it, and she hadn't even managed to listen to the live broadcast on Sameradion. Minna, however, had sat through hours upon hours as the Girjás reindeer collective fought the state to win back the right to control small game hunting in their administrative area.

"Can you really handle a meeting with the police on top of all this?"

"I'm basically your attorney, right?"

Their laughter echoed over the parking lot, and they took a shortcut through the park to get to the police station. But Elsa was anxious inside. Ljungblad had called to say he had tried to contact Mattias, and in lieu of him he was summoning Elsa to the station. And Elsa called Minna, struggling not to sound panicked.

They could glimpse the police station through the birch trees, and Minna stood up straighter.

"Well, we'd better prepare ourselves. What could he want? You said he actually wanted Mattias. And Mattias has already told them what happened, right?"

Yes. They had come to town together, asked to speak to Ljungblad. Mattias hadn't looked up even once as he related, in mechanical tones, how Robert had taken the unsafe waders from him, how he had slipped and fallen into the water, how Mattias had tried to rescue him. Ljungblad had gone to get Henriksson, and Mattias had to tell the whole story again while a recorder captured his monotone voice. Elsa wasn't allowed to stay with him that time. She had taken Ljungblad by the arm before he shut the door.

"He honestly tried to save him. Please, you have to believe that."

Elsa shoved her hands into the pockets of her jeans. Minna's brooches jingled on her chest.

"Yes, Mattias told them everything."

"Then what could they want with you?"

Elsa hadn't wanted to get Minna involved. Now she regretted it.

Minna brushed Elsa's back, sought her gaze.

"I remember when you called me to ask what happens if you walk away from someone who's injured. Why did you do that?"

Elsa grabbed the handle of the door to the police station. She looked up furtively at Minna.

"I was there too," she whispered.

THE SPACE HEATER IN the corner of Ljungblad's office hummed.

"I apologize that it's so cold in here. There's some problem with the heating in the building," he said.

Elsa kept her coat on, but Minna was unbothered in her gákti.

"Thanks for coming on such short notice. How is Mattias? I heard he's in the psych ward?"

"No, it's not the psych ward. He's receiving help from psychologists in Norway who specialize in mental health issues among Sámi folks."

Ljungblad nodded and paged through the piles of paper on his desk.

"You know we've begun an investigation, a proper one. We have found things on Robert's phone and in his home. I can't say more than that right now, but I wanted you to know. Maybe you can pass that on to Mattias as well."

"So are you saying Robert is suspected of a crime now?"

"Unfortunately the truth of the matter is that once a person is deceased he can't be considered a suspect. But even so, it turns out there are reasons to move this forward."

"I told you there would be a lot on Robert's phone. No one listened, in all these years no one ever believed us. We could have been spared so much shit."

"And I don't want to give you false hope—it might be hard to do anything about the older investigations. Plus, some are beyond the statute of limitations."

Minna explained the legal terms, although Elsa understood perfectly without her help. When Ljungblad aimed a weary look at Minna, she pulled an imaginary zipper over her bright red lips. But a second later, she switched tactics.

"If you all had classified those reports as a more serious crime than theft, it wouldn't be too late," Minna said.

"Then I assume you are also aware that we're not the ones who determined that these crimes should be labeled theft. You'll have to take it up with the lawmakers."

"And I will."

Ljungblad sighed and turned to Elsa.

"We've got an empty shell casing that was found near Robert's four-wheeler."

The shell.

"We've tried to call your brother but he doesn't answer. Mattias has a firearms license, we know that," he said, drawing out his words while aiming his steady gaze at Elsa, who didn't dare to blink.

"But why is this of interest? He wasn't shot. The shell casing could have been left behind by some sloppy fowl hunter." Minna couldn't help herself, and Ljungblad pointed at the door.

"I think you should wait outside now."

"Is this an interrogation?"

"I am gathering information by way of questioning. Could you please wait outside?"

Minna stood up, moving slowly on purpose; she adjusted her belt and winked at Elsa, then closed the door behind her.

Elsa shivered and pulled her shawl tighter around her neck.

"He didn't kill him."

"But someone fired a shot, and it could have been meant to strike him. Perhaps the situation wasn't quite as your brother described it."

He was luring her in, speaking softly.

"Does it matter?"

"Maybe. We have to ask, anyway."

"Then I guess you'll have to ask him."

He ran his fingers over his beard.

"I'm thinking he might not have been alone out there, that maybe there were others with him."

Elsa imitated Minna.

"Is this an interrogation?"

He looked at her with disappointment.

"There's a witness who saw your car in the area."

She was struck by dizziness and had to focus on her shoes. She had left it up to Mattias. This would only be about him. She hadn't understood why. Now it was all falling apart.

"Okay, I was there." She looked up. "I found him under the four-wheeler. And I'm the one who fired a shot. But I didn't shoot him."

In her mind's eye she saw the barrel of the gun pointing at his face. The shudder that went through her made her tremble. It had been so close.

"I fired straight up in the air."

"Did you force him to go to the river?"

Ljungblad's voice was tense now.

"No." She paused, and her cheeks flushed. "I left him under the four-wheeler."

"So your brother freed him? You left him with your brother?"

She shook her head and looked him in the eye. It was such a relief to tell the truth. Suddenly she wanted nothing more than to get it all out.

"I didn't know he was by the river, and he didn't know I was in the woods."

"But how did Robert get out? He must have been seriously trapped under the four-wheeler when you showed up, if he was still lying there. Or was he unconscious?"

She couldn't tell him about Lasse. There was no explaining it to people who didn't understand. Or, even more specifically, for those who didn't believe in the possibility. How could she tell him what she knew? Stuff like this, the presence of the dead, wouldn't hold up in court; you couldn't even speak about it openly, and it could never serve as a reasonable explanation. No, they would squirm and shake their heads in disbelief. Call it fantasy and excuses. Once upon a time, Sámi folks were killed for this sort of thing. Silenced with violence. Forced to turn their backs on what was so clear to them. So Ljungblad, like all the others, would look for the logical explanation.

"So Mattias was the one who lifted the four-wheeler?"

"Why would he do that? Only to force him into the waders and shove him into the river?"

She was being sarcastic, and he obviously didn't appreciate it. He was a young officer; he had ambitions. He didn't intend to investigate DUIs and domestic violence for much longer. He would lead high-profile investigations in a bigger city. And here was his chance, Elsa thought. He wanted to solve a murder, uncover an atrocious crime.

"Why didn't you tell us you had been there as well?"

"Mattias thought it was for the best. I wasn't there when Robert went into the river."

"You should have told us. It's a serious matter to lie, especially when a man has died."

"It wasn't a lie—I just didn't mention it."

"But you went out there to kill him, or why else would you have had a gun with you?"

"No, you've got it all wrong! I brought the gun for protection. I was scared. I've been scared all these years, since I was a kid. We're not safe on our own land. Our animals aren't safe."

"You could have made it easy on yourself and said you were going out to hunt fowl."

He was muttering so softly that she could hardly hear him.

"Sure, I could have, but now I want to tell you exactly what happened."

"You're going to have to start again from the beginning, in an official interrogation."

"He drowned. He had water in his lungs. He wasn't dead until he went into the water."

Elsa repeated what Minna had explained to her, and Ljungblad looked at her with his eyebrows raised.

"Yet he ended up in the water and died. Why?"

"He was trying to rescue his dog. Just like Mattias said."

"You've had plenty of time to get your stories straight, you and Mattias."

"And you've had plenty of time to put a stop to what he did to us."

They sat in silence, staring at each other. Neither would yield.

"He killed my reindeer and threatened to kill me when I was nine years old. Do you know what that does to a child?"

CHAPTER EIGHTY-FIVE

Gávccilogivihtta

The article was open on one of the low pine tables in the teachers' lounge at school. But in a flash someone had picked it up again; it circulated among them. Some read it aloud to their colleagues, from the newspaper or from their phones. The headline was big and bold: about the ring of criminals who had supplied pubs and hotels up and down the coast with meat from poached reindeer. Evidence had been found in the homes of two now deceased men, but the police were investigating links to other suspects, including a Finnish branch. At least one restaurateur was also under suspicion of receiving stolen goods. Another stubbornly maintained that he had bought the meat from people he understood to be reindeer herders, but the documentation held by the deceased men said otherwise.

Henriksson gave a statement, saying that they were still interested in more information from the public, and he stressed that the police had never neglected the villages.

"This shows that we get results. We have performed a thorough investigation that has brought very successful results."

That sentence in particular made Elsa's colleagues scoff derisively.

"He should be ashamed of himself!"

Dad too had raised his voice when reading this quote from his phone earlier that morning.

"How can they take credit? Someone simply found Robert's phone, and there sure as hell wasn't any detective work or investigation behind that. If he hadn't died, we'd still be guarding the reindeer around the clock!"

Elsa was waiting for the right moment to tell her parents how it had all gone down. But she had promised Mattias to wait until he could be there to explain. And that's as far as it would go. They would keep it in the family.

She'd told Mattias that he could return to the collective as a hero if the truth came out. But he snapped over the phone, saying she was awfully stupid sometimes.

"We should be grateful that the investigation was closed and that no one but us knew it ever existed."

Yes. Ljungblad had, with a lot of support from Henriksson, tried to reconstruct the last hours of Robert's life. If Ljungblad were to be audited, there would be no aberrations; he had conducted a faultless investigation, followed up on every lead and interrogated the siblings by turns. He was finally able to inform Elsa, with a clear conscience, that the investigation would be closed. Robert had put on the waders and drowned. There was no evidence to suggest otherwise.

"You believe us?" she ventured to ask.

"Yes, actually, I do."

And she had cried.

Elsa leaned back on the red sofa in the staff lounge, sipping her hot tea and listening to the buzz. She wondered if anyone realized she was the person quoted in the article, the anonymous member of the reindeer collective who spoke about the years of harassment and threats and demanded that the laws be reexamined, that the killing of reindeer must bring harsher punishment, be classified differently. It wasn't without risk, to speak out; she was worried about Jon-Isak.

She stood up and went over to his teacher, Karin, who was sitting slightly apart from everyone else. She was stirring her coffee and gazing out at the children, who were playing in the newly fallen snow. Soon it would stay, and it would really be winter.

"Jon-Isak still isn't here."

Karin jumped, and her coffee sloshed. "Oh, you scared me."

"He's been out for weeks now. What are you doing about it?"

"We've called, I've stopped by, and we're in close contact with student health services."

"I'm sure there will be more fights out there." Elsa nodded toward the playground.

Karin gave a heavy sigh. "You know, I've almost given up hope."

"But you can't give up on Jon-Isak."

"His mother isn't so easy to talk to." She looked guilty. "I mean, I don't want to gossip, but it's true. And his father is off with the reindeer basically all of the time; he's never been here."

Elsa hadn't gone back to see Hanna, but each time she passed the hill up to their house on her runs, the thought was there.

"I'll talk to the principal. This can't continue. I don't mean just with Jon-Isak, but in general, everything that goes on between the students," she said.

Karin looked at the clock, stood up, and put a hand on Elsa's arm.

"Jon-Isak doesn't like your working here."

Elsa's shoulders slumped. "I know. But I'll be quitting soon. I'm going to be with Dad full-time now that Mattias is in Karasjok."

"Right."

They never knew what to say about Mattias. It was easier to ignore it or change the subject. *Well, guess I should get going*, they often said. She'd heard it all.

She took out her phone to check if Mattias had sent anything. She texted him every day, tried to read between the lines, spot something that might suggest he was improving. He wrote that he was doing better, but still he hadn't come home. He kept putting his homecoming off, time and again. She wrote that there was nothing to be ashamed of. And then he didn't respond at all.

CHAPTER EIGHTY-SIX

Gávccilogiguhtta

J on-Isak didn't turn around. He straightened his spine and concentrated on finding his rhythm, but still he had to glance down at his skis to make sure they stayed in the tracks.

It was worst coming down the hill from the house, where the incline was steep and there were tufts of grass peeking through the snow. Along the lake there were trails, but they weren't as good as the ones on the ice, where the snowmobiles packed the snow down. He was sure the ice would hold, but Mom had screeched that he was absolutely not allowed to ski there. She immediately regretted raising her voice and pulled him close, whispering an apology. He had shaken himself loose. But inside, he was full of the scent of her.

He poled onward, annoyed that this wasn't going better. It was poor glide, and the snow had hardly enveloped nature yet. But it had to work. He would show them all, once spring came and it was time for the big ski race between the villages. He had plenty of time to practice, since he didn't go to school anymore. He didn't need school; he only needed the reindeer.

ELSA HAD RECENTLY NOTICED the ski tracks coming down the hill from Hanna's house, only to stop at the road and appear again on the other side. So she began to keep watch from the kitchen window, waiting for the little figure to pop up. And today he did. His journey along the river's edge was wobbly, and then he stopped and glanced over his shoulder a few times before sliding a few yards onto the ice. It was still way too thin, and she held her breath. But he backed up and took off on the trail Elsa had broken in.

She put on her skis, sliding them back and forth in place. The sky was white. The air was clear and cold, and she could feel that more snow was on the way.

She gave him a head start, until she could no longer see him from the road. She found her rhythm and glided on, the muscles of her right thigh tightening from yesterday's long run, but she expected it would relax soon.

He was poling evenly and bending his knees to push off. She was catching up, yard by yard. Soon they were at the edge of the woods, where the trail, in the winter, led to the corral. Then she heard him. A bright boyish voice carrying far in the silence of the forest. Was he joiking? It sounded like it. Yes. She could hear whose joik it was. Lasse's. The two of them had never met, yet Lasse had been a constant presence. And now it had come full circle with a joik. Elsa had to stop and let him go.

But Jon-Isak turned around and caught sight of her. The joik stopped suddenly, as it could. Elsa raised her hand in greeting, waving her pole. He nearly fell over, as he turned quickly away from her, and then began to pole fast and jerkily. He vanished into the trees and Elsa stayed put. She took off her mittens, opened the zipper on her pocket, and let her hand slip in, stroking the softness there. She closed the zipper, put on her mittens and tugged her hat down over her ears, which were red from the cold. Then she began to pole, slowly at first, finding her rhythm and her breath. After around a hundred yards she saw his tracks leading straight into the forest, toward the old corral where no real trails had been broken yet. She followed. She could hear him panting and gasping. It was hard work, breaking a trail. The skis got stuck, and there was no glide.

His skis and poles had been abandoned on the ground. She followed his footprints, then stopped to listen.

Now the first flakes of snow were falling, drifting down slowly, doing pirouettes in the air, landing on her cheeks and eyelashes.

The fence was still there; parts of it remained year-round. She looked around for him, took off her skis and leaned her poles against a tree. He was on the other side of the corral, on the highest point, where the fence afforded him a good view. He dangled his legs, not even using his hands to hold on. He made a snowball, patting it with his mittens to make it round and hard. He had to use his calves now and then for balance.

Elsa stepped into the corral and approached him. When she stopped by the fence, she shook it gently so he would have to hold on. She laughed. He didn't.

"You know, when I was about your age, I also skied out here all by myself, and that time your eanu, Lasse, was here. I fed the reindeer with him."

Jon-Isak kept forming the snowball, squeezing it hard.

"Then he towed me behind his snowmobile. He always said it was like going waterskiing in the Mediterranean. Did you know he traveled outside Sweden a lot?"

He didn't want to show that he was curious, but she could tell he was listening as he began handling the snowball more gently.

"There was no one like him in all the village. He traveled all over the world."

Jon-Isak's nose scrunched.

"Well, maybe not *all* over, but he did go to most parts of the world. He came home and showed us things the rest of us had never heard of. But no matter where he went, he didn't stay long. Because I think he missed home."

She leaned against the fence, no longer looking up.

"He helped me. I think he was the only one who understood when I was having a tough time. Even though he didn't say much, he was there."

The snowflakes were coming down faster; soon the visibility would drop to just a few yards.

"He suspected that I had seen something really scary that I was too afraid to tell anyone about. He understood that, but he also didn't make me talk about it. Sometimes you don't want to talk about stuff."

She looked up. Jon-Isak's black hat was white with snow. He blinked rapidly when snowflakes got in his eyes.

"When Lasse died, I planned to bury that secret with him. I thought I would drop something down with him and never have to think about it again. Do you want to see what it is?"

Jon-Isak didn't move; he stared straight ahead.

"It's nothing special, you've seen it before, but it has to do with the worst thing that ever happened to me."

He glanced down at her, and the hand she had in her pocket.

"Do you know why I didn't drop my secret down there with him?"

Jon-Isak waited in silence.

"Because something told me that I would need my secret one more time. For someone else. And I think you're the one who's supposed to have it. But I'm warning you, it's a terrible story."

She waited for him to climb down, but he wasn't giving in to temptation.

"Can I come up?"

When he didn't shake his head, she got a solid hold of the fence and launched her right foot off the bottom board. Using her arms to pull, she took another step. She settled on top, dangling her legs although her stomach lurched when she looked down.

"This is so high. And you're not holding on. Are you crazy?"

She gave a little laugh and made a big show of holding tight to the fence with both hands. A shift in his eyes. He casually tossed the snowball from hand to hand, and she saw the cockiness inside him.

"Right there." Elsa pointed at the entrance in one corner of the corral. "That's where I found my best calf Nástegallu killed. And I saw the man who did it."

Jon-Isak's eyes narrowed and he stared at the fence on the other side. It was hardly visible in the falling snow.

"He had cut off Nástegallu's ears and maybe he was going to take her too, but when I showed up he didn't dare. But you know, he had put one ear in his pants pocket along with his gloves, and when he pulled them out the ear fell out and he drove off. And I took it, but I never showed it to anyone."

Elsa held on tight with one hand and the fence trembled beneath her as she dug in her coat pocket with her free hand. She held out the piece of ear, brushing the snowflakes away with her thumb even though fresh ones kept falling on it.

"You're the first person I've shown it to. And you know what? I think it was meant to be this way. That I was supposed to tell you." She paused for a moment. "The man who killed my calf threatened to kill me if I said anything."

Jon-Isak's eyes went wide.

"Of course you're too afraid to speak up when someone threatens you. I was terrified, so I kept it to myself," she went on.

Suddenly Jon-Isak swung his right arm and the snowball hit a tree trunk with a distinct splat. Elsa gasped.

"You're nuts!" she said, laughing.

He took off his mittens and accepted the ear from her, letting his index finger stroke the soft fur, brushing away the snow. The strands had clumped together with moisture.

"Was it Robert Isaksson who did it?"

"Yes, it was."

Jon-Isak straightened up and thrust out his chin.

"Good thing he's dead now."

Elsa hesitated, unsure of the right thing to say. "I think things are going to get better now. Easier for us all."

"Not at school," he said. "I quit. I'm going to work with the reindeer."

He stroked the piece of ear, cupping his hands around it to protect it from the snow. He had a scar that ran between his thumb and index finger.

"You know, I was scared when I was in school too."

"I'm not scared of anything!"

He stuck out his hand, trying to give the ear back.

"I've got tons of bealljebinnát," he said.

"Then maybe this piece can be part of your collection. I think Lasse would have wanted it that way."

Jon-Isak dropped the ear and let it fall to the ground. They looked at it. Soon it would be covered with snow.

"Maybe you're right. Maybe Nástegallu needed to come home. We'll let her stay here."

The snow let up and soon visibility was good again. When Jon-Isak climbed down, the whole fence shook. She noticed that he carefully spotted his footholds before planting his feet. Elsa climbed down after him. He headed for the skis he had tossed aside.

"See you at separation, then," she said.

"Yup." He looked up, staking his poles in the ground. "Bye."

He poled quickly and vanished down the little slope.

Elsa skied at a leisurely pace, took a right among the pines, broke a trail of her own. She looped around and approached the corral from the back. She stood there, still and quiet.

It didn't take long. The hiss of skis on snow. Creaking poles.

She huddled behind a pine, resting her head against its trunk.

He didn't open the fence; he climbed up, swung over, and jumped down, landing nimbly as a cat. He walked with purpose, knew the exact spot. He bent down, took off his mitten, and closed his hand around Nástegallu. Blew the snow off and stroked her fur with his thumb.

Opening his coat pocket, he put the ear inside and fastened the button carefully. He put his mitten back on and looked up at the sky. And then he waved.

ACKNOWLEDGMENTS

This book has been with me for years. It's taken time to find the right way to tell the story. Help has come from many directions, not least from my maternal grandparents, who are no longer with us. Yet are with us even so.

These things are happening in Sápmi today and have been for a long time. Reality is sometimes worse than fiction. The book is based on real-life events to a certain extent; among other sources I've had access to a hundred police reports.

I've received valuable help when it comes to reindeer herding and police work, but with these facts as a starting point I have, of course, allowed myself the freedom to create a fictional place and story for which I, as the author, bear all responsibility.

With that said, I want to thank everyone who has helped and inspired me throughout the years. For various reasons, not all of them want to be listed by name, but you all know I am deeply grateful and will never forget the time you gave me.

I'd like to direct a big, hearty thanks to the reindeer herders:

Sara Skum for the conversation we had in 2018. It was moving and upsetting and led me onto the right path. Thanks too for the supporting documentation, especially the hundred police reports. Anna-Karin Niia, your reading made a big difference. Thank you so much for all of your clever and amusing comments.

Richard Åström and Anna Kråik Åström for reading the early versions and providing both facts and sensitive feedback.

I'd also like to thank police officers Håkan Alselind and Ulrika Larsson for their conversations about police work in such a vast geographical area.

Big thanks to my Swedish publisher Romanus & Selling, especially my fantastic editor Susanna Romanus, who did everything for my book.

Equally big thanks to my literary agency Ahlander Agency and especially my brilliant agent Kaisa Palo, who made it possible for Elsa to ski out into the world. Thanks to her, *Stolen* is being published in English, among other languages, and that makes me incredibly happy.

I'd like to send a warm thanks to Janie Yoon, Nita Pronovost, Kevin Hanson, and everyone at Scribner Canada, and Emily Polson, Colin Harrison, and their team at Scribner in the U.S., for taking such good care of my book and for making sure it reaches English-speaking readers all over the world. Thank you also to Rachel Willson-Broyles for a fantastic translation.

And last but not least, my dearest thanks go to my family, Micke and Willis—you are always my safe harbor. To my mother Ellen and sister Thérése for reading and helping me make the right choices. And to my father Janne for factual assistance on the topics of firearms, snowmobiles, and life in the forest, which you know inside out.

A NOTE ON THE AUTHOR

ANN-HELÉN LAESTADIUS is an author and journalist from Kiruna, Sweden. She is Sámi and of Tornedalian descent, two of Sweden's national minorities. In 2016, Laestadius was awarded the prestigious August Prize for Best Young Adult and Children's Novel for *Ten Past One*, for which she was also awarded Norrland's Literature Prize. *Stolen* is her first adult novel and was named Sweden's Book of the Year. Connect with her on Twitter @ahlaestadius.

A NOTE ON THE TRANSLATOR

RACHEL WILLSON-BROYLES is a freelance translator based in Saint Paul, Minnesota. She received her BA from Gustavus Adolphus College and her PhD from the University of Wisconsin–Madison. Other authors whose works she has translated include Jonas Hassen Khemiri, Jonas Jonasson, and Malin Persson Giolito.